Recent Research in Psychology

Fletcher A. Blanchard   Faye J. Crosby

Affirmative Action in Perspective

Published Under the Auspices of the Society for the Psychological Study of Social Issues

Springer-Verlag
New York Berlin Heidelberg
London Paris Tokyo

Fletcher A. Blanchard
Faye J. Crosby
Department of Psychology
Smith College
Northampton, MA 01063
USA

With 4 Illustrations

Library of Congress Cataloging-in-Publication Data
Blanchard, Fletcher A.
Affirmative action in perspective / Fletcher A. Blanchard, Faye J. Crosby.
p. cm. — (Recent research in psychology)
Includes index.
1. Affirmative action programs—United States. 2. Discrimination in employment—United States. I. Crosby, Faye J., 1947–
II. Title. III. Series.
HF5549.5.A34B56 1989
331.13'3'0973—dc 19 89-4061

Printed on acid-free paper

Camera-ready copy provided by the authors.
Printed and bound by Edwards Brothers, Inc., Ann Arbor, Michigan.
Printed in the United States of America.

9 8 7 6 5 4 3 2 1

ISBN 0-387-96971-3 Springer-Verlag New York Berlin Heidelberg
ISBN 3-540-96971-3 Springer-Verlag Berlin Heidelberg New York

This volume is dedicated
to
S. W. C. who, through his patient commitment to the understanding of discrimination and prejudice, has shaped the development of generations of social scientists and policy makers
(F.B.)

and to
Catherine, Elga, Etta, Joanne, and all my other friends at the "Committee of 13" with thanks for the beginning lessons in affirmative action.
(F.C.)

Preface

How can society undo the legacy of racial and sexual discrimination in its institutions without engaging in reverse discrimination? Do centuries of injustice -- in which some groups have oppressed others -- require that those who were unfairly advantaged shall now be unfairly disadvantaged? How, in a world of static or diminishing resources, shall some be compensated without unacceptable costs to others?

These questions, difficult in the abstract, become especially problematic when we come to practicalities. For a while, a policy of equal opportunity appeared to be the answer to the racial and gender injustices of American society. But the policy of equal opportunity operates fairly only in a system that does not distinguish between groups either *de jure* or *de facto*, either intentionally or unintentionally, either blatantly or subtly. If racism and sexism exist in America, then equal opportunity is not a feasible policy for American institutions.

That racism and sexism do persist has been documented countless times in a number of ways. Overt and blatant prejudice is no longer acceptable in most circles, but it takes more than a few decades to dismantle the structures that have so relentlessly and so systematically put some groups at a disadvantage relative to others. Imbalances continue, even when they are not intended or attended.

Given the unjust realities of the past, it is not enough to wait passively for a better society. Institutions must go out of their way to assure that their practices are fair. That is why affirmative action can potentially assure a more equitable and efficient society than does a policy of so-called equal opportunity.

The importance of affirmative action for our society is evident from this book. So too are the many problems of the policy. None of the authors hides from the complexities of affirmative action. But while the material here makes abundantly clear the perils of affirmative action, it also demonstrates how effective and fair the policy can be and usually is.

Also abundantly clear is the fact that a book like this involves much good labor from many people whose names do not appear on the pages that follow. We would therefore like to thank several people for their hard work. Michele Wittig deserves credit for originating the book. Kathy Bartus, Janet Lampman, and especially Victoria Dalzell have earned our gratitude for the devotion they showed over several months, helping to transform our project from a set of manuscripts to a finished book. We also thank Richard Parker and Sang-Rang Shin of the Center for Academic Computing at Smith College for their advice and assistance with text preparation. We would also like to shout a hearty thank-you to Travis Crosby who generously gave attention to various drafts of various chapters. For his grace of expression as well as his good graces, we applaud him. Also helpful in reading drafts have been Chi Chi Carson, Susan Clayton, Jack Dovidio, and Edward Etheredge. Finally, we acknowledge the help of Joice Gare. Her sharp eyes helped our weary ones.

Institutional support has been critically important. Smith College's Committee on Faculty Compensation and Development awarded funds to Blanchard and to Crosby. The Dana Foundation also deserves a thank-you for the grant to Janet Lampman that enabled her to work with us on the book.

Northampton, MA
October, 1988

Contents

Contributors

Nijole V. Benokraitis is Professor of Sociology at the University of Baltimore.

Fletcher A. Blanchard is Associate Professor of Psychology at Smith College.

Janet Bokemeier is Associate Professor of Sociology at the University of Kentucky.

Susan D. Clayton is Assistant Professor of Psychology at Tufts University.

Diana Cordova is a graduate student in social psychology at Stanford University.

Faye J. Crosby is Professor of Psychology at Smith College.

John F. Dovidio is Associate Professor of Psychology at Colgate University.

Karen Dwyer is a free spirit living in Whitefish, Montana.

Bernardo M. Ferdman is Assistant Professor of Psychology and of Latin American and Caribbean Studies at the University of New York in Albany.

Samuel L. Gaertner is Professor of Psychology at the University of Delaware.

Melissa Kesler Gilbert is Statistical Analyst and Director of Learning Assessment at Goucher College.

Nancy Goldsmith is Assistant Director of Admissions at Connecticut College.

Frances A. Holloway is the Director of the Affirmative Action Office at Yale University.

Bergen Langlois is an Ada Comstock Scholar at Smith College.

Jeffrey Mann is completing his doctoral studies in social psychology at the University of Delaware.

Rupert W. Nacoste is Assistant Professor of Psychology at North Carolina State University.

Jim D. Newman is an Associate with the law firm of Pettit & Martin in San Francisco, California. He previously served as Senior Attorney in the Office of Regional Counsel for the Internal Revenue Service in San Francisco.

Wessie L. Norris is a Tests and Measurement Specialist at the New York City Department of Personnel.

Maryellen Reardon is a Research Associate at Avon Products, Inc.

Christopher J. Ruhm is Assistant Professor of Economics at Boston University.

Susan Scollay is in the Office of the Vice President for Research and Graduate Studies at the University of Kentucky.

Susan Tabb is a Management Trainee for Continental Cablevision.

Sandra S. Tangri is Professor of Psychology at Howard University.

Dalmas A. Taylor is Dean of the College of Liberal Arts at Wayne State University.

Ann Tickamyer is Associate Professor of Sociology at the University of Kentucky.

Francine Tougas is Professor of Psychology at the University of Ottawa.

Catherine Twiss is a graduate student in social psychology at the University of Connecticut.

France Veilleux is a research analyst at the University of Montreal (GRASP).

Teresa Wood is completing her doctoral studies in sociology at the University of Kentucky.

I: Affirmative Action Policies and Programs

1

Introduction: Affirmative Action and the Question of Standards

Faye J. Crosby and Fletcher A. Blanchard

Racial and sexual inequities characterize the contemporary American economy. Relative to White males, men and women of color and White women are more often unemployed and underemployed. When they do find employment, people of color and women are often relegated to low status, ill-paying occupations. At all occupational levels members of these groups are paid less than comparable White men.

In many respects the current inequities constitute the legacy of centuries of racism and sexism. In North and South alike, racial injustices have taken both subtle and blatant expressions. Sexism, too, has been a general phenomenon, bridging regional and national boundaries (Kirp, Yudof, & Franks, 1986).

The question of remedies arises. How shall we correct the problems of racial and sexual discrimination in the labor force? How should we, today, redress the injustices born of centuries of discriminatory personal attitudes and behaviors and institutional policies? The subtleties of modern prejudice, no less pervasive or influential than its virulent, openly hostile forbearer, obscure easy solutions.

One contemporary remedy is known as affirmative action. Affirmative action programs have been devised and implemented in all sectors of the economy to correct racial and sexual injustices. Affirmative action programs differ widely, ranging from those that simply steer an organization toward vigilance to those that require an organization to attain target quotas of specified categories of underrepresented people.

Affirmative action programs raise issues of feasibility and of fairness for organizations and for society as a whole. Cries of "reverse discrimination" have erupted in response to various types of affirmative programs and, indeed, to the general policy of affirmative action. The controversy alerts us to basic questions. What is affirmative action? How did it evolve? What ought we to expect of affirmative action? The controversy also points us to some specific questions. Why do some people resist affirmative action as a policy? And why, given the resistance, do we need affirmative action?

Standards

Every organization needs standards. Every organization requires some non-elastic yardsticks by which to measure various performances of individuals, of groups within the organization, and of the organization as a whole. The greater the importance of the behaviors to the organization, the more critical it is to establish firm, sensible, and effective standards.

Standards come into play for two types of organizational assessments: those that reward past behaviors and those that predict future behaviors. Rewarding past behaviors and predicting future behaviors sometimes overlap, but not always. The high school student who has an outstanding academic record and who is then awarded a scholarship at an elite university typifies a case where reward and prediction may coincide. Different is the case of the elder scholar whom a university honors on the occasion of her 85th birthday. By conferring on her an honorary doctor of the arts degree, the organization seeks to recognize and reward past performance without making predictions about future performances.

When an organization stresses equity as a dominant form of justice, it needs to reward past behaviors in proportion to their organizational merit. To preserve justice, for example, the car dealership needs to give the largest bonus to the salesperson who has sold the most cars and the smallest bonus to the one who has sold the least. The fair educational institution is one that awards the best grades to the most brilliant papers and the worst grades to the least brilliant papers.

Rewarding past behaviors in proportion to their merit implies that one has a way of gauging merit. The organization that stresses equity must devise standards that allow it to judge merit. If the organization is to be experienced as a fair place, then the standards must be ones that seem correct and effective. Disaffection and anomie prevail when an organization espouses the principle of equity but lacks accepted standards.

Whether or not an organization stresses equity, standards may be crucial for the prediction of future behaviors. Entrance requirements typically exist because an organization needs to hire or admit people who are likely to perform certain sets of behavior (and are, perhaps, likely to refrain from performing certain other behavior). An individual's score on the LSAT, for instance, is generally taken as a fairly reliable predictor of how well or poorly a person will do the work in law school. Given that the demand for places in law school exceeds the supply, it behooves a school to admit students who are likely to perform well and reject those who are not likely to perform. To the extent that they facilitate prediction, then, standards enhance organizational effectiveness. Of course, sensible prediction may or may not contribute to the feeling of fairness in an organization.

Affirmative action programs can appear to compromise both organizational fairness and organizational effectiveness. When a woman with little seniority is promoted rather than an equally able man with much seniority, for example, the promotion will appear to violate the norms of equity, especially if the organization sees seniority (but not gender) as characteristic relevant to job status. If, furthermore, experience helps people function well in the organization, then seniority may serve as a predictor of future performance. Given that seniority is measured in the non-elastic metric of years on the job, then promotion of a woman with few years of seniority rather than a man with many years will appear to threaten effectiveness as well as fairness.

Appearances deceive. A good affirmative action program is one that promotes organizational effectiveness by expanding standards so that they can apply sensibly to individuals who are in some senses nonstandard. Consider organizational effectiveness. Tests that serve as cheap and roughly accurate predictors of the future behaviors of individuals with a "standard" or majority background may be uninformative or -- worse -- misleading when it comes to those with nonstandard backgrounds. SAT scores, for instance, serve as roughly accurate predictors of the academic performance of young people but not of people who are over 30. If a college wishes to admit only people who are likely to perform well, then it should use SAT scores when considering young applicants. But, it should discover or invent better predictors of academic performance by mature students.

Concerning fairness, a good affirmative action program makes an organization more thoughtful about what exactly it wishes to recognize and reward. Sometimes we reward performance, regardless of effort, but oftentimes our reaction to and assessments of the performance of individuals are modified by our understanding of their efforts to perform. The blind student may be given a standing ovation at his graduation from business school while his sighted colleagues are not. We are less impressed by the pupil who turns in a perfect French composition because her francophone grandmother helped her write it than by the pupil who writes her less perfect composition all on her own. So, too, should we be impressed more by the good performance of a female, despite sexism, or of a person of color, despite racism, than by the equally good performance of a White male.

Even in those instances where the organization seeks to reward performance in and of itself, irrespective of effort, good affirmative action programs help assure fairness by fostering self-consciousness about the standards that are used in assessing performance. It is all well and good to say that the trophy should go to the horse that wins the race; but, to be fair, one must specify and justify the criteria by which the winner is determined. Is it the horse that crosses the finish line first? Or the horse that clocks the fastest time? Unless one slants the finish line to compensate for the shorter distance of the inner track, these two criteria may yield different winners. Moreover, the view of the finish line from the club house may produce a different winner than the view from the edge of the track. Similarly, a school can appear to be fair by asserting that the best essays receive the best grades. But what makes an essay good? How much should spelling count? Originality? Organization?

In sum, affirmative action programs may appear to jeopardize fairness and effectiveness by appearing to enjoin organizations to use different standards for different populations. Yet, affirmative action programs can, and should, do just the opposite. Affirmative action programs seek to strengthen, and not to undermine, a just and smoothly organized society. At the very least, affirmative action programs force us to examine the standards we use both when rewarding past performances and predicting future performances. At the most, affirmative action programs promote both true equity and effectiveness.

Present Volume

Issues such as these lie at the core of the present volume. We posit that affirmative action programs are good in principle; but we also recognize that affirmative action programs are not always good in actuality. We suggest, moreover, that affirmative action programs can *appear* unfair, ineffective, or both when, in fact, they are both fair and effective. Peeling away the myths to describe the reality underneath the rhetoric constitutes the aim of this book.

The book contains three sections. The first lays down the basics. Chapters in this section explicate the history of federal legislation, executive orders, and federal court cases regarding the application of the policy of affirmative action. They also include a case study of the New York City firefighters where hiring standards, which imperfectly predicted future performance, appeared to restrict unfairly access to employment. The recent policies of the largest affirmative action employer, the United States government, also come under scrutiny in this first section.

The second section documents people's reaction to various affirmative action programs and policies. It includes a look at the sometimes paradoxical reaction of targeted groups who materially benefit from affirmative action yet resist policies which offer the appearance of inequity. The second section then analyzes the motivational basis for resistance and backlash among those who perceive themselves the victims of reverse discrimination. Also included in this section is an analysis of the perceptions of affirmative action officers in higher education.

Given the difficulties with affirmative action, documented in the second section of the book, we might ask: Why bother? The third section revolves around the question of "why bother" with the several chapters offering various answers. One reason to "bother" with affirmative action programs is because they are needed. Inequities persist in America, appearances to the contrary not withstanding, and individuals systematically underestimate their own victimization. A second major reason to design and implement affirmative action programs is that they can be fair. Finally, affirmative action can work.

Affirmative action programs are problematic, but not irremediably. To recognize the reasons that people resist affirmative action is not to advocate abandonment of the policy. On the contrary we need to improve and strengthen affirmative action programs so that they can both be and appear fair and effective. The book concludes by offering recommendations for the fair and effective design and implementation of affirmative action programs.

References

Kirp, D. L., Yudof, M. G., & Franks, M. S. (1986). *Gender Justice*. Chicago: University of Chicago Press.

2

What Is Affirmative Action?

Frances A. Holloway

The term affirmative action carries many meanings in today's society. Often the term elicits strong feelings -- positive and negative. Frequently these feelings derive from a misunderstanding of what affirmative action is all about.

Executive Order 11246

Most people became acquainted with the term affirmative action in the late 1960's and early 1970's when federal contractors were first required to devise and carry out affirmative action programs. Executive Order 11246, signed by President Lyndon Johnson on September 24, 1965, required that federal contractors "take affirmative action to ensure that applicants are employed, and that employees are treated during employment, without regard to their race, color, religion, sex, or national origin." The order goes on to say:

> Such action shall include, but not be limited to the following: employment, upgrading, demotion, or transfer; recruitment or recruitment advertising; layoff or termination; rates of pay or other forms of compensation; and selection for training, including apprenticeship.

Enforcement of Executive Order 11246 and of the subsequent Executive Orders and federal laws pertaining to affirmative action is the responsibility of the U.S. Department of Labor's Office of Federal Contract Compliance Programs (OFCCP). Equal opportunity specialists in the

OFCCP and affirmative action officers in organizations that have contracts with federal government rely on a thick manual (U.S. Department of Labor, 1979) as well as on the Code of Federal Regulations (Title 41 CFR Chapter 60) to determine whether or not a federal contractor is in compliance with the law.

Executive Order 11246 specifies that affirmative action is one of the conditions of agreeing to do work for the government, but it does not define affirmative action. The OFFCP's manual does. According to the manual, affirmative action consists of:

> Those results oriented actions which a contractor by virtue of its contracts must take to ensure equal employment opportunity. Where appropriate, it includes goals to correct underutilization, correction of problem areas, etc. It may also include relief such as back pay, retroactive seniority, make-up goals and timetables, etc.

Essentially the same definition occurs in Title 41 of Chapter 60 of the Federal Regulations where the regulations outline what constitutes an affirmative action *program*. The language that appears in the regulation states that:

> An affirmative action program is a set of specific and result-oriented procedures to which a contractor commits itself to apply every good faith effort. The objective of those procedures plus such efforts is equal employment opportunity.

Since the onset of affirmative action programs, two groups have been identified as "target groups" -- women and members of minority groups. The definitions of targeted minority groups used by the federal government are:

> American Indian or Alaskan Native -- Persons having origins in any of the original people of North America, and who maintain cultural identification through tribal affiliation or community recognition.

> Asian or Pacific Islander -- Persons having origins in any of the original peoples of the Far East, Southeast Asia, the Indian Subcontinent, or the Pacific Islands. This area includes, for example, China, Japan, Korea, the Philippine Islands, and Samoa.

Black, not of Hispanic Origin -- Persons having origins in any of the Black racial groups of Africa.

Hispanic -- Persons of Mexican, Puerto Rican, Cuban, Central or South American or other Spanish Culture or origin, regardless of race.

What exactly are the requirements of affirmative action? First, the contractor is subject to certain broad ground rules. A contractor must maintain a workplace that is not segregated by race or sex. Subcontractors and vendors with whom the contractor does business must also comply with the nondiscrimination and affirmative action requirements to which the contractor is obligated. The contractor's collective bargaining agreements may not discriminate on the basis of race or sex. Employment selection criteria may not discriminate on the basis of race or sex. This is particularly relevant to required academic degrees such as a high school diploma and to required scores on written tests that the contractor administers to job applicants. In the case of a required degree, the employer must be able to prove that the requirement is job related. In the case of written tests, the employer must conduct periodic analyses of the test performance of women versus men and minority group members versus nonminority group members to determine whether a significantly greater number of women or minority group members are failing these tests. If they are, the employer must either stop using the tests or prove that these tests are job related.

By accepting a federal contract the employer also agrees to permit the federal government to conduct periodic compliance reviews of its employment policies, practices, and affirmative action program. The OFCCP may choose to conduct a compliance review at any time. However, when a contractor negotiates an award of more than $1 million, a pre-award compliance review must be undertaken unless a compliance review has already been completed in the previous twelve months. As a result, many contractors can expect a review every one or two years. Usually the OFCCP finds contractors in general compliance at the end of a review, although specific deficiencies and problem areas may be identified. The contractor must agree to correct any deficiencies and outline specific programs or procedures for resolving the problem areas. Sometimes retroactive pay awards are necessary to correct the deficiencies. If the OFCCP finds a contractor noncompliant and a remedy cannot be negotiated, the OFCCP will debar the contractor from receiving any government contracts. A complaint against a contractor filed by an individual or agency alleging illegal discrimination may also trigger a compliance review.

The OFCCP requires contractors to develop, maintain, and update annually a written affirmative action plan (AAP) targeting the employment of women and members of minority groups. The AAP must contain certain data and data analyses. These data include a workforce analysis, a listing by job title (ranked from lowest paid to highest paid) and by department showing the number of men, women, Blacks, Asians, Hispanics and native Americans for each job title. Job titles are then grouped by job category to permit the employer to perform a utilization analysis. Job categories must contain jobs with "similar content, wage rates and opportunities." For each job group, the contractor identifies the available pool of candidates. The contractor must estimate the percentage of minority group members and women in the pool. For example, in a large university a job group might consist of Junior Faculty Members in the English Department. If the university requires its junior faculty members to have the Ph.D., the pool of candidates will be recent recipients of Ph.D.'s in English.

The percentages of women and of minority group members receiving Ph.D.'s in English during this period provide the availability percentages for the utilization analysis for this job group. The percentages of women and minority group members in each of the availability pools are then compared with the percentages of women and minority group members in the contractor's workforce, again, job group by job group. In those job groups where there are fewer women or minority group members than would be expected based on their availability, the contractor must set a goal or target number of women or minority group members to reduce the discrepancy between workforce underrepresentation and availability. The contractor must also use hiring projections to specify a time period to reach that goal. During a compliance review the OFCCP will not automatically find a contractor to be out of compliance if it has not met a goal in the specified time period. However, the contractor must convince the OFCCP that it made "good faith efforts" to achieve the goal.

Finally, the contractor must monitor employment activity -- e.g. referrals, placements, transfers, promotions and terminations -- for each job group. The contractor must report and analyze these data in its annual affirmative action program report. During a compliance review OFCCP also will analyze the data.

Along with data requirements, the AAP must contain specific policy and procedural commitments. The contractor must formulate a written policy on nondiscrimination and affirmative action and disseminate it widely within the company and the neighboring community. An executive in the organization must be identified as the EEO Coordinator and his or her role made known to employees and potential applicants. The contractor must develop monitoring and reporting systems to measure the progress or lack of progress of its affirmative action program in meeting its goals and timetables.

Other required components of an affirmative action program include the identification of problem areas, the development of action oriented programs, and active support of local and national groups which focus on aiding the employment of women or minority group members. Action oriented programs might include special in-house training for women and minority group members to improve their skills or assist them in acquiring new skills so that they will qualify for higher level, better paying jobs. The contractor may provide training opportunities for all employees while making a special effort to encourage women and minority group members to participate. Many contractors have a committee which focuses on employing, retaining, and promoting women and minority group members. Utilizing special recruitment efforts to identify qualified women and minority group members also falls within this category. Action oriented programs might additionally include mentoring programs, child care programs or assistance, internships for women and minority group members, and contacts with local schools and colleges with high minority enrollments.

Handicapped and Veterans

Legislation enacted in the 1970's broadened the scope of affirmative action originally established by President Johnson's Executive order. The Rehabilitation Act of 1973 and the Vietnam Era Veterans Readjustment Assistance Act of 1974 require federal contractors to develop, maintain, and update written affirmative action plans for the employment of handicapped persons and for disabled veterans and veterans of the Vietnam era. The regulations pertaining to Section 503 of the Rehabilitation Act of 1973 define a handicapped individual as:

> any person who (1) has a physical or mental impairment which substantially limits one or more of such person's major life activities, (2) has a record of such impairment, or (3) is regarded as having such an impairment. A handicapped individual is

"substantially limited" if he or she is likely to experience difficulty in securing, retaining or advancing in employment because of a handicap.

The regulations pertaining to Section 402 define special disabled veterans as:

> persons entitled to compensation (or who but for the receipt of military retirement pay would be entitled to compensation) under laws administered by the Veterans Administration for a disability (i) rated at 30 percent or more, or (ii) rated at 10 or 20 percent in the case of a Veteran who has been determined under Section 1506 of this title to have a serious employment handicap; or persons who were discharged or released from active duty because of a service connected disability.

and Veteran of the Vietnam-era as:

> a person (1) who (i) served on active duty for a period of more than 180 days, any part of which occurred between August 5, 1964, and May 7, 1975, and was discharged or released therefrom with other than a dishonorable discharge, or (ii) was discharged or released from active duty for a service connected disability if any part of such active duty was performed between August 5, 1964, and May 7, 1975.

Although some of the affirmative action requirements of the Rehabilitation Act and the Veterans Readjustment Act diverge from the requirements of the Executive Order, some are similar. A major difference is that the contractor need not provide a workforce analysis, estimate the availability of persons with disabilities and Vietnam-era veterans, determine if it underutilizes them in its workforce, or set goals and timetables for hiring handicapped persons and veterans. Similarities exist in that the contractor must work only with vendors and subcontractors who do not discriminate on the basis of these factors. The contractor is required to notify labor unions with which it has bargaining agreements about its nondiscrimination and affirmative action policies with respect to the relevant protected classes. Also, contractors are subject to compliance reviews as described above, the final sanction for noncompliance being debarment. Individuals may complain to OFCCP alleging discrimination by a contractor on the basis of disability or veteran status.

Regulations concerning persons with disabilities and veterans stipulate that employees and applicants for employment must have the option of identifying themselves as handicapped or veterans. The contractor must invite but not require them to be considered under the company's affirmative action program. The requirements also feature specialized recruitment of members of the two targeted groups. Contractors must contact agencies which work with disabled persons, disabled veterans, and Vietnam veterans. They must identify these agencies, particularly those which emphasize employment, inform them about their affirmative action programs, and establish continuing relationships with them.

The contractor should review and alter any policies and job descriptions which exclude persons from particular positions because of requirements that are unrelated to effective job performance. The OFCCP requires contractors to "make a reasonable accommodation to the physical and mental limitations of an employee or applicant when the individual is generally qualified to do the job." Typical accommodations include ramping entrances to workspaces, raising desks for persons who use wheelchairs, hiring part-time readers for nonsighted persons, providing adaptive equipment for computers, telephones and other mechanical equipment, and job restructuring. In addition, the affirmative action plan will state the contractor's policy on the employment of handicapped persons and Vietnam-era veterans, describe the procedures for community-wide dissemination of this policy, identify the person in charge of the program, identify problem areas relevant to the employment of these targeted groups, describe procedures or programs which address these problems, and outline the procedures designed to monitor hiring and other employment practices.

Affirmative Action and True Equality

Given the lack of definition in the original Executive Order 11246, it may not be surprising that many people have distorted and misinterpreted the meaning of affirmative action. Some people equate the terms affirmative action and equal opportunity. Others think that an employer cannot simultaneously practice affirmative action and equal opportunity because affirmative action means discriminating against or not providing equal opportunity to White males.

It is true that equal opportunity means not discriminating against a particular group because of that group's race, sex, religion, ethnicity, disability, or Vietnam-era veteran status. Employers must evaluate applicants solely by those performance criteria which directly describe the requirements of a particular position of employment or academic program for which they are applying. This sounds easy. The problem arises when persons responsible for hiring or admissions decisions carry with them their own experiences and prejudices. Criteria are often subjective, and people's presumptions affect their judgments. A supervisor may, for example, believe that any blind person is unable to perform secretarial tasks such as typing and filing. A college admissions director may review the high school grades of a dyslexic student in the same way he or she reviews those of a student who is not dyslexic. A supervisor may review the resume of a woman who is returning to the workforce after ten years of staying at home with her young children in the same way he or she reviews that of a man who has had continuous employment. A college admissions officer may review the application of a disadvantaged Black student who has taken care of younger siblings and worked part-time to contribute to the family's income in the same way he or she reviews the application of a more affluent applicant.

A major goal of affirmative action is to alert people to the previously unobserved abilities of members of targeted groups. Targeted group members, such as the hearing-impaired, may perform some job-relevant or educational tasks differently, yet just as effectively as others. In the cases of the woman who interrupts her career in order to care for children and the youth who is unable to participate in extra-curricular activities, the "normal" standards for evaluation may be irrelevant to the demands of the employment position or the school to which the targeted group member seeks entry. By making organizations thoughtful about their standards and about the effects of their management policies, affirmative action promotes equal opportunity.

Affirmative action also goes beyond equal opportunity. When the numbers of qualified members of the targeted groups constitute only a small percentage of the pool, then passively providing equal opportunity will not suffice to undo the effects of years of discrimination. If there are a few (and only a few) qualified women, minorities, or disabled people, then differentially vigorous recruiting efforts may be in order. One way that affirmative action differs from equal opportunity is in the former's differential recruitment of underutilized groups.

A common misunderstanding about the meaning of affirmative action is that a person hired as a result of affirmative action is an inferior employee or student. People with this view operate on the assumption that minority group members in their company are less qualified than Whites, or that minority students are less qualified than White students.

It is not only White men who have this misconception about affirmative action; many women and members of minority groups want it known that they were selected for their conventional qualifications rather than through affirmative action procedures. The presumption that women are continuously inferior to men is also revealed when the rejected male applicant tells his friends that he was not selected for a position because "they had to hire a woman."

There are employment situations where organizations may justifiably hire only members of a targeted group or give special preference to them. If underutilization of targeted groups can be demonstrated, an organization's affirmative action plan may include preferential admission, hiring or promotion. There are also separate programs of a limited duration which differ from an employer's routine hiring procedures and pertain to a specific job group or training program. An employer might for example, provide management internships for minority employees so that they can work with top level administrators and learn the management style of the organization. Or, a company might sponsor a technical training program for all its employees and specify that a minimum number of slots be filled by women. Such special programs are examples of affirmative action.

Affirmative action programs should alert organizations to the presumably unintended discriminatory effects of their policies. For example, many large unionized companies or industries have employed Blacks mainly in departments with low paying positions and no advancement opportunities while Whites tended to be employed in higher paying departments with greater promotional opportunities. Because departmental seniority was a factor in the bidding process, Blacks were effectively kept out of the preferred departments. This practice had an adverse impact on minority employees and was found to be discriminatory.

In the university setting, many institutions would not employ both husbands and wives as faculty members. It once seemed reasonable that a personal relationship might interfere with supervisory or professional responsibilities. However, it has been found that this policy adversely affected women. Because men tend to marry younger women it is likely that wives will be less advanced in their careers than husbands. Thus, a husband would be appointed as an assistant professor ; but, when his wife was on the job market a few years later she would be barred from a faculty position in her husband's department. As in the case of departmental seniority, affirmative action can reveal the pattern of unintended exclusion of a targeted group and lead to its correction.

Most companies now view affirmative action as one of many tools for effective management. In academe the rejection of the "old boy network" for filling faculty positions, and the use of broader advertising networks has probably increased the total quality of the pool of candidates in most disciplines. Also, the statistical requirements of the federal regulations has produced improved personnel data for faculty and staff positions, a key element in the planning function of a college or university. Affirmative action requirements have also forced employers to attend more carefully to the validity of performance criteria in job descriptions and in job interviews. As a result the world of employment has become a fairer place for everyone.

Hope for the Future

Affirmative action has already had an impact on our society. However, the job is not yet finished. We now understand that achieving the goal of true equal opportunity is a much harder task than many people had thought. OFCCP staff members, personnel managers, and affirmative action officers have always believed that affirmative action is a temporary program. Many thought that a contractor simply had to institute some inhouse training for women and open its doors to minority group members and the problem of exclusion would be solved in a few years. Obviously, this has not been the case. Subtle forms of discrimination continue to surface and the contractor has discovered that the prejudices and stereotypes of all its employees contribute to the barriers that block the attainment of equal opportunity.

Affirmative action is just that: action; it is an employer doing something to remedy the effects of past discrimination against women, minority group members, persons with disabilities, the veteran. This action is more than hiring a few more Blacks or women to meet a goal. Affirmative action is a mandate to employers to first discover the barriers to the employment of those underrepresented in the workforce and then to remove these barriers. It is a tool for employers to use in evaluating all their programs and policies and to ensure that their impact on targeted groups is known and understood. Finally, it is a temporary program to guide employment practices and policies only so long as targeted groups are underrepresented in the workforce. Affirmative action will help this country achieve true equal employment opportunity for all persons in our society.

References

Code of Federal Regulations, 41, 60-2.11.

U.S. Department of Labor, Employment Standards Administration, Office of Federal Contract Compliance Programs (1979). *Federal Contract Compliance Manual.* Washington, D.C.: U.S. Government Printing Office.

3

Affirmative Action and Presidential Executive Orders

Dalmas A. Taylor

Any organization that accepts a federal contract must have an affirmative action program: A federal contractor who lacks an affirmative action program breaks the law (Holloway, Chapter 2). Who made the laws concerning affirmative action? Obviously, Congress has played an important part in developing affirmative action, especially when it passed the Civil Rights Act of 1964 and the Equal Employment Opportunity Act of 1972. As influential as Congress has been, the Executive branch of government may have occupied the most crucial role for the policy of affirmative action.

Starting with Franklin Roosevelt, all presidents have had something official to say about affirmative action. Some of the executive orders have strengthened the regulation of employment practices, while others have sought, for example, to replace mandatory practices with voluntary practices. The primary aim of this chapter is to sketch the Executive Orders relevant to affirmative action issued by the nine presidents since Roosevelt. A secondary aim is to argue that affirmative action is an effective policy in combating discrimination. The chapter ends with a brief comment on variability in presidential orientations toward affirmative action.

First Steps

Racial discrimination has always been a feature of American employment practices. It was not until the eve of World War II, however, that discriminatory practices became the focus of official concern. Much of the American manufacturing for the Allied War effort was done by private establishments under contract from the government. Federal contractor establishments typically comprised the best-paying jobs, and competition for those jobs was intense. Those establishments also contained some of the most jealously guarded systems of preference for White males. Minorities were found almost entirely in low-paying, heavy duty jobs. Women were concentrated in clerical occupations in business and industry in general, and in low-paying semi-skilled jobs in women-intensive industries such as garment manufacturing and food processing. Federal contractors were also heavily unionized at a time when union contracts often contained discriminatory features regarding women and minorities. Discriminatory practices characterized many unions, particularly in the skilled trades.

As war approached, the Black community intensified its resentment of unfair employment practices. The U.S. Army included over a quarter of a million Black officers and soldiers by the summer of 1941. It seemed likely that Black men and women were to be killed in war for a country that had not granted them full citizenship. The Black community was virtually unanimous in its reluctance to fight overseas only to be the victims of racism at home.

Black civic leaders, especially A. Philip Randolph, founder of the Brotherhood of Sleeping Car Porters, organized to bring pressure on the White House. In May of 1941 Randolph and other civic leaders threatened the Roosevelt administration with the prospect of 100,000 Blacks marching on Washington, D. C. on the first of July unless the President issued an order banning discrimination in the federal sector. A liberal delegation from the White House tried to persuade the Black leaders to call off the march, but Randolph remained firm. The President invited the men to come to Washington, D.C. to meet with him and with some of his most trusted and powerful advisers.

On June 18, 1941, Randolph and two of his powerful supporters in the March on Washington Movement, Walter White of the NAACP and T. Arnold Hill, Acting Executive of the National Urban League accepted the President's invitation. At the meeting, President Roosevelt challenged the right of the group to put pressure on the White House. Randolph insisted that a march would take place as scheduled unless something could be done. The President replied: "We cannot have a march on Washington. We must approach this problem in an analytical way" (Bennett, 1966, pp. 305-306). Diplomatically turning aside the President's political gambits of appeasement, the leaders forcefully asked for something affirmative -- an executive order making it mandatory that Blacks be integrated into the work force in a more representative manner.

One week later, Randolph got his order. President Roosevelt issued Executive Order 8802 banning discrimination in war industries and armed services -- Randolph called off the March on Washington. President Roosevelt later established a Fair Employment Practices Commission (FEPC) to assure nondiscrimination in all defense contracts and federal training and employment. The order did not deal with segregation in the armed forces, and was eventually weakened by attacks from southern senators. However, the outcome established the precedent of federal intervention in employment discrimination. This precedent represented a significant step in the historical struggle for civil rights by Blacks, and provided the foundation for building an effective remedy for those suffering from harmful institutional practices.

Roosevelt's FEPC marked the beginning of presidential executive orders designed to end discrimination in employment, but, as Table 3.1 shows, it had a short life. In 1943 Roosevelt re-constituted the Committee and broadened its powers to include all government contracts and union membership. The FEPC remained in existence until 1946. When returning veterans reclaimed their jobs, pre-war practices of race and sex discrimination once again became the prevalent norm. The federal contractor monitoring agency reported that the wartime gains of Black, Mexican American, and Jewish workers were receding due to an "unchecked revival of discriminatory practices" (Fair Employment Practice Committee, 1947, p. 5).

Post-War

The Truman administration was active in its efforts to end discrimination in employment. In 1948 Truman called upon Congress to set up a permanent FEPC to prevent discrimination in employment. Congress, not known for its alacrity, delayed in responding thereby causing Truman to bypass the legislative branch. In 1948 Truman issued Executive Order 9980 that established a Fair Employment Board within the Civil Service Commission. Later, he initiated a series of executive orders designed to put an end to all discrimination in federal employment and segregation in the armed forces.

The Truman initiatives died with the change in administration in January 1953. Eisenhower favored the use of "advisory" bodies. Responsibility for monitoring complaints and assuring compliance shifted to the contracting agencies. These were dormant years for federal initiatives in nondiscriminatory employment practices. In January, 1953 the FEPC's successor, the President's Committee on Government Contract compliance, reported:

> The Committee...found the nondiscrimination provision [in Government contracts] almost forgotten, dead and buried under thousands of words of standard legal and technical language in Government procurement contracts (President's Committee on Government Contract compliance, 1953, p. 3).

Renewed interest in equal employment opportunities during the Kennedy-Johnson years resulted in compliance responsibilities being brought back to the federal government. John F. Kennedy spoke more boldly and forthrightly on civil rights than any president before him. He pronounced segregation as morally wrong, and his executive orders reflected his position. The democratic government called on contractors to take special actions to overcome discrimination based on race, creed, color, or national origin.

Further Developments

The individual most committed to affirmative action was probably Lyndon Johnson. In 1961, when he was still Vice President, Johnson convened a meeting of the presidents of the 50 largest government contractors and signed up most of them in a program to promote equal opportunity called "Plans for Progress." It was a program of voluntary effort for equal employment opportunity. Although attempts were made to expand the membership in the program to noncontractors as well, the membership remained predominantly government contractors. Within a short time, it became clear that voluntary efforts to provide equal employment opportunities lacked the impact of mandated programs of affirmative action (Equal Employment Opportunity Commission, 1968).

Increasingly Johnson embraced the need for vigorous measures to correct the country's legacy of discrimination. In the Spring of 1965, he delivered the famed address at the commencement ceremonies of Howard University. "Is it reasonable," asked Johnson, "to start a race between two runners, one of whose legs are shackled at the beginning of the race and unshackled halfway into the contest and declare a fair ending without adjusting for the handicap?"

Johnson answered his own rhetorical question, in deed as well as word, on September 24, 1965, when he signed Executive Order 11246. This was the order that introduced into American law the phrase "affirmative action." It obligated federal contractors to "take affirmative action" and "apply every good faith effort" toward "a set of specific and result-oriented procedures" aimed at assuring true equality in employment (Holloway, Chapter 2).

Presidents since Johnson have continued to issue Executive Orders. As Table 3.1 shows, no president has failed to make a legal statement about affirmative action, but not all orders have the aim of strengthening the federal regulation of non-discriminatory practices. President Reagan, in particular, has sought to make compliance with affirmative action more voluntary than mandatory.

Effectiveness

Differences in presidential support for affirmative action may spring, in part, from differential assessments of the effectiveness of affirmative action as a deterrent to discrimination. There has been a great deal of debate over the efficacy and effectiveness of affirmative action. Documentation is scarce.

The documentation that does exist clearly indicates the positive value of affirmative action. In 1981, the Director of the Office of Federal Contract Compliance Programs (OFCCP) conducted a rather comprehensive study of the issues (Department of Labor, 1984). The study's objective was to determine whether the impact of the Federal Contract Compliance Program could be measured; that is, whether there was any significant difference between the employment and advancement of minorities and women in the work forces of federal contractors and subcontractors and those of employers not covered by the Federal Compliance Program, and if so, whether the difference was attributable to the compliance program.

The study's basic hypothesis was that if the compliance program is effective, federal contractor establishments as a group should, over a period of time, show higher performance in employment and advancement of minorities and women than noncontractor establishments. Further, reviewed establishments as a group might be expected to exceed the accomplishments of unreviewed establishments. Thus, the performance of federal contractors subject to the compliance program was compared to that of non-contractors for the period 1974-1980. This particular period was chosen because it utilized the most reliable current data and coincided with the period of implementation of the requirement of written

Table 3.1

Use of Presidential Executive Orders to End Discrimination in Employment: Roosevelt to Johnson

Order	Year	Agency	Purpose
Roosevelt			
8802	1941	Fair Employment Practices Com	To eliminate discrimination in defense contracts and federal employment & training programs.
9346	1943	Fair Employment Practices Com	Broadened to include all federal contractors and unions.
Truman			
9980	1948	Fair Employment Board (CSC)	To monitor department heads & investigate complaints of discrimination.
9981	1948		To end segregation in the military.
10227	1948	Government Services Adm	Select government agencies instructed to incorporate nondiscriminatory clauses in their procurement contracts.
10231	1951	Tennessee Valley Authority	
10243	1951	Civil Defense Adm	
10281	1951	Materials Procurement Agency	
10298	1951	Department of Interior	
10308	1951	Com on Government Contract Compliance	To assess the effectiveness of nondiscriminatory clauses.
Eisenhower			
10479	1953	Government Contract Com	Advisory and consultative only.
10482	1953	Government Contract Com	To increase size of committee.
10557	1954	Government Contract Com	To assess effectiveness of nondiscriminatory employment provisions.
10590	1954	Com on Government Employment Policy	Advisory to department heads.
Kennedy			
10925	1961	Com on Equal Employment Opportunity	To conduct compliance reviews and impose sanctions where warranted.
11114	1963	Com on Equal Employment Opportunity	Extended to cover employment on federally financed construction projects.
Johnson			
11246	1965	Com on Equal Employment Opportunity/Office of Fed Contract Compliance	Extended sanctions to contractors and subcontractors with contracts over $10,000.
11375	1967	Com on Equal Employment Opportunity	Extended sanctions to contract departments.

Note. Com is Committee; Adm is Administration; Fed is Federal; CSC is Civil Service Commission.

Table 3.1 (continued)

Use of Presidential Executive Orders to End Discrimination in Employment: Nixon to Reagan

Order	Year	Agency	Purpose
Nixon			
11478	1969	Civil Service Commission	States policy of administration continuing federal commitment to equal opportunity. Assuring E.E.O. in a federal department or agency. Directed chairman of CSC to review present efforts in government.
11598	1969	Veterans Adm	Providing for the listing of certain job vacancies by federal agencies, government contractors, and subcontractors to aid veterans seeking employment.
Ford			
11914	1976		Nondiscrimination with respect to handicapped in federal assisted programs.
Carter			
11979	1977		National Commission on the observance of international Women's Year. Organize & convene a National Women's Conference. Appointment of members and presiding officer of the commission (Bella Abzug).
12067	1978	Com on Equal Opportunity	Providing for coordination of Fed Equal Employment Opportunity Programs.
12086	1978		Consolidation of contract compliance functions for Equal Employment Opportunity and functions reassigned to Secretary of Labor from Departments of Defense, Treasury, and Interior.
12106	1978	Civil Service Commission	Transfer of certain equal employment enforcement functions to the Civil Service Commission.
12114	1979	Com on Equal Employment Opportunity	Transfer of certain equal pay and age discrimination in employment enforcement functions.
12125	1979		Competitive status for handicapped federal employees. Permits severely physically handicapped & mentally retarded individuals to obtain civil service competitive status. Amends Civil Service Rule 3.1.
Reagan			
12432	1983		Encouraged, not pressured or compelled, grantees to utilize minority businesses.

Note. Com is Committee; Adm is Administration; Fed is Federal; CSC is Civil Service Commission.

affirmative action programs, which began in 1971, and implementation of compliance activity regarding equal opportunity for women, which began in 1972. Only those establishments which filed reports both in 1974 and 1980 were selected for the study. A total of 77,098 establishments (excluding institutions of higher learning) met this criterion -- 48,981 were federal contractor establishments and 28,117 were noncontractor establishments.

As Table 3.2 shows, in the federal contractor's workforce minority participation increased 20.1 percent while total employment increased only 3.0 percent in those same establishments. Total employment in noncontractors' workforces went up by 8.2 percent, but registered only a 12.3 percent gain for minorities. In the same table, it can be seen that women's participation in the contractors' workforces grew by 15.2 percent, as opposed to 2.2 percent in the noncontractors' workforces.

Table 3.2

Percentage Increase in Employment of Minorities, Women, and Total Workforce for Federal Contractor and Noncontractor Establishments from 1974-1980

Category	Federal Contractors	Non-Contractors
Minorities	20.1	12.3
Women	15.2	2.2
Total Workforce	3.0	8.2

Note. Federal contractors were subject to affirmative action; other establishments were not (Department of Labor, 1984).

In addition to documenting the rising levels of employment of minorities and women, the study shows significant changes in the more complex area of distribution of minorities and women within the workforces compared. The distribution of minorities and women in all establishments has shifted slightly from service worker and lower-skilled blue-collar to white-collar and higher-skilled, blue-collar jobs. The shift has been demonstrably greater among the federal contractors than among other firms.

Conclusions

Given the demonstrated effectiveness of affirmative action as an instrument of social justice, it is distressing to note the uneven support of affirmative action by the executive branch. Conservatives wrap their opposition to affirmative action policies in phrases such as "counting by race is a form of racism," and more than one administration has used this and similar arguments to explain an anti-affirmative action stance. Other administrations, in contrast, have developed and justified affirmative action by noting that the imbalances in our society have continued, do continue, and will continue unless positive steps are taken. In the words of Justice Harry Blackmun: "In order to get beyond racism, we must first take account of race. There is no other way. And in order to treat some persons equally, we must treat them differently" (438 U.S. 407, 1978).

References

Bennett, L., Jr. (1966). *Before the Mayflower: A history of the Negro in America 1619-1964*. Baltimore, MD: Penguin Books.

Department of Labor, Office of Federal Contract Compliance. (1984). *Employment patterns of minorities in federal contractor and noncontractor establishments 1974-1980*. Washington, D.C.: Office of Federal Contract Compliance.

Equal Employment Opportunity Commission. (1968). *Second annual report of the EEOC*. Washington, D.C.: Office of Federal Contract Compliance.

Fair Employment Practice Committee. (1947). *Final report- Fair employment practice committee*. Washington, D.C.: U.S. Government Printing Office.

Holloway, F. A. (1989). What is affirmative action? In F. A. Blanchard & F. J. Crosby (Eds.), *Affirmative Action in Perspective* (pp. 9-19). New York: Springer-Verlag.

President's Committee on Government Contract Compliance. (1953). *Equal economic opportunity - A report by the President's Committee on Government Contract Compliance*. Washington, D.C.: Government Printing Office.

Regents of the University of California v. Bakke, 438 U.S. 407 (1978).

4
Affirmative Action and the Courts

Jim D. Newman

While many feel that affirmative action is necessary to correct centuries of discrimination against women and minorities in the labor force, others believe it is simply discrimination in reverse. The conflicting opinions that exist throughout American society on this issue are mirrored in the decisions of the courts. The federal courts have rendered seemingly contradictory rulings in this area, and many lower court decisions have been reversed by the U. S. Courts of Appeals and the U. S. Supreme Court. The Justices of the Supreme Court have displayed a noticeable lack of unity on questions of affirmative action.

The legal uncertainties surrounding affirmative action put employers in an uncomfortable bind. If employers fail to adopt an affirmative action program, they are subject to attack from women and minority employees. If governmental employers and those who accept government contracts fail to adopt and enforce affirmative action programs, they may be sued by affected employees, the Equal Employment Opportunity Commission, or the Office of Federal Contract Compliance Programs. Yet, employers also need to ensure that their programs do not subject them to liability for reverse discrimination.

How the Supreme Court has ruled on questions of affirmative action is the subject of this chapter. The chapter first reviews basics, setting out the legal definition of affirmative action and outlining how cases reach the Supreme Court. It then summarizes the landmark cases decided by the Supreme Court since 1978. The chapter concludes by discussing three important characteristics of affirmative action programs which emerge in those cases where an employer succeeds in defending challenges against its affirmative action programs.

Basics

Affirmative Action Defined

Most people recognize that affirmative action has both a broad, general meaning and a narrow, legal meaning. For the purposes of this discussion, affirmative action is defined as any race- or sex-conscious employment practices devised with the intention of redressing past racial or gender imbalances and injustices. Affirmative action programs may include preferential treatment to members of a targeted class of people.

The direct and specific beneficiaries of affirmative action need not have been the actual victims of past discrimination in the specific context in which they now benefit. For example, an affirmative action plan may provide that an employer hire a certain percentage of new minority employees on a certain timetable. While the employer may have discriminated against, say, Blacks in the past, new Black hires who had never before applied for a job with the employer need not have been personally the victims of the employer's past discriminatory practices in order to benefit.

The Legal System

The United States has both a federal legal system and state legal systems. Equal employment opportunity is a subject in which both the state and federal governments are involved. States and local governments may enact and enforce anti-discrimination statutes with broader coverage than that provided for by federal law; they may not, however, permit discrimination prohibited by federal law. The U.S. Constitution provides that where federal and state laws conflict, the federal law prevails.

Only certain litigants may bring cases in federal court. Federal courts may consider only those issues which they are authorized, either by federal statute or the Constitution, to hear. Cases concerning employment discrimination and affirmative action may be brought in federal court because such cases concern either the U.S. Constitution or federal anti-discrimination statutes such as Title VII of the Civil Rights Act of 1964 (42 U.S.C. Section 2000e et seq.) or the Age Discrimination in Employment Act (29 U.S.C. Section 621 et seq., 1967).

The federal court system has three levels. At the first level are the district courts. They are trial courts in which single judges preside, sometimes with juries serving as factfinders. At the intermediate level are the Courts of Appeals, arranged into twelve geographical circuits. Most litigants in federal district court have a right to have their cases reviewed on the record by a three judge panel from the appropriate regional United States Circuit Court of Appeals. There is also one circuit court, known as the Federal Circuit, that has exclusive jurisdiction to hear appeals in certain subject matters.

Further review may be obtained before the United States Supreme Court. In most cases the parties can only obtain review by the Supreme Court when the Court grants a petition to hear the case. The Supreme Court accepts only a small percentage of cases in which such a petition is filed. Certain cases may also reach the Supreme Court directly on appeal from the highest court of any state. Every decision by every federal court sets a precedent for some future court or courts, but not all decisions have equal legal significance. Decisions by the Supreme Court bind all federal courts and are, therefore, inherently more significant than decisions by any lower court.

Previous decisions of a court in one district are binding upon courts in that district, as are existing decisions of the reviewing Circuit Court of Appeals and the Supreme Court. Decisions of courts from other federal districts or circuits are not binding and need not be followed. This sometimes leads to different judicial interpretations in different parts of the country. When different Courts of Appeal have contradictory rulings on the same topic, the Supreme Court is more likely to accept review to resolve the disagreement among the circuits than when the Courts of Appeal show no disagreement.

In reality, there are often conflicting decisions within the same district or circuit. Courts and lawyers must attempt to distinguish those cases. Lawyers attempt to analogize their case to favorable precedents and to distinguish it from adverse precedents. Courts, in deciding cases, do the same thing. When it is not possible to distinguish from adverse precedent, but the court feels the precedent is wrong, a court may overrule its previous decision. A classic example is the Supreme Court's decision in *Brown v. Board of Education* (1954) in which the court overruled the longstanding precedent of *Plessy v. Ferguson* (1896). The earlier decision held that separate but equal facilities for different races did not violate the equal protection clause of the Fourteenth Amendment, whereas, in *Brown* the Supreme Court held that racially segregated facilities are inherently unequal.

Just as courts may overturn their own precedent, appellate courts may overturn district court decisions interpreting the Constitution and statutes. Because each court case usually focuses upon just a few issues, it often takes years or decades before a clear body of precedent is established in emerging or changing areas of the law such as affirmative action. Once established, however, this body of law enables organizations and individuals to conduct their affairs with some degree of certainty.

Judicial Decision-making

Most controversial lawsuits which reach the Supreme Court do not result in unanimous decisions by the nine Justices who sit on the Court. In most cases the Court issues both a majority opinion and a dissenting opinion. Often individual Justices prepare separate opinions concurring in the outcome of the case, but presenting different legal rationale for the same conclusion. In unusual circumstances there may be several dissenting and concurring opinions. In the area of affirmative action, multiple dissenting and concurring opinions seem to be the rule rather than the exception. This undermines the value of the decisions as clear precedent for future cases.

In *Wygant v. Jackson Board of Education* (1986), for example, which restricted the scope of affirmative action, Justice Powell wrote a plurality decision in which he was joined by former Chief Justice Burger, Justice Rehnquist, and, only in parts, by Justice O'Connor. Justices O'Connor and White wrote separate concurring opinions. Justice Marshall wrote a dissent in which he was joined by Justices Brennan and Blackmun, and Justice Stevens wrote a separate dissenting opinion. Similarly, in the case of *Johnson v. Transportation Agency* (1987) which expanded the scope of affirmative action, six Justices voted to affirm the lower court's decision, but there were two separate concurring and two separate dissenting opinions.

B. Schlei and P. Grossman comment in the second edition of their classic textbook, *Employment Discrimination Law* (1983) upon the divisiveness that affirmative action has produced among the Justices of the Supreme Court. They note that the trilogy of cases decided by the Court between 1978 and 1980 (*Bakke, Weber,* and *Fullilove*) constituted 15 separate opinions and that the Court's decision attracted as many as five signatures only in the *Weber* case.

Significant Cases

In the late 1970s, the famous *Bakke* case first brought into national consciousness the idea that affirmative action policies might be nothing more than reverse discrimination. In this section I review briefly the *Bakke* case and eight subsequent affirmative action cases. With the exception of the *Bakke* case, all of the cases concern affirmative action in the employment context. Most of the decisions apply by analogy to educational issues such as admissions and evaluations. Inspection of the cases suggests that three issues prominently affect the decisions. These are the remedial character of the programs, their duration, and consideration of those not benefited.

Regents of the University of California v. Bakke, 438 U.S. 265 (1978)

The first significant case in which the Supreme Court squarely addressed affirmative action was the *Bakke* decision (1978). The case reached the United States Supreme Court on appeal from a decision of the California Supreme Court. The plaintiff, a White male, had been denied admission to the medical school at the University of California at Davis. The school had a special admissions program in which a prescribed number of positions were set aside for minority candidates. The plaintiff claimed he was more qualified than some of the minority candidates selected under the special admissions program and that the set-aside prevented his admission by restricting the number of positions available to White applicants. The California Supreme Court found the admissions program to violate the Fourteenth Amendment and directed the plaintiff to be admitted. The California Court also enjoined the school from according any consideration to race in its admission process.

Opinion among the nine Justices on the United States Supreme Court was sharply divided. In several separate written opinions, four Justices voted to affirm and four voted to reverse. Justice Powell voted to affirm the first holding but to overturn the second. His opinion created a different majority for each issue and became the official opinion of the Court.

Therefore, the Court held in *Bakke* that while race could be considered as a factor in admission, it could not be used as a quota to set aside specific positions for minority candidates. Race could be considered as a "plus" factor along with other factors deemed important because in that manner no applicants would be excluded from consideration solely because of their race.

United Steelworkers of America v. Weber, 443 U.S. 193 (1979)

The year following the *Bakke* decision, the Court issued its decision in the *Weber* case. Plaintiff Weber, a White employee had sued his Union, alleging that a collective bargaining agreement with his employer containing an affirmative action plan violated his rights under Title VII. The plan was designed to eliminate conspicuous racial imbalances in the employer's skilled craft workforce. The agreement established a training program for unskilled workers but provided that for every two vacancies in the program one White and one Black would be selected even though Blacks with less seniority were accepted into the training program.

At the time of the agreement, the percentage of skilled workers who were Black was less than 2% even though the local workforce was 39% Black. The employer was under pressure from the Department of Labor's Office of Federal Contract Compliance Programs to increase Black representation among its skilled workforce. The agreement provided that the 50% selection rate was to be maintained until the percentage of Blacks in the skilled trade positions approximated the 39% in the local workforce.

The district court and the Fifth Circuit had found the agreement to be unlawful. The Supreme Court reversed, finding that Title VII did not prohibit the affirmative action plan before it. While the Court did not define the permissible limits of affirmative action plans, it did comment favorably on the temporary duration of the plan, its remedial purpose, its voluntary nature, and the fact that it did not unnecessarily trammel the interests of White workers.

The decision is difficult to reconcile with the decision in *Bakke* and the supposedly distinguishable factor discussed by the Court -- that *Weber* arose under Title VII rather than the Constitution -- has, in more recent cases, been viewed as a meaningless distinction. *Weber* received considerable criticism from legal commentators, but has not been overruled by the Supreme Court and has been followed by the lower federal courts.

Firefighters Local 1784 v. Stotts, 467 U.S. 561 (1984)

The Court took a notable turn in direction in 1984 when it issued its decision in the *Stotts* case. The case arose after a federal district court in Memphis modified a consent decree which contained minority hiring goals by adding provisions to protect against layoffs of minority workers. This overrode a *bona fide* layoff plan which had been negotiated between the city and the Firefighters' Union. *Stotts* held that in so doing, the district court in Memphis had exceeded its powers.

The layoff plan provided that the last hired would be the first fired. Plaintiff Stotts and others petitioned the district court for an injunction to prevent the city from implementing the plan. The plaintiffs argued that the layoffs would reverse all the employment advances achieved by Blacks as a result of a prior consent decree which had required the city to hire and promote greater percentages of Blacks.

The consent decree had provided goals for hiring and promotion of minorities, but was silent concerning layoffs. The district court had granted the injunction, reasoning that it had the authority to modify the consent decree. The Supreme Court disagreed, finding no authority in either the original agreement itself or the inherent powers of the court to justify setting aside the seniority system. The Court felt that the remedy granted went beyond that which could have been awarded had the original case gone to trial and discrimination been found. The Court referred to the Congressional intent behind Title VII "to provide make-whole relief only to those who have been actual victims of illegal discrimination."

The Sixth Circuit Court of Appeals had upheld the injunction on the basis that the court had merely ordered that which the City could have accomplished by adopting an affirmative action program. The Supreme Court, in reversing the Sixth Circuit, refused to decide whether or not the employer could have adopted such an affirmative action plan without violating the law, leaving the question open for future cases.

Wygant V. Jackson Board of Education, 476 U.S. 267 (1986)

Two years later the Supreme Court addressed the question left open in *Stotts*, of whether a voluntary layoff plan which granted preference to minorities could be enforced. The suit in *Wygant* had been filed by White teachers who were laid off pursuant to a Collective Bargaining Agreement which provided that minority layoffs would not exceed the percentage of minority personnel employed at the time layoffs began.

The Court held that the actions of the Board of Education in overriding the seniority of the White teachers violated the equal protection clause of the Fourteenth Amendment. The affirmative action plan had not been implemented after a finding of discrimination, but rather was designed to overcome societal discrimination and ensure that minority teachers remained in the workforce to provide role models for minority students. According to the Court, the state had not articulated a compelling state interest which would justify unequal treatment towards teachers on the basis of race and that, in any event, the remedy was not narrowly tailored to address the state's interest. The Court found that the plan was not narrowly tailored because layoffs are more disruptive of competing interests than are hiring goals. Justice Marshall dissented, writing that the provisions of the Union contract, "forged in the crucible of clashing interests" were the most equitable and narrowly tailored process possible.

Justice O'Connor concurred in the judgment but wrote separately to affirm her belief that "narrowly tailored" affirmative action is permissible even without a finding of past discrimination if there is a sufficient statistical evidence of underrepresentation in the workforce. In the present case she felt the statistical focus had been misdirected because the School Board had adopted the plan to correct the imbalance in the ratio of minority teachers without proper analyses of the qualified applicant pool.

Local No. 28 Sheetmetal Workers v. EEOC, 478 U.S. 421 (1986)

In the *Sheetmetal Workers* case the Court upheld the imposition of affirmative action measures by the district court as a legitimate exercise of its civil contempt powers. In 1975 the district court had found that the almost exclusively White trade union discriminated against minorities in violation of Title VII. In 1982 and 1983 the court found the union to be in contempt because the percentage of Blacks in the skilled trade crafts remained minuscule. The district court then issued an order establishing a minority hiring goal of 29.23% by 1983 and establishing a fund to pay for the training of the minority hires. The Supreme Court found that the pervasive past history of discrimination permitted the ordered relief. The Court found the relief necessary because less restrictive alternatives had proven inadequate and the temporary measures were goals, rather than strict quotas.

Justice O'Connor concurred that Title VII permits affirmative action, but felt that the remedy in this case was a prohibited quota. Justice Rehnquist dissented because he believed Title VII prohibits a court from granting relief to individuals who are not proven victims of discrimination.

Local No. 93 Firefighters v. Cleveland, 478 U.S. 501 (1986)

In the *Firefighters* case, the Court upheld a consent decree between the city of Cleveland and a group of minority firefighters which provided for temporary racial goals in filling promotions. The general membership of the Firefighters Union voted against the agreement, but it was enacted over their objection. The consent decree required the promotion of Black and Hispanic firefighters to higher ranking positions. However, the goal was to be accomplished by filling a greater number of positions than originally planned. Furthermore, only those minority employees who met the qualifications for the position could be promoted.

The Court found that the promotion plan was permissible even though it benefited non-victims. It held that Title VII is not a bar to private, voluntary, race-conscious efforts to abolish discrimination and suggested that any limits which might apply to a court's power to unilaterally remedy past discrimination by awarding benefits to non-victims, would not apply to voluntary agreements.

The Court distinguished its decision in the *Firefighters* case from *Stotts* because *Stotts* involved layoffs rather than promotions. The plan in this case provided for the promotion of minorities who would not have been promoted in its absence because their test scores were lower than the White employees'. However, no one was promoted who was not qualified and none of the White employees who would have received promotions at that time was denied promotion. Justice Rehnquist dissented arguing that the consent decree in this case could not be distinguished from the modification which was prohibited in *Stotts*.

United States v. Paradise, 480 U.S. 149 (1987)

In *Paradise,* the Court reaffirmed that affirmative action relief may be imposed to remedy judicial findings of past discrimination even though the relief benefits non-victims. The case arose from a suit filed by the National Association for the Advancement of Colored People (NAACP) against the State of Alabama Department of Public Safety. The plaintiffs established a pattern and practice of blatant and pervasive discrimination by the Department. The district court issued an order requiring the Department to hire one Black trooper for each White trooper hired until Blacks constituted approximately 25% of the state trooper force.

After a protracted history of non-compliance and further litigation, the Court issued an order concerning promotions within the Department: For a nonspecific "limited period of time" at least 50% of the promotions to corporal had to be awarded to Black troopers, if qualified Black candidates were available.

The Reagan Administration challenged the order, claiming it violated the Equal Protection Clause of the Fourteenth Amendment. The Court found, however, that the relief was narrowly tailored to serve a compelling interest. It upheld the promotion goal as flexible and temporary, noting that no layoffs were required and that only qualified Blacks could be promoted. Justices O'Connor, Rehnquist, and Scalia dissented on the basis that the district court had imposed a promotion quota without consideration of available alternatives.

Johnson v. Transportation Agency, 480 U.S. 616 (1987)

The Court's decision in the *Johnson* case provides considerable guidance to employers seeking to fashion a permissible affirmative action plan. Plaintiff Johnson, a White male, sued his employer, the Santa Clara County Transportation Agency, after he was not selected for a promotion to road dispatcher. The plaintiff alleged reverse sex discrimination because the employer selected a woman who, the plaintiff argued, was less qualified.

The selection involved a screening process which included interviews and numerical ranking of the candidates. The applicable civil service rules permitted the selecting official to pick any of seven qualified candidates. Plaintiff Johnson received the recommendation of the interview panel, but the employer's Affirmative Action Officer recommended that a woman be selected. Considering all relevant factors, including affirmative action goals as well as the candidates' experience and other qualifications, the agency director selected the female candidate.

The district court found that the employer had discriminated against the plaintiff. The Ninth Circuit Court of Appeals reversed, and the Supreme Court affirmed the Court of Appeals. The Court held that the existence of a valid affirmative action plan provided a nondiscriminatory rationale for taking gender into account in promotion decisions. The Court then analyzed the validity of the Santa Clara plan.

First the Court held that a prior finding of discrimination was not necessary so long as there was a manifest imbalance in traditionally segregated job categories. While women comprised approximately 36% of the area labor market, only 22% of the employees at the Transportation Agency were women. Furthermore, most of the women occupied clerical jobs traditionally held by women. Less than 10% of the administrative, professional and technical positions were held by women and in the applicable job category -- skilled craft workers -- women occupied none of the 238 positions prior to the challenged selection. Nevertheless, the Court favorably commented upon the fact that the Santa Clara plan before it did not rely solely upon general population statistics in determining underrepresentation, but looked to the pool of candidates with the necessary qualifications.

The Court then held that the plan did not unnecessarily trammel the rights of male employees, noting that the plaintiff had no absolute entitlement to the promotion, had retained his salary and seniority, and remained eligible for other promotions. Finally, the Court found that the plan was temporary even though it had no specific end date, because it was directed towards gradually attaining a racial and sexual balance, rather than permanently maintaining one. The Court pointed out that specific deadlines may be required where a plan sets aside positions in fixed numbers or percentages, as in the *Firefighters* case. The Court also pointed out that because Congress had not amended Title VII after the *Weber* decision, its interpretation could be presumed correct.

Justice O'Connor concurred in a separate opinion. She criticized the majority for following an "ill-defined approach to voluntary affirmative action" and the dissent for failing to address the reality of the Court's precedents upholding affirmative action. Specifically, she argued for a more precise measure of manifest imbalance: that used to establish a *prima facie* case of discrimination. She also reaffirmed her belief that affirmative action may be used as a plus factor but that blind quotas are impermissible.

Justice Scalia wrote a well-considered dissent which challenged the basic tenets of affirmative action. After reciting the language of Title VII he wrote "The Court today completes the process of converting this from a guarantee that race or sex will *not* be the basis for employment determinations, to a guarantee that it often *will*." His opinion provides persuasive argument for why affirmative action may be unfair, but as Justice O'Connor points out, in so doing provides no guidance for employers who accept the need for affirmative action and wish to implement a program which is legal and as fair as possible to employees.

Martin v. Wilks, ___ U.S. ___, 108 S. Ct. 2843 (Cert. granted June 20, 1988)

Recently the Court agreed to review the standing of White employees affected by a consent decree to later challenge the consent degree in a collateral proceeding. In this group of cases, several White plaintiffs filed lawsuits against their employer alleging that actions taken by the employer in accordance with the terms of a consent degree constituted reverse discrimination. The plaintiffs in these cases were not parties to the original suit in which the consent decree was entered, but they had been notified and given an opportunity to intervene before the entry of the decree. The Court of Appeals for the Eleventh Circuit held that the White employees are permitted to bring a separate action.

The issue before the Supreme Court is a question of legal procedure. However, if the Court affirms the Eleventh Circuit's holding, it may have a significant impact: If employers know that they can be subjected to reverse discrimination suits at any time, they will be discouraged from providing affirmative action relief in settlement of discrimination suits. Although previous cases have held that the law permits employers to voluntarily provide relief to non-victims, employers may no longer be willing to do so.

Characteristics of Defensible Affirmative Action Programs

The review of specific cases makes clear that affirmative action precedents have been evolving rapidly. At first glance, the Court appears almost fickle. What may be less immediately evident is the fact that courts tend to look with favor on some types of affirmative action programs and not on others. More specifically, three characteristics affect the vulnerability of affirmative action program.

Remedial in Nature

The courts have long recognized their inherent authority to order preferential treatment for identified victims of past discrimination as a remedy to violations of the victims' civil rights. Discrimination can be argued in two ways: disparate treatment and disparate impact. In order to prove disparate treatment, an employee must prove, either directly or by inference, that the employer intended to discriminate. To argue disparate impact, in contrast, the plaintiff need not show an intent to discriminate. It is sufficient to show that an employee has been adversely affected by seemingly neutral employment practices (e.g., tests of physical strength that are irrelevant to the work and that exclude women).

Whether disparate treatment or disparate impact forms the basis of the argument, a case concerning employment discrimination requires that the plaintiff prove that he or she was personally discriminated against. This is true even for a class action lawsuit. In a class action discrimination case, for example, an employer can escape liability with respect to any plaintiff by demonstrating that even if others in the class were discriminated against, that specific plaintiff was not.

In affirmative action, by contrast there is no burden to show that the beneficiaries of the program were themselves personally discriminated against. The underlying premise to affirmative action is that, absent some form of discrimination, individual or systemic, gross disparities in workforce representation would not exist. In some instances, it may be possible to prove that an employer's discriminatory practices have had an adverse impact on the protected minority groups. However, even where employment practices cannot be proven discriminatory, it may be proper to infer discrimination to be the cause of gross statistical disparities. If it is not possible to determine the victims, such as when the discrimination is systemic rather than specific to individual employees, then a remedy may be fashioned to benefit the entire class.

For example, in many organizations where women are employed in proportion to their general workforce population there is a significant underrepresentation of women in the upper ranks of management. While it may be reasonable to infer this to be the result of past discriminatory practices, it remains impossible to determine which women in the organization would have risen to the top, absent any discrimination.

Of course, there are many factors other than discrimination which may result in statistical disparities in workforce representation. The courts are generally unwilling to uphold affirmative action plans that seek to establish a workforce which mirrors the general population but does not take outside factors into consideration. In *Wygant*, the Court stated that "societal discrimination, without more, is too amorphous a basis for imposing a racially classified remedy" (476 U.S. 267 at 276, 1986).

In determining whether an affirmative action plan is remedial in nature, the courts will look to the cause and the scope of any statistical disparities which the plan seeks to correct. Not surprisingly, the situation in which courts will most likely find a plan to be remedial in nature is when the plan has been adopted after a previous judicial finding of discrimination. Similarly, courts will uphold plans premised upon an administrative finding of discrimination by an outside agency or the organization itself.

However, for fear of liability and other obvious reasons, few employers are willing to admit past discrimination even though they may be willing to undertake remedial affirmative action. Thus, the courts are willing to imply an administrative "finding" by virtue of the employer's adoption of a plan when there is a significant statistical disparity in the employer's workforce population. Under such circumstances, as in the *Johnson* case, a plan may be found to be remedial even though there has been no previous finding of discrimination.

The statistical disparity in *Johnson* was glaring, notwithstanding the dissenter's observation that most women themselves would not view road maintenance work as desirable. Future cases will decide the specific level of statistical disparity sufficient to support a determination that a plan is remedial in nature.

Limited in Duration

Courts are more likely to uphold temporary measures which result in preferential treatment than long-term plans. The limited duration of the challenged plan has been favorably cited as a basis for affirmance of the plan by the Court in a number of cases (e.g., *Weber, Johnson*). This is consistent with the holding discussed above that affirmative action plans must be remedial in nature. Ironically, in some cases it may conflict with the holding discussed below that such plans may not unnecessarily trammel the interests of other employees. For instance, a plan that seeks to promote Blacks more rapidly than Whites but which is limited to a short time period may result in greater immediate loss of job opportunities for qualified Whites than a similar plan which is more gradual, and as a consequence, longer in duration.

The requirement that a plan have a limited duration is based upon the theory that the purpose of affirmative action is to attain a balanced workforce rather than to maintain one. However, the duration of the plan need not be for a fixed period of time. Courts will uphold plans that are self-canceling in nature. In some cases, the courts will uphold a plan by implying a condition of limited duration to be a part of the plan.

Consideration of the Rights of Those not Benefited

The factor of greatest concern to the courts is the extent to which affirmative action adversely affects the rights and interests of non-benefited employees. The additional job opportunities created for women and minorities by affirmative action will necessarily reduce some employment opportunities for those in the majority. However, the method by which this transfer of opportunity is accomplished is crucial to whether an affirmative action plan will survive legal attack.

The decisions of the Supreme Court make it clear that affirmative action that unnecessarily trammels the rights of non-benefited employees will be struck down. To determine whether the rights of non-benefited employees have been trammeled, they must also determine what rights those employees legitimately hold. The rights employees hold in their positions vary widely, depending upon such diverse factors as whether the position is in the public or private sector; whether the workforce is unionized; and any state laws concerning at-will employment. In legal parlance, the focus of the inquiry is on whether the displaced rights or opportunities of the majority employees are vested as opposed to contingent rights. The more vested the majority employees' rights are, the more likely a court will overturn the affirmative action. In lay terms, two principles can be articulated.

The first principle is that employees have more of a right to keep their present jobs than to gain new jobs. While the courts may permit preferential hiring and promotion plans, they universally reject plans which grant similar preferences in layoff situations. The distinction is straightforward.

The second principle is that while employees have the right to expect reasonable opportunities for advancement, the general expectation of promotion is not the same as the expectation of promotion to one or another specific job. For this reason, the courts do not uphold affirmative action plans that impose an absolute bar to the advancement of non-benefited employees, but have held that consideration of race or sex as a "plus factor" is permissible.

Whether the consideration of race or sex operates as a plus factor or as a bar depends largely upon the selection process utilized by the employer. In the *Johnson* case, the challenged promotion was made pursuant to a civil service system which permitted the selecting official to pick from a number of qualified candidates. The Court held that it was permissible to consider the candidates' sex among the other criteria such as education and experience.

However, many employers do not utilize selection procedures which permit discretion in choosing among qualified applicants. For example, some civil service systems utilize selection procedures which require the candidate receiving the highest score in an examination process to be selected. Similarly, many private employers have negotiated labor agreements which require advancement to be based absolutely upon factors such as seniority. Employers operating under such selection systems have sometimes adopted affirmative action plans which establish a separate pool of minority candidates and set aside a number of positions to be filled separately from the minority pool. This type of program is analogous to the admissions procedure struck down in *Bakke,* and is unlikely to withstand legal challenge.

As a general rule, the more rigid the selection system, the less likely it will be found reasonable to take race or sex into account in the selection process. However, for other reasons, it is desirable that employers adopt selection systems that are as objective as possible. One possible way to incorporate affirmative action goals into rigid selection systems may be to grant examination or experience credits based upon race or sex, similar to the preference granted to veterans in the federal civil service. That preference system gives "bonus points" to candidates with veteran's status and requires employers to document and explain their reasons if they choose to bypass veterans in favor of non-veteran candidates eligible for selection but with a lower adjusted score. A similar combination of "bonus points" and bypass protection for minorities might obviate the need to set aside positions for minorities.

Where specific positions are set aside for women or minorities, they are not available to others and the policy will impose a total bar to those vacancies. Such set-asides have often been viewed by the courts as prohibited blind quotas. The use of the term quota by the courts has not been consistent and has created considerable confusion. In the *Sheetmetal Workers* case, for instance, the Court upheld a hiring goal of 29.23% prompting the question: If 29.23% isn't a quota, what is (Newsweek, 1986)? The answer lies not in the precision of the numerical goal set, but in the method by which the goal is to be achieved. Where positions are merely targeted for minorities but may be filled by majority employees if insufficient minority candidates are qualified and available, the program is more likely to survive judicial scrutiny. So long as opportunities for advancement of majority employees are only limited and not eliminated, a goal will probably not be viewed as a quota.

These principles concerning employment rights help to clarify and justify many of the Court's seemingly inconsistent decisions. They help explain why the Court will not allow quotas, but will allow precise numerical hiring goals and the consideration of race and sex as "plus factors."

Parting Thoughts

Clayton and Tangri (Chapter 15) argue that affirmative action is a just policy. Persuasive as their arguments are about the justice of affirmative action, they do not touch on constitutional issues. Affirmative action programs must be legal as well as just. Guidelines do exist for helping an organization assure the constitutionality of its practices (Holloway, Chapter 2), but legal challenges occur with some frequency.

Predicting which affirmative action plans will withstand legal challenge has become somewhat easier over the last decade. Precedents have been set, especially by the Supreme Court. It is now possible to identify some principles that will help an affirmative action plan withstand legal challenge. Yet uncertainties persist.

We might ask why. Lawyers and the courts often cite the inherent conflict between affirmative action policy and the intent behind Title VII of creating a "color-blind" American workplace. The issue becomes characterized as a question of whether the end justifies the means. Opponents argue that any race- or sex-conscious remedy sanctioned by the legal system promotes rather than eradicates racism and sexism. Social science research suggests, however, that the conflict may just reflect our national ambivalence about racial and gender justice (Kinder, 1986; Kirp, Yudof, & Franks, 1986). As Dovidio, Mann, and Gaertner (Chapter 7) argue about opposition to affirmative action among the general population, such opposition among jurists may simply be a more subtle and contemporary form of racism or sexism.

The disagreements among judges about affirmative action may stem, in part, from differences in political attitudes. Some of the Justices on the Supreme Court have voted consistently in favor of or against affirmative action. Justice Marshall, the only Black Justice, consistently supports affirmative action. Justice Scalia, a conservative Reagan appointee, has emerged as the most formidable critic of affirmative action. Justice O'Connor, also a Reagan appointee but the only female Justice, appears disposed to upholding affirmative action programs so long as they do not contain blind quotas. While legal scholars generally choose to ignore the social and political bases of judicial decisions, it is virtually impossible to do so with respect to this issue. It is reasonable to assume that these influences, visible in the decisions of the Supreme Court, are even more prevalent among other federal and state courts.

Even if we admit that politics affect judicial decisions, however, we are left wondering: Why do they seem more influential in this area of law? The answer may lie in the reactive nature of the judicial system. The role of the judiciary in our form of government is to define what behavior is prohibited, not to speculate upon what behavior may be most desirable. In contrast, the policy of affirmative action is by its very name and nature *pro*active rather that *re*active. The legislature has noticeably failed to perform its function is this area. During the last ten years, Congress has not enacted any major legislation to restrict or expand the scope of affirmative action. The courts have been left to fulfill the functions of two branches of government. The role of formulating and shaping national policy, normally performed by the legislature, is inherently political. Therefore, it really should not be surprising that the decisions of the judiciary are unusually political in the area of affirmative action.

Eventually, Congress will step in or the courts will develop a sufficient body of precedent to provide employers and employees alike a clearer definition of the requirements and boundaries of affirmative action. For the time being, we will all have to rely upon the sometimes confusing and contradictory guidance that the courts have, so far, provided.

References

Age Discrimination in Employment Act, 29 U.S.C. Section 621 et seq. (1967).

Brown v. Board of Education, 347 U.S. 483 (1954).

Clayton, S. D., & Tangri, S. S. (1989). The justice of affirmative action. In F. A. Blanchard & F. J. Crosby (Eds.), *Affirmative Action in Perspective* (pp. 177-192). New York: Springer-Verlag.

Dovidio, J. F., Mann, J., & Gaertner, S. L. (1989). Resistance to affirmative action: The implication of aversive racism. In F. A. Blanchard & F. J. Crosby (Eds.), *Affirmative Action in Perspective* (pp. 83-102). New York: Springer-Verlag.

Firefighters Local 1784 v. Stotts, 467 U.S. 561 (1984).

Fullilove v. Klutznik, 448 U.S. 448 (1980).

Holloway, F. A. (1989). What is affirmative action? In F. Blanchard & F. Crosby (Eds.), *Affirmative Action in Perspective* (pp. 9-19). New York: Springer-Verlag.

Johnson v. Transportation Agency, 480 U.S. 616 (1987).

Kinder, D. (1986). The continuing dilemma: White resistance to racial change 40 years after Myrdal. *Journal of Social Issues*, *42*(2), 151-171.

Kirp, D. L., Yudof, M. G., & Franks, M.S. (1986). *Gender Justice*. Chicago: University of Chicago Press.

Local No. 93 Firefighters v. Cleveland, 478 U.S. 501 (1986)

Local No. 28 Sheetmetal Workers v. EEOC, 478 U.S. 421 (1986).

Martin v. Wilks, ___ U.S. ___, 108 S. Ct. 2843 (Cert. granted June 20, 1988).

Newsweek (1986, July 4). *A Yes for Affirmative Action*. 74.

Plessy v. Ferguson, 163 U.S. 537 (1896).

Regents of the University of California v. Bakke, 438 U.S. 265 (1978).

Schlei, B., & Grossman, P. (1983). *Employment Discrimination Law* (2nd Ed.). Chi-

cago: American Bar Association Press.
Taylor, D. A. (1989). Affirmative action and presidential executive orders. In F. A. Blanchard & F. J. Crosby (Eds.), *Affirmative Action in Perspective* (pp. 21-29). New York: Springer-Verlag.
Title VII of the Civil Rights Act of 1964, 42 U.S.C. 2000e et seq.
United States v. Paradise, 480 U.S. 149 (1987).
United Steelworkers of America v. Weber, 443 U.S. 193 (1979).
Wygant v. Jackson Board of Education, 476 U.S. 267 (1986).

5

Employment Screening, Qualifications, and Gender Discrimination: A Case Study of the New York City Firefighters

Wessie L. Norris and Maryellen Reardon

Most affirmative action programs operate in environments where the number of women or minorities have traditionally been small. But what happens when the representation is so small that it is non-existent? Fire-fighting is an occupation that until recently included no women whatsoever. In many areas of the country it has seemed as if gender were an unstated but universally accepted prerequisite of the job. Over a decade ago people began to question the exclusion of women from the occupation of firefighter. In 1973, the City of New York began to change its policies, and the celebrated case of the New York City Firefighters began. The aim of this chapter is to present the story, without taking one side or another in the battle to integrate women into the force. Much of the story revolves around the question of employment testing, and so it is there that we begin.

Occupational Screening Tests

Testing as a means of identifying qualified candidates for employment is a common practice in American life. Although the testing movement contrasts favorably with older, less formal systems which emphasized the privileges of race, ethnicity, sex, social class, and political affiliation, it has not yet achieved the meritocratic goals upon which it was predicated. In principle good tests fairly identify suitable and qualified job candidates. In practice bad tests confer a veil of fairness, but neither distinguish among the qualified candidates nor produce an equitable distribution of employment opportunities. All too frequently invalid and irrelevant tests have contributed to the subtle perpetuation of the older systems of privilege and advantage which they are intended to replace.

Validity is an important prerequisite of good employment screening tests. Validity describes the extent to which scores on a test faithfully represent the characteristic they intend to measure. The *Standards for Educational & Psychological Tests* (American Psychological Association, 1974) suggests that "questions of validity are questions of what may be properly inferred from a test score..."(p. 25). For example, systematic observation of a new driver's performance in a driving simulator might provide an index for predicting that person's performance in a car on the open road. The driving test may be valid if its scores correlate highly with other measures of actual driving performance.

Relevance is the other important prerequisite of good employment screening tests. A valid test may accurately measure a characteristic which is irrelevant to job performance. Knowing how well a person drives a car may be important, for example, if one is hiring taxi cab drivers, but not if one is hiring dispatchers or mechanics. The driving test may be relevant if a job analysis, a detailed study of the important tasks of a job, suggests that driving is a major component of the job.

Validity and relevance have become key concepts in the debate surrounding fair testing (Doverspike, Barrett, & Alexander, 1985). In *Griggs v. Duke Power* (1971) the Supreme Court held that employment practices which reduce minority opportunities are discriminatory unless it can be shown that those practices validly predict criteria which are specifically relevant to job performance, regardless of how fair the practices appear. Relevance can be demonstrated by establishing a logical relationship between test scores and job performance (Doverspike et al., 1985). Three types of employment screening strategies are emphasized in the federal *Uniform Guidelines on Employee Selection Procedures* (1978): (1) criterion validity, where test scores must correlate with measures of performance on the job; (2) content validity, where the test itself must consist of components of the job for which it is designed to select; and (3) construct validity, where the test must measure an underlying characteristic which is thought to be paramount to job performance. When the validation criteria are job-related, relevance and validity converge.

Among the most committed advocates of the use of testing to promote fair hiring have been governmental agencies. New York City, like many other cities, screens prospective employees and candidates for promotion largely on the basis of test performance. Candidates are tested to determine their knowledge, skills, and abilities relative to the position's requirements. This is true for both entry-level and promotional positions in the Fire, Police, Sanitation and Corrections Departments. The tests are developed and administered by the City's Department of Personnel.

After a test is administered, candidates' scores are combined in some predetermined fashion with other relevant information, e.g., psychological tests, seniority, military credit. A ranked eligibility list is then developed reflecting each candidate's total score. Job offers are made starting at the top of the eligibility list and proceeding down the list until the positions are filled. This system attempts to ensure that hiring and promotion decisions are based upon fairness and merit, rather than upon such nonvalid criteria as nepotism, bribery, racism, or sexism.

In recent years, however, a number of the City's tests have been criticized for being neither fair nor valid. A particularly informative example involved Examination #3040, an entry-level Firefighter examination for the New York City Fire Department (FDNY). The controversy and subsequent litigation led to the hiring of women as firefighters for the first time in the history of the New York City Fire Department.

New York City Firefighters Admit Women to Their Ranks

Firefighting is a profession which encompasses a range of responsibilities. A firefighter may spend the day battling fires in hot, smoky, life-threatening conditions or performing building inspections to ensure compliance with fire regulations. The time spent on tasks does not always indicate their importance. For example, the extremely important task of fighting fires occurs infrequently compared to the other tasks, and an "average" fire can usually be extinguished in less than one hour. By integrating information across such dimensions as frequency, time spent, and importance of tasks, job analysts determine the degree and kind of physical fitness and cognitive ability required to perform successfully as a firefighter.

A unique and strong culture exists among traditionally male, blue-collar firefighters. During their shifts, they live together in the firehouse, cooking and cleaning, almost as a family. Because they function as a team during life-threatening situations, they must be able to trust and rely upon each other. In New York City the male-oriented, firefighter comraderie had been evolving for 100 years prior to the inclusion of women.

Examination #3040

In 1973 the City of New York hired the American Institute for Research (AIR) to develop a valid examination for the entry level position of Firefighter. AIR contracted to develop both the written and physical test components of this examination, known as number 3040.

The competitive written test, consisting of 100 multiple choice questions, was administered in December, 1977 to 24,758 male and 410 female candidates. About 98% of the males and 95% of the females received passing scores. Those who passed the written test were permitted to proceed to the physical test. Because the majority of the subsequent legal controversy focused on the physical test component, the remainder of this chapter will focus on its development, legal issues, and ramifications.

The physical test was based primarily upon Fleishman's human abilities taxonomy of physical fitness (Fleishman & Stephenson, 1970). One technique used during the job analysis of the abilities required in the position of Firefighter was the Physical Abilities Analysis (PAA) (Fleishman, 1977). This instrument requires professionally trained individuals to rate the amount of each ability required in the performance of specific tasks. In preparation for Examination #3040, the PAA was administered to a panel consisting of 23 firefighters and 12 officers in November, 1973. They were asked to rate the amount of each ability needed in the many tasks performed by firefighters. As a result of the panel's ratings, nine physical abilities were ranked in the following descending order of importance: stamina; static strength; explosive strength; gross body equilibrium; extent flexibility; gross body coordination; dynamic strength; dynamic flexibility; and speed of limb movement. There had been, however, some evidence that the panel members were confused about the proper use of the PAA.

A second panel composed of 19 firefighters and 12 officers was asked by AIR to complete the Physical Demands Analysis (PDA) (Hahn, Trittipoe, Trittipoe, & Johnson, 1972). This panel was asked to rate the frequency and time spent by firefighters on various physical activities such as sitting, crawling, and carrying very heavy objects. The panel also gave specific information about such things as the tools used in each activity and the particular circumstances in which the activity might be required. The information was used in an attempt to substantiate the ranking results of the PAA.

Following the two panels, AIR selected physical tests from among those previously developed by Fleishman (1964). Eleven physical tests, each of which theoretically measured one of the ranked abilities, were pretested in December, 1973 to determine the scoring for, weighting of, and degree of overlap among the tests. These eleven tests were: (1) one mile run/walk; (2) five minute free-style stepping; (3) hand grip (preferred hand); (4) hand grip (non-preferred hand); (5) free style broad jump; (6) balancing; (7) twist and touch; (8) cable jump; (9) push ups; (10) leg lifts; and (11) bend/twist/touch. The subjects for the pretest were 100 men (including Blacks, Hispanics, and Whites) who were either in training to take the Firefighter examination or who had been New York City Firefighters for less than one year.

At this time the Fire Commissioner asked AIR to examine the appropriateness of retaining the previously established height requirement (5′7") for New York City Firefighters. In January and February of 1974, 200 men (including 100 Firefighters) were asked by AIR to perform several tasks, such as positioning a ladder, in order to determine whether height affected performance. After combining the results of the pretest with the results of the height requirement tests, and with professional judgment, AIR recommended a physical test plan in February, 1974. It consisted of a one mile run/walk subtest of stamina; a handgrip subtest of static strength; a freestyle broadjump subtest of explosive strength; a balance subtest of gross body equilibrium; a twist and touch subtest of flexibility; a push-up subtest of dynamic strength; an obstacle course agility subtest of explosive and dynamic strength, stamina, and gross body equilibrium; and a rescue dummy carry subtest of strength and gross body equilibrium. AIR did not make clear why they included the dummy carry and agility tests, as opposed to tests which more clearly measured a single ability. It appeared, however, that their selection did not result from a systematic job analysis.

Upon receiving AIR's proposal, individuals in both the New York City Fire Department and the New York City Department of Personnel criticized the inclusion of some of the tests (*Berkman v. City of New York*, 536 F Supp 177, 1982). For example, questions about the appropriateness of the twist and touch test and the balance test were raised. Despite the fact that AIR objected and no additional research was conducted, the plan was revised. The revision omitted the balance, twist and touch, and push-up tests. It added a flexed arm hang test, a ledge walk test, and an additional component to the agility test. The addition of the flexed arm hang appeared to result from an observation of the physical test used to select Firefighters in the city of Chicago. The agility test was expanded to include both an obstacle course (including the scaling of 8′ and 5′ walls) and a window-ladder-window test which required the candidate to crawl through a window, across a horizontal ladder, and through a second window. The ledge walk test was a new, unstudied test which replaced the purportedly non-face valid balance test. The new components of the physical test and the dummy carry were pretested with 75 firefighters in November, 1974.

Scoring the physical test. With the exception of hand grip and broad jump, all test scores were a function of completion time. Hand grip scores were a function of dynamometer readings in kilograms. Broad jump scores were a function of distance. Because the physical test was competitive in nature, scores were rank ordered, rather than categorized on a pass/fail basis.

Scoring norms were determined in a variety of ways. Norms for the agility test, for instance, were originally based upon the scores for the similar agility test used in the 1971 Firefighter examination and were subsequently revised to include norms based upon the November, 1974 pretest of the window-ladder-window test, but norms for other subtests came from a variety of pretests. Some norms, such as those for the mile run, were made more stringent when officials complained they were too lenient. In addition to being individually normed, each physical test was assigned a weight. Initially, the mile run was given the highest weight of 200 points, since it measured the ability with the highest ranking on the PAA (stamina). Each of the pure ability tests (hand grip, broad jump, ledge walk, flexed arm hang) was given a weight of 100 points. Each of the mixed ability tests (agility test, dummy carry) was initially given a weight of 150 points. However, an additional 100 points was given to the agility test when the window-ladder-window test was added, thus giving the agility test the largest weight of 250 points.

Minimum standards were also established for each physical subtest. For example, if a candidate did not jump at least 6 feet in the broad jump test, a score of zero was received. Due to the City's criticism of leniency, however, AIR's initially suggested minimum requirements were made more stringent, e.g., the 6 ft minimum requirement for the broad jump was increased by 2 inches. The passing score for the physical test was set at 70%. Raw scores, not standard scores, of the physical and written tests were averaged to yield a final test score for each candidate.

Test administration and results. Prior to the administration of the physical test, the City of New York took several steps to attract candidates and enhance their performance. First, the City recruited female candidates through the New York University system and encouraged female relatives of current FDNY personnel to take the Firefighter examination. Second, all persons who registered to take Examination #3040 were sent descriptions of both the written and physical test components, and information on how to prepare for the physical test. Third, a physical test familiarization program was conducted by the City. Independent of the City's efforts, FDNY personnel organized private "schools" where candidates could practice performing the subtests and could learn techniques to improve their performance.

The physical test was administered to 18,060 male candidates and 88 female candidates from February to April, 1978. This group represented about 74% of the men who passed the written test and 23% of the women. About 43% of the men and none of the women received passing grades. Thus, the eligibility list for the position of Firefighter excluded female candidates.

Berkman Lawsuit

In 1979 Brenda Berkman filed a lawsuit (*Berkman v. City of New York*, 536 F Supp 177, 1982) on behalf of herself and the class of women who took and passed the written test component of Examination #3040 and later either took and failed or allegedly were deterred from taking the physical test component as a result of sex discrimination by the defendants. The defendants were the City of New York and its Mayor, the New York City Fire Department and its Commissioner, the New York City Department of Personnel and its current and former Directors, and the Civil Service Commission of the City of New York. The lawsuit alleged that there was discrimination against women in the selection of New York City Firefighters in violation of Title VII of the Civil Rights Act of 1964, the fourteenth amendment to the United States Constitution, and other legislative acts. The plaintiff challenged the physical test component on the grounds that the test had disparate impact on women resulting in a 43% pass rate for men and a zero pass rate for women. The plaintiff also challenged the physical test on the grounds that it was not job-related.

Approximately two years later the court determined that Examination #3040 did discriminate against women in the selection of New York City Firefighters. Because the court found that the screening procedure resulted in disparate impact for women, it scrutinized carefully the relevance and validity of the tests. It determined that the test was not content valid because the abilities measured were not the most observable abilities of significance to the job. It determined that neither construct nor criterion validity had been adequately demonstrated, in part because the expert test developers were subject to interference from the Fire Department and the NYC Department of Personnel. Finally, it found that the scoring procedure of rank ordering candidates was not justified by a job analysis, the physical test itself, or its validation procedures.

The court ordered a number of remedies. The FDNY was to make conditional use of the Firefighter eligibility list based upon compelling staff needs of the Fire Department. It was to hire women who had passed both the written component of Examination #3040 and a special qualifying physical test agreed upon by all parties involved in the lawsuit. The court issued a supplemental order directing the parties to cooperate in an effort to reach an accord on new selection procedures. The parties agreed upon a special qualifying physical test that closely reflected on-the-job conditions. The qualifying test consisted of subtests which precisely simulated the hose and ladder handling, forcible entry, and rescue tasks actually performed by engine and ladder companies of the Fire Department.

A considerable amount of publicity surrounded the lawsuit against the Fire Department and the City; and an adversarial atmosphere developed. The Uniformed Firefighters' Association (UFA), representing the approximately 10,000 men in the Fire Department, charged that the special qualifying physical test discriminated against men who were subjected to the "more rigorous standards" of the earlier physical test. Further, there were charges that the qualifying physical test could pave the way for appointing women who were not physically capable of performing the duties of a firefighter. The UFA unsuccessfully sought an injunction against the test. A group of male candidates who had failed the competitive physical test filed a lawsuit to be admitted to the special qualifying physical test. This attempt was also unsuccessful.

In September, 1982, seventy-eight female candidates took the special qualifying physical test for Examination #3040. These 78 women represented 20% of the 389 women who passed the written test and were subsequently eligible to take this special qualifying test. Fifty-two of the female candidates passed the qualifying physical test, a pass rate of 67%. Thirty-eight of these women were appointed to the Fire Department of New York City. Consistent with standard procedures, the women entered the Fire Department at the level of probationary firefighter. Probationary status lasts for a period of one year, beginning with a six-week training program.

New York City Firefighters Integrate Women into Their Ranks

The charges of female inadequacy were not abated by the initial performance of the first class of female candidates at the Fire Department Training Academy. At the end of the six week training period, only twenty-eight women (73.6%) had passed the training and ten women were permitted to repeat training. After this second training period, five additional women passed and five others were fired on the last day for failing to meet required standards of upper body strength under simulated conditions.

Tensions also arose concerning the assignment of women to firehouses. Renovations to physical facilities were required. Out of concern for the possibility of harassment charges, the traditional hazing of male probationary firefighters was reevaluated. The women were treated as intruders in the previously all-male domain (Daly, 1982; Greenberger, 1983). In addition, the presence of women in the firehouse sparked an angry response from some of the wives of the male firefighters. The wives were not only concerned about the living and sleeping arrangements, but also about the ability of women to perform adequately fighting fires, which could put their husbands at risk. Given the conditions under which the women were hired, feelings persisted among the men that most women could not perform the demanding physical tasks required of firefighters and were unequipped to handle the emotional issues of death and disaster that are prevalent in the job. Many remained unchanged in the belief that the dangerous nature of the job made it unsuitable for women.

Contributing to the tension was the dismissal from the Fire Department in September, 1983, of Brenda Berkman and another female probationary firefighter for inadequate job performance during their probationary period. The two women successfully sued to be reinstated. The court found that the termination had been the result of intentional discrimination on the part of the Fire Department (*Berkman v. City of New York*, 580 F Supp 226, E.D.N.Y., 1983).

New Examinations

Although resistance to the inclusion of females continued in New York's firehouses, some progress was being made in the creation of new, nondiscriminatory exams. A new written examination (Examination #1162) was administered in December, 1982, followed by a physical test offered between July 1983 and the Spring of 1984. The passing rates for the written test were 98.65% for male candidates and 97.8% for female candidates.

The competitive physical test component for Examination #1162 was a modified version of the special qualifying physical test for Examination #3040. The subtests for the 1162 physical test again simulated the hose and ladder handling, forcible entry, and rescue tasks actually performed by engine and ladder companies of the Fire Department. The passing rates for the physical test component were 95.42% for the male candidates and 46.67% for the female candidates.

A disparate impact challenge to Examination #1162 was brought on two grounds (*Berkman v. City of New York,* 626 F Supp 591, E.D. N.Y. 1985). First, it was alleged that the physical test component emphasized a candidate's speed rather than pacing which biased it in favor of men and allegedly was not representative of how the job is actually performed. The second argument challenged the appropriateness of the written test. The written test was so easy, contended the plaintiffs, that it did not differentiate among candidates, and, consequently, ranking on the eligibility list was determined almost solely by the results of the physical test. This was contrary to the 50-50 weight that the City had accorded to the two components of the examination. It also resulted in low combined scores for women. No women placed in the top 4,000 scores on the eligibility list, meaning that few, if any, women would be hired from the list.

U.S. District Court Judge Charles P. Sifton agreed that the physical test component of Examination #1162 did emphasize speed and aerobic energy over pacing and anaerobic energy because the test scores were a function of completion time. He further ruled that the proposed scoring system for the physical test placed "too great an emphasis on the aerobic capacities of candidates with too little regard for those aspects of firefighting that call upon prudent, paced performance." Finally, Judge Sifton ruled that the scoring system should be revised to present the least adverse impact on women and to reduce the undue emphasis on the physical test component due to the "extraordinarily indiscriminate" written test component (*Berkman v. City of New York,* 626 F Supp 591, E.D. N.Y. 1985). The City of New York appealed the decision, however, and the use of Examination #1162 was upheld in the Second Circuit Court of Appeals. The plaintiffs next appealed to the United States Supreme Court. The Supreme Court refused, without comment, to hear the appeal. An eligibles list was developed based upon the combined scores from the written and physical test components of Examination #1162.

While there are some women included on the eligibles list, their positions suggest that they will not be hired before the list expires.

Yet another new Firefighter examination (Examination #7022) was recently created. The written test component was administered in December, 1987, and administration of the physical test component began in the spring of 1988. The large percentage of women who passed the written test component of Examination #1162 (but who then did not take the physical test component) are now being allowed to take the physical test component of Examination #7022.

Conclusions

The story of the New York City Firefighters and how they included women in their ranks reveals both the problems and the promise of change. Are the gains worth the trouble? We believe so, not only for the benefits gained but also for the lessons learned.

Benefits

There are many positive outcomes of the struggle. First, there has been improved recruitment of female candidates for the position of firefighter. Women are now recruited by Fire Department personnel at high schools, colleges, health clubs, street fairs, and shopping malls. Recruitment posters and public service radio announcements are widespread. A good faith attempt is being made by the Fire Department to find women who are physically capable of performing the tasks required of the firefighter's job.

Second, the presence of women has positively affected the firefighter culture. For example, there has been a reduction in the amount of hazing which a probationary firefighter experiences. Third, there has been some examination of alternative firefighting techniques which rely upon a collaborative approach emphasizing a team member's particular strengths. For example, shorter and smaller male firefighters have been known to discuss with female firefighters techniques for holding a charged hoseline in ways that minimize the use of upper body strength and maximize the use of leg strength.

Not all the changes in the organizational culture are unplanned. Currently the FDNY conducts sensitivity training programs for all Fire Department personnel. The purpose of the program is to make individuals aware of issues which may be of particular concern to female firefighters. The programs are usually moderated by outside consultants and female Fire Department personnel. The Fire Department is also placing more responsibility on the officers to show equitable treatment of all firefighters regardless of gender.

Finally, there have been substantial improvements in the manner in which both the New York City Department of Personnel and the Fire Department of New York City approach the development of selection tests and promote the inclusion of women. First, the importance of job relevance and test validity has been reaffirmed. Physical tests administered by the Department of Personnel now usually include simulations of the job tasks which have been determined by job analysis to be the most critical and important. Job analyses are typically more thorough than in the 1970s.

Lessons Learned

The chronicle of events surrounding the hiring of the first women Firefighters by the New York City Fire Department underscores the difficulty of achieving fairness in occupations which have historically restricted their ranks to men. The construction of fair employment screening procedures is a challenging task, even when the experts who design them are well-intentioned. Validity and relevance are demanding, yet appropriate standards. However, there remain serious questions concerning the criteria of validity and the scope of relevance.

At first glance, the ideal criteria of validity for employment screening procedures would emphasize the skills, abilities, and job performance of those who already work in that occupation. Minimum screening standards for abilities might be set no higher than the lowest scores of those functioning effectively in the occupation. On the other hand, when the ranks of a profession are so narrowly circumscribed by a history of exclusion of large classes of people, it may be impossible to ascertain the range of relevant abilities which underlie effective performance in that occupation. It is rare for employment screening procedures to acknowledge the possibility that there may be ways of functioning effectively in an occupation which have not yet been observed precisely because the persons possessing those strengths have never been hired before.

It is clear that the scope of effective affirmative action programs must include scrutiny of the cultures of organizations which evolve out of long traditions of exclusion. While valid and relevant employment screening procedures can open the doors to new groups of people, every feature of subsequent training, operating procedure, and promotion will warrant scrutiny as the newcomers demonstrate innovative ways of performing effectively the important tasks of the organization. It will be difficult to anticipate all of the necessary adjustments. We can be confident, however, that adjustments will be necessary -- in individuals and in organizations. We expect that both individuals and organizations will be the ultimate beneficiaries of the changes.

References

American Psychological Association. (1974). *Standards for Educational & Psychological Tests.* Washington, D.C.: American Psychological Association.

Berkman v. City of New York, 536 F Supp 177 (1982).

Berkman v. City of New York, 580 F Supp 226 (E.D. N.Y. 1983).

Berkman v. City of New York, 626 F Supp 591 (E.D. N.Y. 1985).

Civil Rights Act of 1964 as amended by the Equal Employment Opportunity Act of 1972 (Public Law 92-261). Washington, D.C.: U.S. Government Printing Office, 1972.

Daly, M. (1982, January 10) Fire Women. *New York Magazine,* 22-29.

Doverspike, D., Barrett, G. V., & Alexander, R. A. (1985). The feasibility of traditional validation procedures for demonstrating job-relatedness, *Law and Psychology Review,* 9, 35-44.

Fleishman, E. A. (1964). *Structure and Measurement of Physical Fitness.* Englewood Cliffs, N.J.: Prentice Hall.

Fleishman, E. A. (1977). *Physical abilities analysis manual.* Washington, D.C.: Advanced Research Resources Organization.

Fleishman, E. A., & Stephenson, R. W. (1970). *Development of a taxonomy of human performance: A review of the third year's progress.* Washington, D.C.: American Institute for Research.

Greenberger, R. S. (1983, February 3). Burning Issue: Women Firefighters Still Spark Resentment in Strongly Macho Job. *Wall Street Journal,* 1, 25.

Griggs v. Duke Power, 401 U.S. 424 (1971).

Hahn, C. P., Trittipoe, T. G., Trittipoe, W. J., & Johnson, P. R. (1972) *Application of Self-Instructional and Programmed Learning Procedures to the "Physical Demands Analysis" Portion of Job Analysis Training.* Washington, D.C.: American Institute for Research.

Uniform Guidelines on Employee Selection, 43 Fed. Reg. 38,290 (1978).

6

Women In Federal Government Employment

Nijole V. Benokraitis and Melissa Kesler Gilbert

The federal government is the nation's largest employer, with nearly 3 million civilian employees. Almost 81 percent of these workers are in white-collar jobs; of these, women accounted for 47.6 percent of the federal white-collar workers in 1986. Over one and a half million women work for the federal government in white-collar jobs. The question arises: How well does the government, as a major employer, meet its affirmative action obligations?

The answer, as we shall see, is one of rather mixed success. The number of women who work for the federal government has been increasing very slowly in recent years. Both in terms of job status and pay, however, women in the federal system still remain disadvantaged relative to men.

After reviewing the statistics on gender and employment in the federal government, we examine explanations of the obvious gender differentials. Attitudinal barriers block the advancement of women. Affirmative action programs, which ought to remedy some of the problems, have suffered under the Reagan administration. The ineffectiveness of affirmative action programs also arises, in part, from the fact that affirmative action as a policy aims to correct blatant discrimination and does not attack the subtle and covert discrimination that affects so many organizations today.

General Characteristics of the Federal Female Workforce

Table 6.1 indicates that although both total and federal female employment decreased slightly between 1972 and 1976, women's employment has increased slowly, 4.5 percent from 1966 to 1986. Most of this increase has occurred since 1982 when affirmative action and equal employment policies were discouraged by the Reagan administration. The increase has probably arisen, therefore, from unprecedented numbers of women entering the workforce rather than the federal government's commitment to recruit, hire and promote women.

Table 6.1
Women in Federal Employment from 1966-1986

Year	Federal Employment	Percent Women
1966	2,303	33.6
1972	2,542	33.7
1976	2,418	35.9
1982	2,550	35.1
1986	2,703	38.1

Note. Full-time employment in thousands for all pay systems (Civil Service Commission, 1969,1976; Equal Employment Opportunity Commission, 1986).

Table 6.2 shows the percentage of women employed in 18 major federal agencies (with 500+ employees) in 1966, 1976, and 1986. Between 1966 and 1976 the percentage of women increased in ten agencies and decreased in eight. The greatest losses occurred in three of the largest agencies -- Army, Navy, and Air Force (-3.8%, -4.6%, and -5.7%, respectively). By 1986 women's employment declined in four agencies -- Government Printing Office (GPO), -20.9%; Navy, -2.3%; Air Force, -1.7%; and Labor, -2.9% -- and increased in fourteen agencies. In five agencies -- Treasury, Housing and Urban Development (HUD), Veterans Administration (VA), Office of Personnel Management (OPM), and the Equal Employment Opportunity Commission (EEOC) -- more than half of those employed were women.

It is not clear why the percentage of women employed has fluctuated so widely across the major agencies. The increase in some agencies (e.g., Treasury, HUD, OPM, VA, EEOC) probably reflects women's

Table 6.2
Female Employment in White-Collar Positions in Selected Federal Agencies: 1966, 1976, 1986

Agency	Percent Women 1966	Percent Women 1976	Percent Women 1986	Percent Change 1966-1976	Percent Change 1976-1986	Total Full-Time Employees 1986
GPO	53.3	51.7	32.4	-1.6	-20.9	5,081
State	35.4	36.8	40.9	1.4	5.5	11,655
Treasury	42.5	47.5	54.6	5.0	12.1	119,715
Army	46.7	42.9	46.9	-3.8	0.2	242,311
Navy	43.6	39.0	41.3	-4.6	-2.3	186,972
Air Force	49.8	44.1	48.1	-5.7	-1.7	148,011
Justice	35.1	34.2	38.6	-0.9	3.5	62,287
Interior	29.7	32.2	36.9	2.5	7.2	48,636
Agriculture	25.4	24.3	34.9	-1.1	9.5	86,181
Commerce	31.7	35.3	42.5	3.6	10.8	27,723
Labor	46.7	45.1	43.8	-1.6	-2.9	16,593
HUD	40.7	44.4	53.9	3.7	13.2	11,309
GSA	39.2	41.8	46.4	2.6	7.2	14,578
NASA	23.2	19.8	27.9	-3.4	4.7	20,534
USPS	12.3	16.2	30.0	3.9	17.7	744,630
VA	49.6	56.8	62.2	7.2	12.6	171,364
CSC/OPM	52.6	56.9	60.3	4.3	7.7	5,130
EEOC	45.7	56.3	59.9	10.6	14.2	2,945
Total	33.6	35.9	38.1	2.3	4.5	2,703,466

Note. GPO is Government Printing Office; HUD is Housing & Urban Development; GSA is General Services Administration; NASA is National Aeronautics & Space Administration; USPS is U.S. Postal Service; VA is Veterans Administration; CSC is Civil Service Commission which became the Office of Personnel Management (OPM) in 1979; EEOC is Equal Employment Opportunity Commission. Civil Service Commission (1969, 1976); Equal Employment Opportunity Commission (1986).

entry into low-paying clerical positions. Technological changes may account for some of the decreases, as in the GPO (where women's employment decreased by 20.9 percent between 1976 to 1986). Women in low-level, low seniority jobs are often displaced by computers (Hacker, 1982). Also, the military agencies (where women's employment has decreased) traditionally have not received gold medals for advocating women's rights (Holm, 1982). These explanations are speculative, however, and merit future research.

Women's employment across pay grade ranges has shifted somewhat during the last two decades (see Table 6.3). Between 1966 and 1986,

Table 6.3

Full-Time White-Collar Federal Employment of Women by General Schedule and Equivalent Grades (Excluding U.S. Postal Workers): 1966, 1976, 1986

Grade Group	Total Employment	Number of Women	Percent Women in Grade Group	Percent of Total Women Employed
1966				
1-4	424,260	295,097	69.5	48.5
5-8	804,049	254,887	31.7	41.9
9-12	414,829	52,093	12.5	8.5
13-15	138,595	5,045	3.6	.8
16-18	9,073	150	1.6	.02
Total	1,790,806	607,272	33.9	99.7
1976				
1-4	294,486	227,534	77.2	37.8
5-8	429,052	259,686	60.5	43.2
9-12	482,866	102,621	21.1	17.0
13-15	198,067	10,960	5.5	1.8
16-18	6,987	198	2.8	.03
Total	1,411,458	600,999	42.5	99.8
1986				
1-4	204,821	156,315	76.3	22.6
5-8	448,363	309,731	69.1	44.8
9-12	567,129	195,389	34.5	28.2
13-15	216,956	29,183	13.5	4.2
16-18	7,291	603	8.3	.08
Total	1,444,560	699,579	48.4	99.8

Note. Percentages were calculated from Civil Service Commission (1969, p. 19; 1976, p. xiii) and Equal Employment Opportunity Commission (1986, p. 53). Percentages do not equal 100.0 due to rounding.

there was a decrease in the total employment, female employment, and the percentage of women distributed in the lowest grades (1-4). However, the percentage of women in this grade group increased from 69.5 percent to 76.3 percent during this period. The greatest increases have been in the middle grades (9-12). In 1966, 8.5 percent of all women employed were concentrated in the 9-12 grades compared to 28.2 percent in 1986. This grade range also increased the most (36.7%) in terms of total employment. Although the greatest decrease in the percentage of all females employed was at the lowest grades (1-4), total employment in these grade levels also decreased from 424,260 in 1966 to 204,821 in 1986. Gains at the higher ranks have been less impressive. In grades 13-15 the percentage of all females employed increased from .8 percent in 1966 to 4.2 percent in 1986. At the highest ranks (16-18), however, the percentage of females employed increased from .02 percent in 1966 to .08 percent in 1986. Thus, in 1986, approximately 67 percent of the women were still clustered in the lowest-paying grades (1-8), even though the total employment in these levels decreased by almost 50 percent since 1966.

Women's overrepresentation in the lower-status categories is especially pronounced when we examine federal employment by both race and sex. Compared to men, both minority and nonminority women are disproportionately overrepresented in the lower-paying categories (see Table 6.4). Except for Asian American women, as the job level increases, the percentage of women decreases. In contrast to previous years, women in clerical positions earned slightly more than men. At the other three levels, however, not only are women's annual salaries lower than those of men, but the gap increases at the higher levels (U.S. Office of Personnel Management, 1986, Table 3):

	Men	Women
Professional	$40,081	$29,170
Administrative	35,937	28,686
Technical	23,515	18,537
Clerical	14,580	15,375

Detailed studies of different organizations in the federal government corroborate the statistics. Like the gross statistics, the detailed studies reveal deep gender asymmetries. As DiPrete and Soule (1986) point out, the work performed in the federal government by some administrators and clerical workers is similar. However, the maintenance of separate career lines gives administrators greater control in the promotion process. Because many men have veterans' preference and are less likely to be sexually harassed, they face fewer structural constraints.

In a recent study comparing supervisory positions in the OPM in 1974 and 1982, Lewis and Emmert (1986) found few improvements in the last decade. Controlling for race, grade rank, educational level, major field of study in college, length of federal experience and age, Lewis and Emmert concluded that the general pattern is discouraging because women are not rising to supervisory positions as White men retire. Another study of gender and career advancement also documented obstacles to women seeking promotion. In the Milwaukee District Office of the Internal Revenue Service, Vertz (1985) found that the women in the high-level positions started their careers earlier than their male counter

Table 6.4
Percentage Distribution of White-Collar Federal Employees Across Occupational Categories for Men and Women in Each Minority Group in 1986

Minority Group	Occupational Category					Total %	Total N
	Prof	Adm	Tech	Cler	Other		
White							
Men	34.6	38.0	19.1	4.3	4.0	100.0	635,738
Women	14.5	24.0	21.0	40.1	.3	99.9	485,109
Black							
Men	14.7	31.7	27.2	17.9	8.4	99.9	71,771
Women	7.6	19.8	26.1	46.0	.5	100.0	155,297
Hispanic							
Men	20.8	33.6	25.6	11.0	9.0	100.0	34,032
Women	10.0	20.4	20.6	48.3	.7	100.0	30,288
Asian							
Men	51.0	21.8	15.9	7.8	3.6	100.1	21,363
Women	28.3	17.6	17.9	35.6	.6	100.0	17,975
Native							
Men	17.2	37.3	31.2	7.0	7.4	100.1	7,692
Women	9.3	17.0	31.5	41.8	.4	100.0	10,910

Note. Prof is Professional; Adm is Administrative; Tech is Technical; Cler is Clerical. Some percentage totals do not equal 100.0 due to rounding. Equal Employment Opportunity Commission (1986, p. 55).

parts and often began their careers outside of the federal civil service. Thus, to be upwardly-mobile in the federal government, women have to work longer than men and, ironically, *not* work for the federal government as a first employer.

Obstacles in Women's Employment

What accounts for the sluggish rate of change? A common justification for the low participation of women in federal employment -- especially in high status positions -- is that they lack the necessary "qualifications" (Huckle, 1985). Typically, it is argued, women do not have the experience, education, or skill required to compete for jobs and promotions.

Several studies indicate, however, that this is not the case. In a recent analysis of a one percent random sample of the Central Personnel Data File of the Office of Personnel Management, Lewis and Emmert

(1986) found that federal white-collar employment is highly segregated by sex -- even after the effects of race, education, and experience have been taken into account. Lewis and Emmert conclude that "at the rate of the last 16 years it would take nearly a century to achieve perfect integration in sex-segregated occupations" in the federal government (p. 155). In a study of 129,385 randomly-sampled, full-time Government Service employees in 22 major occupational groups, Taylor (1977) controlled for education, number of degrees, years of service, age, supervisory status, location, veteran's preference, and government training and still found that substantial salary differences between minority/sex groups and non-minority males. Taylor pointed out that, even equating for these factors, minority women are paid $4,276 less then White men; and White women earn $3,798 less than White men.

If women's qualifications do not differ from men's, perhaps their attitudes inhibit them from career advances. MacLennan (1973) suggests that "women conspire by their attitudes and behavior to perpetuate institutional sexism" (p. 11). That is, women fill out applications poorly, accept positions several grades below their rating, do not fight for salary and promotion increases, accept additional responsibilities without remuneration, are modest and nonaggressive about competing for awards and publicizing their achievements, are more critical of and less helpful to women than to men, and "are too unwilling to risk the security they have for a more respected position for women in the future" (p. 11).

Women's alleged lack of competitiveness may reflect realistically low expectations about job mobility. For example, in a study of federal executive positions at grades GS 15-18, Lepper (1974) found that women do not compete for choice positions because of a deep-seated pessimistic belief that attempts to further their careers will prove futile. Thus, feeling that job prospects are limited because of sex, some women may have lower aspirations regarding job mobility. The data presented in Tables 6.3 and 6.4 support such realistic pessimism. Women's initial exclusion becomes a self-fulfilling prophecy.

Much more important than the attitudes of women in subordinate roles are the attitudes of men -- and perhaps women -- in supervisory roles. In a study of middle-management in Pennsylvania's state government, Bocher (1982) found that "negative traditionalism" functions to automatically appoint men, rather than women, when vacancies occur at supervisory levels. Supervisors often justify not promoting women into high positions because "no one wants women bosses," even though several studies show that it is men, and not women, who are prejudiced toward female supervisors (Ferber, Huber, & Spitzer, 1979; Statham,

1988) and that women encounter more prejudice in employers' rather than co-workers' or subordinates' attitudes (Goodman, 1975).

Although some gatekeepers support the principles of affirmative action and equal employment opportunity, they are unwilling to implement specific mechanisms that place women in higher ranks. Some supervisors assume that affirmative action is synonymous with promoting unqualified women and do not take women applicants seriously. Others -- especially older and more conservative male supervisors -- oppose targets and timetables, resent the paperwork involved, or believe that the government should not interfere with recruitment efforts (Slack, 1987). Thus, women may not get the same training, on-the-job experience or information about promotion opportunities as do men (Deaux, 1984).

In a study of federal personnel systems, Zashin (1980) concluded that the OPM's first loyalty to the merit system, rather than equal employment opportunity, also severely limits women's (and minorities') chances for promotion. First, experience is an important criterion, but women and minorities are less likely to meet these requirements. Second, women suffer because promotion panels and committees from comparable grades are usually composed of White males who have been mentored by other men about the kinds of training necessary to qualify for managerial positions. Third, because promotions for women are frequently based on technical competence in contrast to peer relations for men, women may be seen as less desirable candidates for supervisory positions. Men are still uncomfortable with women as co-workers and professional peers (Franklin & Sweeney, 1988). Finally, government-wide evaluations of "outstanding," "satisfactory" and "unsatisfactory" are ambiguous, and thus supervisors have great latitude in promoting friends rather than qualified applicants.

Affirmative Action and Women

Some research suggests that pressure to conform to affirmative action can produce positive results for women and minorities. For example, in a study of state and federal equal employment opportunity and affirmative action policies in New York and Oregon, Eberts and Stone (1985) found that enforcement of Title IX resulted in a decline of discrimination. In a study of the 15 largest agencies of the federal government during 1962-1977, DiPrete (1987) found that equal employment policies benefited the entry of women and minorities into administrative positions at grades 5-7. Leonard (1985) compared the employment and occupations of minorities and women in federal contract establishments which were subject to affirmative action regulations and those that were not (between 1974 and 1980) and concluded that the federal affirmative action effort improved hiring in higher-level occupations.

It may be the case that women have made some progress *despite* affirmative action and equal employment opportunity policies. Affirmative action enforcement and compliance problems are just as persistent in the 1980s as they were in the 1970s. In 1981, the Commission on Civil Rights published a report which was based "primarily upon fact finding meetings in 10 cities around the country, interviews with knowledgeable people, and an examination of the laws and regulations under which the major federal enforcement agencies discharge their responsibilities in the area of equal employment opportunity" (U.S. Commission on Civil Rights, 1981, p. iii). The report cited a variety of problems in some of the most important agencies which have responsibility for implementing, supervising and enforcing affirmative action policies.

The Federal agency that is responsible for ensuring equal employment opportunity by federal contractors is the Office of Federal Contract Compliance Programs (OFCCP) of the Department of Labor. Representatives of minority and women's groups have cited such problems as inadequate monitoring, lack of readily available and comprehensible information about Federal requirements and procedures, and a general failure to "deliver the goods" to those who are supposed to benefit from these programs (U.S. Commission on Civil Rights, 1981).

The EEOC is primarily responsible for enforcing Title VII of the Civil Rights Act of 1964 which was enacted to eliminate employment discrimination. The problems attributed to the EEOC included the following: duplication and conflicts between EEOC and other agency requirements; inadequate technical assistance; inactivity in terms of the number of Title VII lawsuits brought by the agency; inadequate resources available for EEOC to do its job; and failure to provide adequate information for community groups to educate themselves and monitor equal employment opportunity activities aimed at eliminating employment discrimination (U.S. Commission on Civil Rights, 1981, pp. 26-28).

The Office of Personnel Management (OPM) plays a significant role in promoting and meeting equal employment obligations in the federal government. Among other problems, the OPM has been faulted with having little authority to apply sanctions against recalcitrant agencies or managers, meting out inadequate sanctions, not keeping current statistics, and developing goals at the national level which ignore regional and local underrepresented groups (U.S. Commission on Civil

Rights, 1981, pp. 38-40).

In 1982 the Ad Hoc Committee on Affirmative Action Statistics of the American Statistical Association published a critique of some of the Federal requirements for statistical procedures used to detect problems attaining equal employment opportunity (Notes, 1982). Recommendations for procedural improvements in the EEOC and OFCCP included substituting one uniform report for the dozen or more slightly different forms then in use; replacing the "visual" identification strategy with reliable methods for categorization of employee race and ethnicity; stopping the practice of counting minorities and women twice; expanding the definition of the labor market recruitment area to include professional and highly skilled workers rather than limiting them almost exclusively to unspecialized and unskilled labor; and instituting much greater correspondence between Census of Population and agency classifications of occupations.

Despite these problems and recommendations, the Reagan administration attempted, in 1981 and 1983, to establish only voluntary compliance in the OFCCP and more lenient rules for federal contractors. Women's and civil rights groups tried to halt some of the proposed dilutions, but the OFCCP has significantly reduced the impact of affirmative action:

> The ... [OFCCP] has narrowed the standards for eligibility for backpay by limiting the period of harm for which backpay is sought. It has also made it more difficult to prove patterns and practices of discrimination by statistical evidence. It has instituted the national self-monitoring reporting system, a program under which large multifacility contractors may effectively monitor their own affirmative action performance with little or no oversight by the OFCCP. (Withers, 1985, p. 214)

The Department of Justice has also been accused of trying to undermine the affirmative action gains of the last two decades. According to Goldsmith (1985), the Department of Justice's attacks on affirmative action throughout the 1980s have both created confusion among employers and supervisors and legitimized opposition to race- and sex-based numerical relief.

Subtle and Covert Sex Discrimination

Affirmative action and equal employment opportunity were set up to attack the most blatant, open, and virulent forms of sex discrimination. Thus, definitions of inequality typically focus on results or outcomes. Although an analysis of results is important, it would be a mistake to focus *only* on results and *only* on blatant sex discrimination because an understanding of process, and especially *subtle* process, helps explain why the slow progress of remedying overt discrimination is even slower than might be expected.

Subtle Sex Discrimination

There are many forms of subtle sex discrimination that affect women, especially minority women, in all types of employment (Benokraitis & Feagin, 1986; Dovidio, Mann, & Gaertner, Chapter 7). Subtle sex discrimination involves intentional and unintentional sex inequality. It may be visible, but often goes unnoticed because it has been built into our society's norms, values, and ideologies. It is communicated both verbally and behaviorally, is usually informal rather than formal, and is most visible on individual rather than organizational levels (Benokraitis & Feagin, 1986). A few examples will illustrate the subtle barriers that women encounter in federal government employment.

"Supportive discouragement" refers to a form of subtle sex discrimination in which women receive mixed messages about their abilities, capabilities, intelligence, performance, or accomplishments. For example, a middle-level (GS-10) female federal employee, a computer programmer in the Army, said she was denied a promotion because the (all-male) evaluation team focused on her stereotypically female high evaluations of being "supportive," "following directions," and being "thorough" while ignoring such traditionally nonfemale characteristics (on which she was also evaluated highly) as leadership, innovation, and original contributions to the division (Benokraitis & Feagin, 1986, p. 69).

"Liberated sexism," another type of subtle sex discrimination, refers to the process that, at face value, appears to actively and self-consciously treat women and men equally but which, in practice, increases men's freedom while placing greater burdens on women (Benokraitis & Feagin, 1986, p. 83). Perhaps one of the best examples of liberated sexism is "double days" where "liberated" women now have two full-time jobs -- one inside the home and one outside the home. In 1978 Congress passed the Federal Employees Flexible and Compressed Work Schedules Act to help working parents. Because, however, it is women and not men who are expected to care for children, such alternative work patterns have reinforced women's child-care responsibilities. The Federal Part-Time Career Employment Act of 1978 opened up some 20,000 part-time professional and managerial positions in federal employment by 1982. Part-time jobs carry no job security and minimal fringe benefits (as paid vacations, sick leave, health insurance, retirement plans, etc.), and are filled by women who are balancing double days. Thus, part-time work proliferates job ghettos for women (Stoper, 1988).

Covert Sex Discrimination

Covert sex discrimination refers to unequal and harmful treatment of women that is hidden, clandestine, and maliciously motivated. This barrier is difficult to document because victims are frequently unaware of being targeted and are often ignorant of the means to secure, track, and record evidence of covert discrimination (Benokraitis & Feagin, 1986; Twiss, Tabb, & Crosby, Chapter 13). Two types of covert discrimination are especially harmful to women in federal employment.

The first is tokenism. Because male quotas are high -- 95 to 99 percent -- it is not difficult to fill the low percentage of slots allocated to "token" women. A typical form of tokenism is "numerical exclusion" which uses quotas to maintain a predominantly male workforce -- especially at higher salary levels. Some women are even told by recruiters that they are being hired as tokens. A recent college graduate, who was a mathematics major, related the following to one of the authors:

> My friend, Susan, and I got similar [high] grades in college and were interviewed by [Mr. X, a recruiter for the Army] a few months before graduation. We applied for the same department. I found out later that Susan would probably get a job offer from a different engineering department and not the one we applied for because a woman had retired and they needed "another woman" to replace her.

The respondent was angry because she felt that they were being placed in job slots not because of their interests or qualifications, but just because "a token woman" was needed in a department.

Even in those situations where women are not tokens, accusations of tokenism are effective strategies for keeping women in their place (Benokraitis & Feagin, 1986). Such accusations create suspicion, raise doubts about women's intelligence, abilities, and achievements, and decrease competition among women.

"Containment" refers to the unwritten and usually unspoken policy or practice of restricting women's entry into designated jobs and positions so as not to threaten or displace the composition of dominant -- that is, White male -- group members (Benokraitis & Feagin, 1986). Often, women are allowed to enter traditionally male-dominated areas but run into rules that preclude their promotion. For example, when the draft ended in the early 1970s, the military recruited women to meet projected human resource shortages. The typical route to high ranks in the military is through combat. Because women are not allowed to serve in combat, promotion opportunities are limited to command of support units and other peripheral positions. In the Navy, for instance, the 175 women surface-warfare officers who were preparing for sea duty could serve on only 33 of the Navy's 527 ships, and those 33 operate only on the fringes of the fleet -- as repair vessels, research ships, tenders (small ships that service larger ships), and the like. As one female officer stated, "To spend twenty years to get to be a captain of a tender isn't enough incentive" (Schwadel, 1985, p. 33).

Documenting overt structural discrimination to eliminate sex inequality in federal government employment is important. As these examples suggest, however, a variety of subtle and covert sex discrimination processes are also impeding women's progress. These subtle and covert processes of discrimination will require closer examination in the future.

Conclusion

The federal government, as a major employer, does not meet its affirmative action obligations. Despite widespread popularized rhetoric about "quotas," "reverse discrimination," and "preferential treatment," women's progress in federal government employment during the last two decades has been excruciatingly slow. Women are unable to penetrate the higher-paying, higher-status jobs. Many structural and attitudinal barriers have not changed much since 1966. Others are being reinforced or replaced by more subtle processes of sex discrimination. Instead of playing a leadership role to ensure greater job equality, the federal government has recently moved to dilute and dismantle affirmative action policies and enforcement. It would be a serious mistake to assume that the few gains women have made in federal employment cannot or will not be reversed by their employer in the future.

References

Benokraitis, N. V., & Feagin, J. R. (1986). *Modern sexism: Blatant, subtle, and covert discrimination*. Englewood Cliffs, NJ: Prentice-Hall.

Bocher, R. B. (1982). Does tradition affect affirmative action results? How Pennsylvania achieved changes at the middle management level. *Public Administration Review, 42*, 475-478.

Deaux, K. (1984). Blue-collar barriers. *American Behavioral Scientist, 27*, 287-300.

DiPrete, T. A. (1987). The professionalization of administration and equal employment opportunity in the U.S. federal government. *American Journal of Sociology, 93*, 119-140.

DiPrete, T. A., & Soule, W. T. (1986). The organization of career lines: Equal employment opportunity and status advancement in a federal bureaucracy. *American Sociological Review, 51*, 295-309.

Dovidio, J. F., Mann, J., & Gaertner, S. L. (1989). Resistance to Affirmative action: The Implications of Aversive Racism. In F. A. Blanchard & F. J. Crosby (Eds.), *Affirmative Action in Perspective* (pp. 83-102). New York: Springer-Verlag.

Eberts, R. W., & Stone, J. A. (1985). Male-female differences in promotions: EEO in public education. *The Journal of Human Resources, 20*, 504-521.

Ferber, M., Huber, J., & Spitzer, G. (1979). Preference for men as bosses and professionals. *Social Forces, 58*, 466-476.

Franklin, W. F., & Sweeney, J. L. (1988). Women and corporate power. In E. Boneparth & E. Stoper (Eds.), *Women, power and policy: Toward the year 2000* (pp. 48-65). New York: Pergamon Press.

Goldsmith, J. (1985). Testimony of the National Organization of Women. Pp. 227-234 in U.S. Commission on Civil Rights, *Selected affirmative action topics in employment and business set-asides*, Washington, D.C.

Goodman, N. C. (1975). *Women and management*. Cambridge, MA: Radcliffe College.

Hacker, S. L. (1982). Sex stratification, technology and organization change: A longitudinal case study of AT&T. In R. Kahn-Hut, A. K. Daniels & R. Colvard (Eds.), *Women and Work: Problems and perspectives* (pp. 248-266). New York: Oxford University Press.

Holm, S. L. (1982). *Women in the military: An unfinished revolution*. Novato, CA: Presidio Press.

Huckle, P. (1985). Whatever happened to affirmative action? Employment of women in the Los Angeles city department of water and power, 1973-1983. *Review of Public Personnel Administration, 6*, 44-58.

Leonard, J. S. (1985). What promises are worth: The impact of affirmative action goals. *The Journal of Human Resources, 20*, 3-20.

Lepper, M. M. (1974). A study of career structures of federal executives: A focus on women. In J.S. Jaquette (Ed.), *Women in politics* (pp. 109-130). New York: John Wiley.

Lewis, G. B., & Emmert, M. A. (1986). The sexual division of labor in federal employment. *Social Science Quarterly, 67*, 143-155.

MacLennan, B. W. (1973). Women's part in institutional sexism. Speech given at the New York Academy of Sciences.

Morrison, A. M., White, R. P., & Van Velsor, E. (1987). Executive women: Substance plus style. *Psychology Today, 21*(8), 18-32.

Notes. (1982). Summary notes on the statistics of federal affirmative action programs. *The American Journal of Economics and Sociology, 41*, 321-332.

Schwadel, F. (1985, March 14). Women move up in the military, but many jobs remain off limits. *Wall Street Journal*, 33.

Slack, J. D. (1987). Affirmative action and city managers: Attitudes toward recruitment of women. *Public Administration Review, 47*, 199-206.

Statham, A. (1988). Women working for women: The manager and her secretary. In A. Statham, E. M. Miller & H. O. Mauksch (Eds.), *The Worth of Women's Work* (pp. 225-243). New York: SUNY Press.

Stoper, E. (1988). Alternative work patterns and the double life. In E. Boneparth & E. Stoper (Eds.), *Women, Power and Policy* (2nd ed., pp. 93-112). New York: Pergamon Press.

Taylor, P. A. (1977). Equal employment opportunity in the federal government: An examination of the available evidence. Paper presented at the 72nd annual meeting of the American Sociological Association, Chicago.

Twiss, C., Tabb, S., & Crosby, F. (1989). Affirmative action and aggregate data: The importance of patterns in the perception of discrimination. In F. A. Blanchard & F. J. Crosby (Eds.), *Affirmative Action in Perspective* (pp. 159-167). New York: Springer-Verlag.

U.S. Civil Service Commission, Bureau of Manpower Information Systems. (1969). *Federal civilian personnel statistics: Study of employment of women in the federal government*. Washington, D.C.: Government Printing Office.

U.S. Civil Service Commission, Bureau of Personnel Management Information System. (1976). *Federal civilian work force statistics: Equal employment opportunity statistics.* Washington, D.C.: Government Printing Office.

U.S. Commission on Civil Rights. (1981). *Promises and perceptions: Federal efforts to eliminate employment discrimination through affirmative action.* Washington, D.C.: Government Printing Office.

U.S. Equal Employment Opportunity Commission. (1986). *Annual report on the employment of minorities, women & individuals with handicaps in the federal government.* Washington, D.C.: Government Printing Office.

U.S. Office of Personnel Management, Federal Civilian Workforce Statistics.

(1986). *Affirmative employment statistics*. Washington, D.C.: Government Printing Office.

Vertz, L. L. (1985). Women, occupational advancement, and mentoring: An analysis of one public organization. *Public Administration Review, 45*, 415-423.

Withers, C. (1985). Statement of the women's legal defense fund. In U.S. Commission on Civil Rights, *Selected affirmative action topics in employment and business set-asides* (pp. 209-218). Washington, D.C.: Government Printing Office.

Zashin, E. M. (1980). Affirmative action and federal personnel systems. *Public Policy, 28*, 351-380.

II: Reactions to Affirmative Action

7

Resistance to Affirmative Action: The Implications of Aversive Racism

John F. Dovidio, Jeffrey Mann, and Samuel L. Gaertner

America is a country of paradoxes. The American ideology is strongly egalitarian, and yet the history of our country includes centuries of institutionalized inequality. Even today, persistent racial injustice in the face of democratic ideals truly remains the "American Dilemma" (Myrdal, 1944).

Nationwide polls show that White citizens are becoming increasingly non-prejudiced and racially tolerant. More and more Whites have expressed support for the assertion that Blacks "should have as good a chance as White people to get a job" (Schuman, Steeh, & Bobo, 1985): The percentage of Whites agreeing with this statement has risen from 45% in 1944, to 49% in 1946, 85% in 1963, and 89% in 1966. In 1972, virtually all of the Whites surveyed (97%) supported this view. Racial tolerance is also evident in other polls. In 1972, only 31% of Whites agreed that "Blacks come from a less able race and this explains why Blacks are not as well off as Whites" (Sniderman & Hagen, 1985). In 1988 only 29% of Whites reported feeling that the reason "poor Blacks have not been able to rise out of poverty...[is]...mainly the fault of Blacks themselves" (Newsweek, 1988). Instead, the majority of Whites, 72%, believe that "generations of slavery and discrimination have created conditions that make it difficult for Blacks to work their way out of the lower class" (Sniderman & Hagen, 1985).

Given the current pro-equality and apparently non-racist ideology, it would seem logical to find White citizens supporting affirmative action programs. Yet, White Americans appear deeply ambivalent about affirmative action. On the one hand, 76% of Whites agree that "affirmative action programs that help Blacks and other minorities to get ahead should be supported" (Kluegel & Smith, 1986). On the other hand, there is resistance to the *implementation* of affirmative action programs. Approximately 80% of Whites oppose giving *preference* to a Black worker over a White worker of equal ability (Lipset & Schneider, 1978). In 1988, only 14% of Whites felt that "because of past discrimination...qualified Blacks [should] receive preferential treatment over equally qualified Whites in such matters as getting into college or getting jobs" (Newsweek, 1988). The weak support among Whites for preferential treatment contrasted with moderate support among Blacks, 40% of whom favored it. Overall, 35% of Whites view preferential treatment for Blacks as fair, but only about 10% support it (Kluegel & Smith, 1986). Thus, there appears to be a discrepancy between how White Americans react to affirmative action in principle and in practice.

Apparently, some of the negative reaction to affirmative action involves the assumption by Whites that affirmative action is synonymous with preferential treatment in which less qualified minorities are selected over more qualified White males. Garcia, Erskine, Hawn, and Casmay (1981) demonstrated that successful minority candidates to graduate school were judged to be less qualified when evaluators believed that the institution had an affirmative action policy than when they believed that it did not. Furthermore, other research reveals that women leaders are responded to more negatively when subordinates believe that leader selection is sex-based rather than merit-based (Jacobson & Koch, 1977).

In terms of self-perceptions, a correlational study (Chacko, 1982) found that women's perceptions that they were hired because of their sex were related to low job satisfaction, low job commitment, and high role stress. Similarly, Heilman, Simon, and Repper (1987) demonstrated in an experimental study that when women believed that their selection as leader was on the basis of sex rather than merit, they devalued their leadership performance, took less credit for successful outcomes, and were less interested in continuing as leader. Finally, Nacoste (1987) showed that persons who benefited from preferential treatment were more attracted to the agency controlling their selection when they perceived the selection procedure as fairer. Thus, there appears to be a strong stigma associated with category-based rather than merit-based treatment.

Explanations

What accounts for our American ambivalence about affirmative action policies and programs? One explanation, proposed by Lipset and Schneider (1978), is that the ambivalence involves the conflict between two core American values, individualism and egalitarianism. Support for the principle of affirmative action represents the egalitarian value; the opposition to the implementation of affirmative action programs reflects the individualism value: "Many Whites deeply resent efforts to force racial integration on them, not because they oppose racial equality, but because they feel it violates their individual freedom" (Lipset & Schneider, 1978, p. 43).

Although Lipset and Schneider's (1978) explanation of the data is suggestive, we believe that it does not provide a complete account. We propose that race is an important element in this value conflict. The conflict between egalitarianism and individualism can and does play itself out in many arenas of policy -- from public health to government involvement in environmental protection. With questions of affirmative action, however, the issue of race becomes much more prominent than in other policy issues, such as environmental protection.

We contend that one important factor in the resistance to affirmative action programs is subtle, modern racism. Like Kluegel and Smith (1986), we argue that "opposition to equal opportunity programs stems from the threat these programs present to an economic order that is believed to be just in principle and to work well in fact" (p. 212). Thus, although racist traditions may have initially produced social inequalities, many Whites who truly believe that they are non-prejudiced and non-discriminating may presently be participating in the continued restriction of opportunities for Blacks and other minorities by opposing programs that threaten their own advantaged status.

The central purpose of this chapter is to develop the case that White opposition to affirmative action programs grows, in part, from subtle but pervasive racism. After defining our terms, we review some evidence that documents the persistence of "aversive racism" among White people who genuinely endorse egalitarian values and who appear racially tolerant on attitude surveys. Both survey and experimental data on subtle racism have been extensively reviewed (see Crosby, Bromley, & Saxe, 1980; Kinder, 1986); consequently, for this chapter, we focus mainly on our own research. We then describe some empirical data that link aversive racism to resistance to the implementation of affirmative action and conclude by outlining strategies, suggested by the present perspective, for facilitating the increased acceptance of affirmative action policies. While our focus is on racism, our discussion also concerns sexism. We believe that many of the critical elements of modern racism relate to sexism (see Feagin & Feagin, 1978), and together they contribute to opposition to affirmative action.

Modern Racism

A number of studies and surveys have revealed consistent decreases in expressed negative racial attitudes (Dovidio & Gaertner, 1986; Kluegel & Smith, 1986; Schuman et al., 1985). Some scholars interpret these changes in public opinion to mean that White Americans no longer feel deeply anti-Black (Poskocil, 1977). Other researchers, ourselves included, are less sanguine. We contend that some of the decrease in overt anti-Black prejudice among White Americans is more apparent than real. Racism has not gone away; rather, its expression has become more subtle, indirect, and rationalizable.

Aversive Racism

One form of subtle racism is *aversive racism* (Gaertner, 1976; Kovel, 1970). We conceive of aversive racism as an attitudinal adaptation resulting from an assimilation of an egalitarian value system with prejudice and with racist beliefs (Gaertner & Dovidio, 1986a). The aversive racist perspective assumes that cognitive and motivational biases and the historically racist culture of the United States have led most White Americans to develop biased beliefs and feelings of superiority to Blacks and other minorities. Because of traditional cultural values, however, most Whites also have convictions concerning fairness, justice, and racial equality. The existence, both of almost unavoidable racial biases and of the desire to be egalitarian and racially tolerant, forms the basis of the ambivalence that aversive racists experience.

Because aversive racists endorse egalitarian values and regard themselves as racially tolerant, generally they will not discriminate against Blacks in situations in which norms prescribing appropriate behavior are clear and unambiguous. To discriminate against Blacks in these situations would directly threaten the egalitarian self-image. When the normative structure within the situation is weak, ambiguous, or conflicting, or if a White person can justify or rationalize a negative response on the basis of some factor other than race, negative feelings toward Blacks will be manifested. Thus, an aversive racist can discriminate against Blacks without challenging his or her egalitarian self-image.

Related Conceptions of Modern Racism

The concept of aversive racism bears a similarity to other conceptions of modern racism. In interpreting survey data, Jackman (1978) has made a distinction between "general" and "applied" measures of racial tolerance and suggests that the divergent trends for responses to principle and implementation items reflect "superficial racial tolerance." General measures involve endorsement of abstract values, whereas applied measures relating to implementation of affirmative action policies involve a genuine commitment to integration. Thus, Jackman interprets the positive relationship between education level (which correlates with liberalism) and support for integration in principle as a reflection of the recognition and acceptance of popular, egalitarian ideals. She views the lack of correlation between education and support for the implementation of integration policies as an indication that more educated people do not actually have a greater commitment to that position when real-life issues are at stake (Jackman, 1978; Jackman & Muha, 1984).

Another related concept is "symbolic racism" (Kinder, 1986; Kinder & Sears, 1981; McConahay & Hough, 1976; Sears, Hensler, & Speer, 1979; Sears & Allen, 1984) or "modern racism" (McConahay, 1986). Whereas aversive racism focuses on subtle racism among liberals, symbolic racism "rests upon anti-Black socialization and conservative political and value socialization" (McConahay & Hough, 1976, p. 23). According to symbolic (and modern) racism theory, Whites acquire negative feelings toward Blacks early in life. These feelings persist into adulthood but are expressed indirectly and symbolically, in terms of opposition to busing or resistance to preferential treatment, rather than directly or overtly, as in support for segregation. Given that the material conditions of people's lives change over time, the existence of symbolic racism explains the lack of correspondence between narrow self-interest (e.g., having a child who might be biased) and political behavior in adult life. Also, because modern racism involves the rejection of traditional racist beliefs and the displacement of anti-Black feelings onto more rationalizable abstract social and political issues, modern racists, like aversive racists, are relatively unaware of their racist feelings (McConahay, 1986).

Evidence for Aversive Racism

A substantial number of experiments demonstrate the subtle expression of prejudice and discrimination (see Gaertner & Dovidio, 1986a). White subjects, typically college students, do not behaviorally differentiate between White and nonwhite others when differentiation would clearly signal prejudice. While overt racism is generally absent in these studies, however, covert racism is clearly evident.

Blacks Are Not Worse, But Whites Are Better

Aversive racists resist believing that Blacks are bad or even that Blacks are worse than Whites, remarks easily interpreted as indicating racial bias. Subtle bias is displayed, however, in respondents' willingness to entertain the belief that Whites are better than Blacks. This apparent lapse in logic was discovered in a series of studies with White college students.

White subjects asked to evaluate Black and White people on bipolar adjective scales (e.g., Good-Bad), demonstrated no differences in evaluative ratings of Blacks and Whites. A biased response ("Bad") is obvious, and subjects consistently rated both Blacks and Whites on the positive end. When we varied the measurement instrument slightly by placing positive and negative characteristics in separate scales (e.g., Bad, from "not at all" to "extremely"), we found that bias does exist -- but in a subtle form. Although ratings of Blacks and Whites on the negative scales showed no racial bias. The ratings on the positive scales did reveal a significant difference ($p < .05$). Whereas Blacks were not rated more negatively than Whites, Whites were evaluated more positively than Blacks.

Similarly, Gaertner and McLaughlin (1983, Study 3) replaced conventional positive-negative scales with negative-negative scales (e.g., Unambitious-Lazy) and positive-positive scales (e.g., Ambitious-Not Lazy). Discrimination did not occur on the negative-negative scales but did appear on the positive-positive scales. For example, Blacks were not rated as more lazy than Whites, but Whites were evaluated as more ambitious than Blacks.

Further evidence of the subtlety of modern racism comes from a study in which White Colgate University students were asked to evaluate on negative-positive 6-point scales (e.g., bad-good) either the "typical White Colgate student" or the "typical Black Colgate student." Then, subjects were asked to evaluate themselves on the same scales. The results indicated that if only the ratings of the typical Black or White student were compared, no bias was found. The ratings were all quite positive. However, when other- and self-ratings were compared, bias became evident. Specifically, our White subjects evaluated themselves somewhat more positively than the typical White Colgate student, but significantly more positively than the typical Black Colgate student.

Categories of Judgment

Clearly, self-report is susceptible to evaluative concerns and impression management motivations (Sigall & Page, 1971). Consequently, we followed up these self-report studies with a lexical decision task and a priming task in order to provide measures that are more free of evaluative concerns. By measuring reaction times in decision-making, the lexical decision task assesses the extent to which two words are associated in memory, whereas the priming paradigm assesses the extent to which attributes are associated with a category (or group) label. In a lexical decision task, subjects are presented simultaneously with two strings of letters and are asked to decide (yes or no) if both strings are words. Meyer and Schvaneveldt (1971) reported that highly associated words (e.g., doctor, nurse) produced faster reaction times than did unassociated words (nurse, apple). In applying this paradigm to race, Gaertner and McLaughlin (1983) paired the words "Blacks" and "Whites" with positive and negative attributes. In a priming task, subjects are presented with a category name and then are asked to decide if the instances that follow are members of that category. Rosch (1975) found that the presentation of the name of a category, such as "fruit," facilitates decisions (i.e., reduces reaction times) about typical instances (e.g., "orange") more than atypical instances (e.g., "prune"). In our study, subjects were first presented with the primes of "Black" and "White," representing the racial groups. These primes were then followed by positive and negative characteristics. The subject's task was to decide if the characteristic could ever describe the primed social category. Faster reaction times are assumed to reflect greater category association.

The results of our two reaction time studies were consistent. In both studies, negative characteristics were equally associated with Blacks and Whites; in both experiments, positive characteristics were more associated with Whites than with Blacks (*ps* < .05). As in our self-report studies, bias exists, but in a subtle, less obvious form.

Race and the Evaluation of Competent and Incompetent Candidates

The next stage of our research examined how modern biases pertaining to the racial *categories* of Black and White affect responses to *particular* Black or White persons with varying competencies. One study involved students in college admissions decisions (Kline & Dovidio, 1982). White students at Colgate rated applicants who, on the basis of transcript information (e.g., SAT scores), were strongly qualified, moderately qualified, or weakly qualified. The race of the applicant (Black or White) was manipulated by varying a photograph that accompanied the transcript.

When the applicant had weak qualifications, there was no discrimination between Black and White applicants: Both were rated unacceptable for admission to Colgate. When the applicant had moderate qualifications, Whites were evaluated slightly, but not significantly more positively than Blacks. When the applicant had strong qualifications, however, Blacks were evaluated significantly less positively than Whites who had the same qualifications ($p < .05$). Consistent with the previous research presented in this chapter, bias did not occur at all levels; it occurred only at the "high" (i.e., positive) end.

The stimulus materials included individual items that contributed to the overall evaluative score. We scaled the items according to how directly they related to the information presented in the applicant's transcript. The less directly related the item was to the transcript information, the greater was the racist bias ($r = .69$). These results corroborate the finding that Whites tend to evaluate Blacks less favorably than Whites on subjective dimensions of work performance (Kraiger & Ford, 1985) and support Goddard's (1986) observation in applied settings that "vague, ill-defined, subjective criteria lend themselves to all kinds of biased judgments" (p. 34).

In a related experiment, the target of evaluation was not a student but rather a faculty member. White subjects listened to a tape recording of a lecture presumably given by a Black or White applicant (manipulated with a photograph) for a teaching position at Colgate. After listening to the lecture, subjects were quizzed on the content. The quizzes were allegedly graded. Actually, subjects were randomly assigned positive feedback (scores of 87% or better), negative feedback (scores of 63% or worse), or no feedback. Before the conclusion of the session, subjects completed teaching evaluation questionnaires.

Subjects who received negative feedback rated the professor lower, on a 7-item composite index, than did subjects who received no feedback or positive feedback ($p < .01$). In addition, subjects who received the negative feedback rated the Black teacher significantly lower than the White teacher ($p < .02$). Subjects who received no feedback did not discriminate against the Black candidate, whereas subjects who received positive feedback tended to rate the Black teacher more positively ($p < .10$) than the White teacher. Thus, subjects seemed to use an "indirect attitudinal process" whereby information about the other person's race differentially enhanced the salience and potency of *non-race-related* elements, in this case the teacher's effectiveness, that would justify a negative response even if a White person were involved (Gaertner & Dovidio, 1977).

To examine how the indirect attitudinal process can relate to resistance to affirmative action, we conducted another study (Dovidio & Gaertner, 1981). Although Whites who protest affirmative action may express the concern that *qualified* Whites will be disadvantaged relative to *less qualified* Blacks (e.g., *Regents of University of California v. Bakke,* 1978), it is possible that the greatest threat comes not from Black inferiority but from being subordinated to a Black person. The traditional role relationship is one in which Whites have occupied positions of superior status. To change the tradition is to threaten some Whites. The purpose of the study was to investigate the possibility that the generally articulated issue of relative competence is a rationalization in which a nonracial factor, competence, is used by Whites to object to affirmative action programs that increase the likelihood that they will be subordinated to Blacks.

In our study, White male undergraduates were introduced to a Black or White male confederate who was presented as either the subject's supervisor or subordinate. In addition, the confederate was described as being higher or lower than the subject in an intellectual ability that was relevant to the dyad's task. The dependent measure was an incidental helping task, picking up pencils that the confederate "accidentally" knocked to the floor. This situation provided subjects with an opportunity to offer assistance which was not absolutely necessary but which could connote affiliative and friendly feelings.

Overall, subjects helped Black partners more than White partners ($p < .05$). The effect of race, however, was moderated by status and ability (interaction $ps < .05$). Specifically, the results indicated that relative status, rather than relative ability was the primary determinant of helping behavior toward Blacks. Regardless of ability, Black supervisors were helped less ($p < .05$) than Black subordinates (58% vs. 83%), whereas White supervisors were helped somewhat more than White subordinates (54% vs. 41%). Relative ability, in contrast, did not affect prosocial behavior toward Blacks. Collapsing across status, high and low ability Blacks were helped equally often (70% each), whereas high ability White partners were helped more frequently ($p < .05$) than were low ability White partners (67% vs. 29%). Thus ability, not status, was instrumental in determining helping toward Whites; but status, not ability, was the major factor influencing prosocial behavior toward Blacks.

How could people in this experiment rationalize not responding positively to competent Blacks? Subjects' post-experimental evaluations of their partners revealed that their behaviors may have been mediated by perceptions of relative intelligence (competence). Subjects' ratings indicated that they accepted high-ability White partners as being somewhat more intelligent than themselves, but subjects described even high-ability Black partners as significantly less intelligent than themselves ($p < .05$). Thus, even when the competence of Black supervisors surpasses that of Whites, Whites appear to perceive the situation as if Blacks of lower competence than themselves are being given preferential treatment. Identical patterns of results were revealed for helping and competence ratings in a subsequent study using sex rather than race as the manipulated social category (Dovidio & Gaertner, 1983).

Aversive Racism and Affirmative Action

We believe that the aversive racism framework has important and direct implications for the implementation of affirmative action-type policies. Affirmative action has often been interpreted as "when all things are equal, take the minority person." Our research suggests that even when things are equal, they may not be perceived as equal -- particularly when the minority person is well-qualified and the situation has personal relevance to the nonminority person. Because Whites tend to misperceive the competence of Blacks relative to themselves, resistance to affirmative action may appear quite legitimate to the protesters. Insufficient competence, not race, becomes the apparent rationale justifying resistance. Similarly, deficiencies in prerequisite qualifications (relative to one's own), not racial antipathy, become the dominant articulated theme for protesting special admissions policies for minorities. Thus, Whites may support the principle of affirmative action in the abstract but may oppose the actual implementation of affirmative action on the basis of an apparently non-race-related rationale.

The connection between opposition to affirmative action, on the one hand, and racism, on the other, has been suggested by several authors (see Benokraitis & Feagin, 1978), and this relationship, in terms of old-fashioned racism, has been empirically verified (Kinder & Sears, 1981). With respect to modern racism, in particular, Jacobson (1985) found that symbolic racism was a stronger predictor of negative attitudes toward affirmative action than old-fashioned racism, stereotyping, or self-interest. In addition, symbolic racism was the best predictor of negative reactions to a concrete instance of the implementation of affirmative action: Respondents were asked to state their approval or disapproval of the Supreme Court's dismissal of a case involving a claim of reverse discrimination. Thus, although there may be a number of reasons for opposing affirmative action, modern racism appears to be among the most important (Kinder, 1986; Kluegel & Smith, 1983).

Facilitating Acceptance of Affirmative Action

Our research indicates that modern racism is, unfortunately, alive and well among well-intentioned Whites. Modern forms of racism are more subtle and indirect than the old-fashioned form, and support for policies that perpetuate the different status of Blacks and Whites is often justified on the basis of issues that are ostensibly non-race-related (Gaertner & Dovidio, 1986a; Pettigrew & Martin, 1987). Because of the increased salience of these nonracial factors in interracial situations, Whites may discriminate against Blacks and still perceive themselves as being egalitarian.

Given that resistance to affirmative action can be understood, at least partially, in terms of racial bias, what strategies should be used to implement affirmative action programs? We offer two concrete suggestions. First administrators should articulate in the clearest way possible that affirmative action is a fair policy, and resistance to affirmative action is non-egalitarian and racist. Second, effective implementation of affirmative action can be supported by changing perceptions of personal relevance in the situation. To the extent that increased opportunities for minorities due to affirmative action policies have negative consequences on the opportunities for oneself and one's own group, these policies will be resisted. It may be possible, however, to develop decategorization or recategorization strategies that produce a redefinition of self- and group-interest and consequently facilitate acceptance of affirmative action policies.

Clarifying Egalitarianism

Egalitarianism is a core American value, rooted in philosophical, social, and political systems, that can prime pro-Black sentiments (Katz & Hass, in press) and thus can be used productively for implementing affirmative action programs. Because affirmative action often involves *preferential* treatment of minorities and women, common objections are that it is unfair, *non*-egalitarian, and, paradoxically, discriminatory.

Nevertheless, what appears to be unfair at the micro level of a particular instance may be seen as very fair at a more macro level that considers broader social, legal, and moral issues. In this volume, Clayton and Tangri (Chapter 15) and Holloway (Chapter 2) strongly argue that affirmative action should be evaluated at this more macro level because: (1) equity, narrowly defined, perpetuates and exacerbates the disadvantaged status of people who already possess disproportionately fewer resources; (2) equal opportunity and colorblind procedures are not sufficient to reverse the effects of years of personal and institutional discrimination; (3) the effects of discrimination are more clearly seen at the societal level than at the individual level; and (4) the focus on microjustice, which may involve a specific instance that implicates particular individuals, unnecessarily and erroneously personalizes the more general issue. Thus, Clayton and Tangri assert that "a precise analysis of fairness, one that acknowledges the complexity of the multifaceted construct of justice, yields the conclusion that affirmative action is fair under any principle of justice" (Chapter 15, p. 179).

To the extent that administrators and top management strongly and persuasively present affirmative action as an egalitarian policy, aversive racists should embrace it in practice as well as in principle. Resisting affirmative action under these circumstances could readily be interpreted as a racially biased reaction. Our research on aversive racism indicates that when norms for appropriate behavior are clearly defined, and a biased response can be recognized, Whites are consistently as positive in their behavior toward Blacks as toward Whites (Gaertner & Dovidio, 1986a); in fact, when people who endorse egalitarian values are confronted with the possibility that they may be prejudiced, they often respond more favorably to Blacks than to Whites (Dutton, 1976). In addition, the fairer a procedure is perceived to be, the more satisfied the participants are -- regardless of whether the outcome is personally desirable or undesirable (Lind, Kurtz, Musante, & Thibaut, 1980; see also Nacoste, Chapter 8). Consistent with this reasoning, corporate research has revealed that commitment to affirmative action by top management and higher administration is a key factor for successfully implementing affirmative action (Hitt & Keats, 1984; Marino, 1980).

Decategorization and Recategorization

Whereas our first proposed strategy of clarifying egalitarianism necessarily involves recognition of existing racial (or gender) category membership, other strategies for implementing affirmative action programs focus on minimizing or redefining social categories. Theoretically, factors that draw attention to distinct category memberships (such as Black-White or male-female), rather than to the qualities shared between groups, lead people to overemphasize differences between groups and similarities within groups. Group memberships become separated and simplified so that members within a category seem interchangeable and members between groups seem non-interchangeable. When this happens, group members tend to compare themselves with other groups in a way that consistently portrays one's own group members more positively than members of other groups (Brewer, 1979; Tajfel & Turner, 1979; Turner, 1987). Thus, according to the social categorization perspective, the ingroup favoritism that characterizes Whites' aversive reactions to Blacks is partly the normal consequence of categorizing people into groups. Given the integral role of categorical perceptions in prejudice (Hamilton & Trolier, 1986; Messick & Mackie, in press; Stephan, 1985), attempts to reduce bias have focused on decreasing people's reliance on social categories in intergroup situations.

One strategy for producing decategorized perceptions has focused on providing individuating information about outgroup members (Wilder, 1978). Ingroup favoritism decreases, for example, when outgroup members are portrayed as differing in opinion from one another (Wilder, 1978, Study 1). In theory, individuation decreases bias because people previously seen as interchangeable group members come to be seen as individuals. With respect to employment settings, Crocker and Park (in press) propose that stereotypes have the strongest effects when the least information is available about the candidate, for example in hiring decisions. When more individuating information is available, however, the effect of stereotyping diminishes (Heilman, 1984; Terborg & Ilgen, 1975).

Another strategy for establishing decategorized perceptions involves inducing members of different groups to discuss personalized, intimate information in a context that stresses attention to personal qualities (Miller & Brewer, 1984). Whereas individuation primarily operates by increasing perceptions of outgroup variability, personalization has its effect by establishing personal, intimate interactions. For example, when group members disclose unique characteristics about themselves that they believe make them particularly qualified for a task, ingroup favoritism decreases and egalitarian evaluations generalize to other outgroup members who do not share personalizing information (Miller & Brewer, 1984). Dipboye (1985) argued that in employment settings personal feelings toward an employee affect evaluations of him or her, independent of social stereotypes arising from social categorization. Thus, to the extent that individuating or personalizing information can be made salient in interview and work settings, social prejudices and ingroup favoritism should be reduced. These positions suggest, on a practical level, that employment interviews should be structured to focus on the personal and unique aspects of the applicant, as well as the more categorical information about the applicant.

Interventions that involve *re*categorization rather than *de*categorization can also reduce intergroup bias (Turner, 1981; Worchel, 1979). In particular, we have attempted to reduce intergroup bias by changing group members' cognitive representations from two groups to one group (Gaertner, 1985; Gaertner & Dovidio, 1986b; Gaertner, Mann, Murrell, & Dovidio, 1988). We have varied the spatial arrangement of members of different groups in a room and the presence of symbols that highlight either separate group memberships or a superordinate group identity, and we have found that evaluations of former outgroup members significantly improve as these individuals become identified with the ingroup.

We view the recategorization of two groups into one group as a particularly powerful and pragmatic strategy for improving reactions to affirmative action. One reason is the recognition that humans' limited cognitive processing capacity strongly encourages the maintenance of social categories in lieu of more individualistic, personalized perceptions. Also, because ingroup members favor their own group and assume within-group similarity (Linville, Salovey, & Fischer, 1986), a superordinate identity should especially facilitate the development of positive personalized evaluations. Such ingroup favoritism and personalized evaluation should facilitate accurate evaluation and acceptance of high ability minority members.

A third reason that a common group identity should be effective at facilitating acceptance of affirmative action is that it promotes the self-sacrificing behaviors that affirmative action apparently requires for an advantaged majority to yield its privileges to a disadvantaged minority. Meindl and Lerner (1983) found that subjects were more likely to put themselves at risk for a stranger perceived to be a member of their ingroup than they were for a stranger perceived to be simply another individual. Consistent with this evidence, Kramer and Brewer (1984) found that subjects were more likely to suspend their short-term self-interest and to cooperate with strangers for long-term benefits when the strangers involved were portrayed as ingroup members rather than as unrelated individuals. Moreover, we hypothesize that in assigning jobs or in deciding admissions, people would be more willing to use a need-based rule than an equity-based rule (Deutsch, 1975) when applicants are perceived to be members of a common salient ingroup rather than individual strangers or members of some delineated outgroup. Furthermore, in general, people tend to be more helpful to ingroup members than to other people (Hornstein, 1976; Piliavin, Dovidio, Gaertner, & Clark, 1981).

Fourth, a common group identity should be effective because it contributes to the development of cooperative interaction, which, in turn, can independently have beneficial consequences. Slavin and Madden's (1979; also Slavin, 1985) review of school practices that improve interracial attitudes revealed that participating on interracial sports teams and in cooperative learning groups were activities most related to students having positive interracial attitudes. Similarly, the "jig-saw" classroom method of introducing interdependence in problem-solving situations seems to capitalize on the enhanced salience of common group membership (Aronson, Blaney, Stephan, Sikes, & Snapp, 1978).

Conclusion

In summary, despite apparent widespread increases in racial tolerance and support for affirmative action in principle, modern racism continues subtly to undermine equal opportunity for Blacks and other minorities and to motivate resistance to affirmative action (see also Pettigrew & Martin, 1987). While the expression may be more subtle, the consequence of modern racism is comparable to that of old-fashioned racism -- the continuation of a system that provides Whites advantaged status relative to Blacks and other minorities. In addition, modern racism perpetuates the American paradox: It allows Whites to identify themselves with the solution rather than the problem of racism. The aversive racist sees himself or herself, for instance, as excluding Blacks from certain organizations not because of any anti-Black sentiment but rather because of a devotion to abstract standards. Because of this subtle but insidious form of racism, people's good intentions cannot be relied on to provide true equal opportunity. Strong and vigorous programs mandated by law, such as affirmative action, are required to reverse centuries of individual, institutional, and cultural racism.

References

Aronson, E., Blaney, N., Stephan, C. W., Sikes, J., & Snapp, M. (1978). *The jigsaw classroom*. Beverly Hills, CA: Sage.

Benokraitis, N. V., & Feagin, J. R. (1978). *Affirmative action and equal opportunity: Action, inaction, reaction*. Boulder, CO: Westview Press.

Brewer, M. B. (1979). In-group bias in the minimal intergroup situation: A cognitive-motivational analysis. *Psychological Bulletin, 86*, 307-324.

Chacko, T. T. (1982). Women and equal employment opportunity: Some unintended effects. *Journal of Applied Psychology, 67*, 119-123.

Clayton, S. D., & Tangri, S. S. (1989). The justice of affirmative action. In F. A. Blanchard & F. J. Crosby (Ed.), *Affirmative Action in Perspective* (pp. 177-192). New York: Springer-Verlag.

Crocker, J., & Park, B. (in press). The consequences of social stereotypes. In R. Cardy, J. M. Newman, & S. Puffer (Eds.), *Advances in information processing in organizations* (Vol. 3). Greenwich, CT: JAI Press.

Crosby, F., Bromley, S., & Saxe, L. (1980). Recent unobtrusive studies of Black and white discrimination and prejudice: A literature review. *Psychological Bulletin, 87*, 546-563.

Deutsch, M. (1975). Equity, equality, and need: What determines which value will be used as a basis for distributive justice? *Journal of Social Issues, 31*, 137-149.

Dipboye, R. L. (1985). Some neglected variables in research on discrimination in appraisals. *Academy of Management Review, 10*, 116-127.

Dovidio, J. F., & Gaertner, S. L. (1981). The effects of race, status, and ability on helping behavior. *Social Psychology Quarterly, 44*, 192-203.

Dovidio, J. F., & Gaertner, S. L. (1983). The effects of sex, status, and ability on helping behavior. *Journal of Applied Social Psychology, 13*, 191-205.

Dovidio, J. F., & Gaertner, S. L. (1986). Prejudice, discrimination, and racism: Historical trends and contemporary approaches. In J. F. Dovidio & S. L. Gaertner (Eds.), *Prejudice, discrimination, and racism* (pp. 1-34). Orlando, FL: Academic Press.

Dutton, D. G. (1976). Tokenism, reverse discrimination and egalitarianism in interracial behavior. *Journal of Social Issues, 32*(2), 93-107.

Feagin, J. B., & Feagin, L. B. (1978). *Discrimination American style: Institutional racism and sexism*. Englewood Cliffs, NJ: Prentice-Hall.

Gaertner, S. L. (1976). Nonreactive measures in racial attitude research: A focus on "Liberals." In P. Katz (Ed.), *Toward the elimination of racism* (pp. 183-211). New York: Pergamon Press.

Gaertner, S. L. (1985, March). *When groups merge: Reducing the salience of group boundaries*. Paper presented at the American Educational Research Association Annual Meeting, Chicago.

Gaertner, S. L., & Dovidio, J. F. (1977). The subtlety of white racism, arousal, and helping behavior. *Journal of Personality and Social Psychology, 35,* 691-707.

Gaertner, S. L., & Dovidio, J. F. (1986a). The aversive form of racism. In J. F. Dovidio & S. L. Gaertner (Eds.), *Prejudice, discrimination, and racism* (pp. 61-89). Orlando, FL: Academic Press.

Gaertner, S. L., & Dovidio, J. F. (1986b). Prejudice, discrimination, and racism: Problems, progress, and promise. In J. F. Dovidio & S. L. Gaertner (Eds.), *Prejudice, discrimination, and racism* (pp. 315-332). Orlando, FL: Academic Press.

Gaertner, S. L., Mann, J., Murrell, A., & Dovidio, J. F. (1988). *Reduction of intergroup bias: The benefits of perceiving the memberships as one group or as separate individuals.* Manuscript submitted for publication.

Gaertner, S. L., & McLaughlin, J. P. (1983). Racial stereotypes: Associations and ascriptions of positive and negative characteristics. *Social Psychology Quarterly, 46,* 23-30.

Garcia, L. T., Erskine, N., Hawn, & Casmay, S. R. (1981). The effect of affirmative action on attributions about minority group members. *Journal of Personality, 49,* 427-437.

Goddard, R. W. (1986). Post-employment: The changing current in discrimination charges. *Personnel Journal, 65,* 34-40.

Hamilton, D. L., & Trolier, T. K. (1986). Stereotypes and stereotyping: An overview of the cognitive approach. In J. F. Dovidio & S. L. Gaertner (Eds.), *Prejudice, discrimination, and racism* (pp. 1-34). Orlando, FL: Academic Press.

Heilman, M. E. (1984). Information as a deterrent against sex discrimination: The effects of applicant sex and information type on preliminary employment decisions. *Organizational Behavior and Human Performance, 33,* 174-186.

Heilman, M. E., Simon, M. C., & Repper, D. P. (1987). Intentionally favored, unintentionally harmed? Impact of sex-based preferential selection on self-perceptions and self-evaluations. *Journal of Applied Psychology, 72,* 62-66.

Hitt, M. A., & Keats, B. W. (1984). Empirical identification of the criteria for effective affirmative action programs. *Journal of Applied Behavioral Science, 20,* 203-222.

Holloway, F. A. (1989). What is affirmative action? In F. A. Blanchard & F. J. Crosby (Ed.), *Affirmative Action in Perspective* (pp. 9-19). New York: Springer-Verlag.

Hornstein, H. A. (1976). *Cruelty and kindness: A new look at aggression and altruism.* Englewood Cliffs, NJ: Prentice-Hall.

Jackman, M. R. (1978). General and applied tolerance: Does education increase commitment to racial integration? *American Journal of Political Science, 22,* 302-324.

Jackman, M. R., & Muha, M. J. (1984). Education and intergroup attitudes: Moral enlightenment, superficial democratic commitment, or ideological refinement? *American Sociological Review, 49,* 751-769.

Jacobson, C. K. (1985). Resistance to affirmative action: Self-interest or racism? *Journal of Conflict Resolution, 29,* 306-329.

Jacobson, M. B., & Koch, W. (1977). Women as leaders: Performance evaluation as a function of leader selection. *Organizational Behavior and Human Performance, 20,* 149-157.

Katz, I., & Hass, R. G. (in press). Racial ambivalence and American value conflict: Correlational and priming studies of dual cognitive structures. *Journal of Personality and Social Psychology.*

Kinder, D. R. (1986). The continuing American dilemma: White resistance to racial change 40 years after Myrdal. *Journal of Social Issues, 42*(2), 151-171.

Kinder, D. R., & Sears, D. O. (1981). Symbolic racism versus threats to "the good life." *Journal of Personality and Social Psychology, 40,* 414-431.

Kline, B. B., & Dovidio, J. F. (1982, April). *Effects of race, sex, and qualifications on predictions of a college applicant's performance.* Paper presented at the annual meeting of the Eastern Psychological Association, Baltimore.

Kluegel, J. R., & Smith, E. R. (1983). Affirmative action attitudes: Effects of self-interest, racial affect, and stratification beliefs on whites' beliefs. *Social Forces, 61,* 797-824.

Kluegel, J. R., & Smith, E. R. (1986). *Beliefs about inequality: American's views of what is and what ought to be.* New York: Aldine de Gruyter.

Kovel, J. (1970). *White racism: A psychohistory.* New York: Pantheon.

Kraiger, K., & Ford, J. K. (1985). A meta-analysis of ratee effects in performance ratings. *Journal of Applied Psychology, 70,* 56-65.

Kramer, R. M., & Brewer, M. B. (1984). Effects of group identity on resource use in a simulated commons dilemma. *Journal of Personality and Social Psychology, 46,* 1044-1057.

Lind, E. A., Kurtz, S., Musante, L., & Thibaut, J. W. (1980). Procedure and outcome effects on reactions to adjudicated resolution of conflicts of interest. *Journal of Personality and Social Psychology, 39,* 643-653.

Linville, P. W., Salovey, P., & Fischer, G. W. (1986). Stereotyping and perceived distributions of social characteristics: An application to ingroup-outgroup perception. In J. F. Dovidio & S. L. Gaertner (Eds.), *Prejudice, discrimination, and racism* (pp. 165-208). Orlando, FL: Academic Press.

Lipset, S. M., & Schneider, W. (1978). The Bakke case: How would it be decided at the bar of public opinion? *Public Opinion, 1,* 38-44.

Marino, K. E. (1980). A preliminary investigation into behavioral dimensions of affirmative action compliance. *Journal of Applied Psychology, 65,* 346-350.

Messick, D. M., & Mackie, D. M. (in press). Intergroup relations. In M. R. Rosenweig & L. W. Porter (Eds.), *Annual Review of Psychology*.

McConahay, J. B. (1986). Modern racism, ambivalence, and the modern racism scale. In J. F. Dovidio & S. L. Gaertner (Eds.), *Prejudice, discrimination, and racism* (pp. 91-125). Orlando, FL: Academic Press.

McConahay, J. B., & Hough, J. C., Jr. (1976). Symbolic racism. *Journal of Social Issues, 32*(2), 23-45.

Meindl, J. R., & Lerner, M. J. (1983). The heroic motive: Some experimental demonstrations. *Journal of Experimental Social Psychology, 19*, 1-20.

Meyer, D. E., & Schvaneveldt, R. W. (1971). Facilitation in recognizing pairs of words: Evidence of dependence between retrieval operations. *Journal of Experimental Psychology, 90*, 227-234.

Miller, N., & Brewer, M. B. (1984). The psychology of desegregation: An introduction. In N. Miller & M. B. Brewer (Eds.), *Groups in contact: The psychology of desegregation* (pp. 1-8). Orlando, FL: Academic Press.

Myrdal, G. (1944). *The American dilemma: The Negro problem and modern democracy.* New York: Harper.

Nacoste, R. W. (1987). But do they care about fairness? The dynamics of preferential treatment and minority influence. *Basic and Applied Social Psychology, 8*, 77-191.

Nacoste, R. W. (1989). Affirmative action and self-evaluation. In F. A. Blanchard & F. J. Crosby (Ed.), *Affirmative Action in Perspective* (pp. 103-109). New York: Springer-Verlag.

Newsweek, (1988, March 7).

Pettigrew, T. F., & Martin, J. (1987). Shaping the organizational context for black American inclusion. *Journal of Social Issues, 43*(1), 41-78.

Piliavin, J. A., Dovidio, J. F., Gaertner, S. L., & Clark, R. D., III. (1981). *Emergency intervention*. New York: Academic Press.

Poskocil, A. (1977). Encounters between black and white liberals: The collision of stereotypes. *Social Forces, 55*, 715-727.

Regents of the University of California v. Bakke (1978). *U. S. Law Weekly, 46*, 4896.

Rosch, E. (1975). Cognitive representations of semantic categories. *Journal of Experimental Psychology: General, 104*, 192-233.

Schuman, H., Steeh, C., & Bobo, L. (1985). *Racial attitudes in America: Trends and interpretations*. Cambridge, MA: Harvard University Press.

Sears, D. O., & Allen, H. M., Jr. (1984). The trajectory of local desegregation controversies and whites' opposition to busing. In M. B. Brewer & N. Miller (Eds.), *Groups in contact: The psychology of desegregation* (pp. 123-151). New York: Academic Press.

Sears, D. O., Hensler, C. P., & Speer, L. K. (1979). Whites' opposition to "busing": Self-interest or symbolic politics? *American Political Science Review, 73*, 369-

384.

Sigall, H., & Page, R. (1971). Current stereotypes: A little fading, a little faking. *Journal of Personality and Social Psychology, 18*, 247-255.

Slavin, R. E. (1985). Cooperative learning: Applying contact theory in desegregated schools. *Journal of Social Issues, 41*(3), 45-62.

Slavin, R. E., & Madden, N. A. (1979). School practices that improve social relations. *American Educational Research Journal, 16*, 169-180.

Sniderman, P. M., & Hagen, M. G. (1985). *Race and inequality: A study in American values*. Chatham, NJ: Chatham House.

Stephan, W. G. (1985). Intergroup relations. *In* G. Lindzey & E. Aronson (Eds.), *The handbook of social psychology* (3rd ed., Vol. 2, pp. 599-658). New York: Random House.

Tajfel, H., & Turner, J. C. (1979). An integrative theory of intergroup conflict. *In* W. G. Austin & S. Worchel (Eds.), *The social psychology of intergroup relations* (pp. 33-48). Monterey, CA: Brooks/Cole.

Terborg, J. R., & Ilgen, D. R. (1975). A theoretical approach to sex discrimination in traditionally masculine occupations. *Organizational Behavior and Human Performance, 13*, 352-376.

Turner, J. C. (1981). The experimental social psychology of intergroup behavior. In J. C. Turner & H. Giles (Eds.), *Intergroup behavior* (pp. 1-21). Chicago: University of Chicago Press.

Turner, J. C. (1987). *Rediscovering the social group: A self-categorization theory*. New York: Basil Blackwell.

Wilder, D. A. (1978). Reduction of intergroup discrimination through individuation of the out-group. *Journal of Personality and Social Psychology, 36*, 1361-1374.

Worchel, S. (1979). Cooperation and the reduction of intergroup conflict: Some determining factors. In W. G. Austin & S. Worchel (Eds.), *The social psychology of intergroup relations* (pp. 262-273). Monterey, CA: Brooks/Cole.

8

Affirmative Action and Self-Evaluation

Rupert W. Nacoste

Some of the most troubling criticisms of the policy of affirmative action have suggested that the policy may cause subtle, harmful consequences to those whom the policy is intended to benefit. Some policy analysts have argued, for example, that affirmative action delegitimizes the achievements of women and minorities because others presume that those hired through affirmative action are underqualified (Decter, 1980; Roberts, 1981). Explains Loury (1986):

> If it is known that differential selection criteria are used for different [groups], and if it is ... known that the quality of performance depends on how one did on the criteria of selection, then ... it is a rational statistical inference to impute a lowered quality of performance to persons of the [group] ... preferentially favored in selection (p. 170).

Worse yet, say some analysts, affirmative action can undermine the self-confidence of the direct beneficiaries of the policy (Boxill, 1984) and create a sense of dependency among them (Eastland & Bennett, 1979; Howard & Hammond, 1985). In an organization where the affirmative action program appears to operate unfairly, White males may not be the only ones to question the qualifications and to underestimate the accomplishments of targeted groups; members of the targeted groups also may question their qualifications and their performance. In the long run the under-evaluation of one's own accomplishments could have the pernicious effect of a self-fulfilling prophecy, and the impostor syndrome can develop among minority members and women working in organizations that have affirmative action policies. People suffering from the impostor syndrome tend to overcompensate for imagined in-adquacies so that they are initially productive but frazzled in the long run.

Policy analysts who oppose affirmative action are no doubt correct when they point to the potential long-term detrimental effects of the impostor syndrome. But are the analysts justified in assuming that affirmative action programs always foster an impostor syndrome? Probably not. Several studies have shown that affirmative action does not influence organizational productivity (Leonard, 1984; Lovrich, Steel, & Hood, 1986; Steel & Lovrich, 1987). Studies at the organizational level, however, have limited value because they may mask the effect on the individuals.

What is needed is a test of the proposition that affirmative action programs lead to an impostor syndrome for all individuals. Within that focus, it would be important to begin by asking questions, rather than stating conclusions. We could ask, for example, if it is possible that affirmative action sometimes leads to the impostor syndrome and sometimes does not. Could it be that affirmative action selection produces self-doubt only if the member of the benefited group does not believe in the fairness of the policy? These questions point to a contingency hypothesis. Responses to affirmative action are no doubt contingent on a person's evaluations of the fairness of the policy.

To investigate the contingency hypothesis, we analyzed data from part of a large two-phase panel study administered by the Institute for Research in Social Science at the University of North Carolina. The analysis focused on part of the panel study concerned with the effects of procedural structure on feelings of competence and productivity among the beneficiaries of affirmative action. In the first phase we assessed the attitudes toward, conceptions of, and evaluations of the fairness of affirmative action among 49 female and 48 male participants. Males and females did not differ from each other in their attitudes toward affirmative action. Using a median split (separately among males and females) on our measure of the perceived fairness of affirmative action procedures, we then divided the sample into two groups. The former group contained 20 females and 24 males who thought the procedure of affirmative action a fair procedure; the later, 29 females and 24 males who thought the procedure of affirmative action unfair.

Approximately four months later, participants were presented the experimental phase of the study. In the experimental phase, participants were led to believe that they were going to take part in an investigation of the relationship between a test of creativity and creative behavior. Participants were told that in one of the many questionnaires they had completed over the course of the larger panel study, there had been a test of creativity and that the researchers were interested in the relationship between scores on the test and creative behavior.

Participants were randomly assigned to one of two conditions. In the *standard selection condition* a fictitious criterion score -- 80 points out of 100 -- was set and was used to evaluate individuals. Participants in this condition were told that everyone who had been selected had met this test score criterion. In the *affirmative action selection condition,* participants were also told of the use of a criterion score of 80 out of 100. However, those in this condition were told:

> When we looked at the test scores, we discovered that we didn't get as many [members of the participant's sex] as anticipated. Because we wanted to have approximately equal numbers of males and females to do this task, we included some [members of the participant's sex] whose scores fell below the original minimum score of 80. You are one of the individuals chosen to participate in this [study].

Three aspects of the affirmative action selection method merit comment. First, no indication was provided about how much "violation" of the test score criterion was needed to balance for gender. Second, the method seemed to parallel strongly the stereotype of actual affirmative action procedures. Finally, and most importantly, no subject was told that his or her own score fell below the score of 80; subjects in the affirmative action condition were only told that the scores of *some people* of their own gender fell below the minimum score of 80.

After they were "selected" for the creativity task, participants worked on two computer-controlled brainstorming tasks. They were required to come up with as many uses as they could for two objects -- a burnt match and an empty coke can. Tasks appeared in different orders and independently. For each object, participants were given up to five minutes to create a list of uses. Once they elected to stop generating uses for the two objects, participants independently completed a questionnaire designed to assess emotional and cognitive responses to their participation. In that questionnaire, a measure of each subject's estimates of their score on the "creativity criterion tests" was obtained. For the purposes at hand, we focused on the subjects' self-evaluations and looked at the amount of uses they generated for the two objects (i.e., their productivity) and at the time they spend on the tasks (i.e., effort).

Fairness and Self-doubt

What results might we expect? If the opinions of some policy analysts are correct, we should find that the subjects who were selected through the affirmative action procedure would have a poor self-evaluation, whether or not they think affirmative action a fair policy. We might also find diminished productivity and diminished effort among them. According to the contingency approach, we ought to find that subjects selected in the affirmative action condition should have a poor self-evaluation if and only if they also think that affirmative action is an unfair policy.

Table 8.1 displays the mean self-evaluations of participants who were selected according to the affirmative action procedure or the standard procedure, organized by whether the subjects had previously indicated that they thought the procedure of affirmative action is fair or unfair. As is apparent from the table, participants who thought affirmative action unfair in principle and who were selected by an affirmative action procedure during the experimental phase of the study evaluated their criterion "creativity" scores more harshly than did any other group. It is important to remember that the people in the affirmative action selection condition were not told that they individually had scored below the 80-point cut-off, but they were free to assume that they had. People who thought affirmative action unfair made that assumption; people who thought affirmative action fair also made the assumption, on average, but to a much lesser degree than the others.

Statistical analyses corroborate the impression that Table 8.1 presents so clearly. An analysis of variance in which opinion (affirmative action is fair; affirmative action is unfair), selection procedure (standard, affirmative action), and sex of subject (male, female) are included as independent variables reveals a main effect for opinion, $F(1, 81) = 3.87, p < .05$, and for selection method, $F(1, 81) = 3.87, p < .05$, and two interaction effects. The first interaction effect concerns selection procedure and sex. Males in the standard selection procedure evaluated their creativity scores as 83.8, on average, while males in the affirmative action condition placed themselves at 57.5 on average. Among the females, the average scores were 76.0 and 65.0, respectively. The second interaction effect,

Table 8.1
Self-evaluation: Participants' Estimates of Own Score on "Creativity Test"

	Pretested Opinion About Affirmative Action			
	Affirmative Action is Fair		Affirmative Action is Unfair	
Selection Procedure	*n*	Mean	*n*	Mean
Standard	24	79.7	26	80.6
Affirmative Action	20	70.6	27	54.7

Note. The highest attainable score on the "Creativity Test" was 100. Scoring 80 or above on this test was described as the criterion for selection in the Standard Condition.

between opinion selection procedure, is marginally significant, $F(1, 96) = 3.11$, $p = .08$, but the planned comparisons show the expected contingency effect. Specifically, among those who feel affirmative action is fair, the self-evaluations do not vary as a function of selection method, $F(1, 96) = 2.22, p > .10$. Among those who think affirmative action an unfair policy, in contrast, method of selection has a large and significant effect, $F(1, 96) = 21.8, p < .001$.

What about productivity and time spent on the task? Overall, summing across the two creativity tasks, participants produced about 15 uses for the objects and spent about 8 minutes on the task. There was not much variation on either measure among the conditions of the study, and no statistically significant effects obtained. If we look at the one cell of especial interest, the 27 participants who thought affirmative action unfair and who were selected by affirmative action criteria, we find an average of 16 uses produced in an average of 7.8 minutes.

Further analyses show that the participants in the special cell (i.e., those who think affirmative action unfair and who were selected through affirmative action) were more efficient than others. When we calculated efficiency by dividing the number of items produced by the time spent on the task, the following averages occurred: standard procedure, positive opinion, 3.9; standard procedure, negative opinion, 3.4; affirmative action procedure, positive opinion, 3.6; and affirmative action procedure, negative opinion, 4.4. An analysis of variance confirmed that the effect was reliable, $F(1, 93) = 5.1$, $p < .05$. It was as if the participants who were placed in an anomalous position were compensating for some possible injustice.

Lessons

Affirmative action is an important but delicate policy. Clearly, persistent sex and race discrimination needs to be corrected. In several instances, affirmative action has been shown to be a good corrective for factors that have had adverse impact on women and Blacks. Yet affirmative action practices must be well designed and carefully implemented to avoid unintended "adverse psychological impact" on beneficiaries and others. In the laboratory, we have seen that affirmative action procedures can generate self-doubt. Outside the laboratory, such self-doubt among women and minorities might often be matched with equal disrespect from White males. It is easy to understand how a negative cycle could begin and continue.

If caution is one lesson of our study, hope is another. It is important to remember that the pernicious effects of affirmative action procedures occurred only among some participants and not among all participants in our study. When people think affirmative action is a fair policy, they do not assume that everyone who benefits from the policy is below par. That pattern is consistent with our other research. In that research, we have focused more directly on the influence of the procedure of affirmative action selection methods. The procedure of affirmative action was defined as the weights placed on universalistic (e.g., education) and particularistic (e.g., applicant sex) criteria. There we found the policy-procedure to have powerful influences on perceived fairness and other psychological responses of beneficiaries (Nacoste, 1985; Nacoste, 1987; Nacoste & Lehman, 1987). More analyses of this type will be important because there is so much variation in the actual procedures used to implement affirmative action (Combs & Gruhl, 1986; Rosenbloom, 1984). Now the task for policy analysts is to document the outcomes of different strategies of implementation. If we can do that, we can hold at bay the biased pontifications of both the nay and yea sayers and move toward keeping what is good about affirmative action, and throwing out what is bad.

References

Boxill, B. R. (1984). *Blacks and social justice.* Totawa, NJ: Rowman & Allanheld.

Combs, M. W., & Gruhl, J. (1986). *Affirmative action: Theory, analysis and prospects.* Jefferson, NC: McFarland & Co., Inc.

Decter, M. (1980). Benign victimization. *Policy Review, 13,* 65-72.

Eastland, T., & Bennett, W. J. (1979). *Counting by race: Equality from the founding fathers to Bakke and Weber.* New York: Basic Books.

Howard, J., & Hammond, R. (1985, September 9). Rumors of inferiority: The hidden obstacles to black success. *The New Republic,* 17-21.

Leonard, J. S. (1984). Antidiscrimination or reverse discrimination: The impact of changing demographics, Title VII, and affirmative action on productivity. *Journal of Human Resources, 19,* 145-174.

Loury, G. (1986). Beyond civil rights. In J. D. Williams (Ed.), *The state of black America - 1986* (pp. 163-174). New York: National Urban League.

Lovrich, N. P., Steel, B. S., & Hood, D. (1986). Equity versus productivity: Affirmative action and municipal police services. *Public Productivity Review, 39,* 61-72.

Nacoste, R. W. (1985). Selection procedure and responses to affirmative action: The case of favorable treatment. *Law and Human Behavior, 9,* 225-242.

Nacoste, R. W. (1987). But do they care about fairness: The dynamics of preferential treatment and minority interest. *Basic and Applied Social Psychology, 8,* 171-191.

Nacoste, R. W., & Lehman, D. R. (1987). Procedural stigma. *Representative Research in Social Psychology, 17,* 25-38.

Roberts, L. W. (1981). Understanding affirmative action. In W. E. Block & M. A. Walker (Eds.), *Discrimination, affirmative action and equal opportunity,* (pp. 147-182). Vancouver, B.C.: The Fraser Institute.

Rosenbloom, D. H. (1984). What have policy studies told us about affirmative action and where can we go from here? *Policy Studies Review, 4,* 43-48.

Steel, B. S., & Lovrich, N. P. (1987). Equality and efficiency tradeoffs in affirmative action - real or imagined? The case of women in policing. *Social Science Journal, 24,* 53-70.

9

Who Likes Affirmative Action: Attitudinal Processes Among Men and Women

Francine Tougas and France Veilleux

Gender asymmetries in employment are a matter of contemporary concern. Opinion polls show that the majority of North Americans have come, over the last two decades, to favor gender equity in the workplace (Kahn & Crosby, 1985). In contrast to the definite changes in public opinion are the uncertain changes in the actual conditions of the workplace (Colwill, 1982; Etaugh & Kasley, 1981; Hopkins Lattin, 1983; Kaschak, 1981; Labour Canada, 1983; Simpson, McCarrey, & Edwards, 1987; U.S. Department of Labor, 1978a, 1978b). Statistics show that women are still disadvantaged in North American labor markets.

Affirmative action programs offer one well-recognized means of diminishing sex inequalities in the labor force. Given that popular sentiment now favors gender equality in the labor force, the question arises: Who likes affirmative action? More precisely, what are the processes that govern the endorsement of affirmative action programs among women and men? This chapter presents a three part answer. First, we look at women's reactions to affirmative action. Three theories figure prominently in the first section. Taken together, they help explain why some women favor affirmative action while others do not. The second part of our chapter extends the analysis to men. In it we present and empirically test a predictive model of men's attitudes. Men's reactions are as important as women's for two reasons. Ideally, employment equity ought to be a joint venture; and practically, the managerial corps responsible for affirmative action policies and programs includes men. Drawing on the first two sections of the chapter, the third and final part offers a tentative, integrative answer to the question: What are the processes by which people come to support affirmative action?

Women's Responses to Affirmative Action

Some women endorse affirmative action programs more than do others. A complete understanding of the variation in women's attitudes toward affirmative action seems to lie at the juncture of relative deprivation theory, social identity theory, and procedural justice theory. More specifically, we propose that a woman will endorse affirmative action if she feels discontented with the position of women and also feels that affirmative action offers a fair remedy. We also propose that women who strongly identify as employed women will feel especially discontented about the position of women in the economy and be very favorably disposed toward affirmative action programs.

Social change has often been explained by reference to the concept of relative deprivation (Crosby, 1982; Martin, Brickman, & Murray, 1983; Useem, 1980). Runciman (1966, 1972) has distinguished between deprivations felt on behalf of oneself and deprivations felt on behalf of one's reference group -- which he calls fraternal and we call collective. Collective relative deprivation (CRD) refers to the feeling of discontent experienced as a result of a disadvantageous comparison between one's group and an outgroup. Collective relative deprivation should be experienced whenever women feel dissatisfied with the fact that men and women are treated unequally in the work force.

Feelings of collective relative deprivation are influenced by the strength of one's attachment to the disadvantaged group. According to Tajfel (1978) and others (Taylor & Dubé, 1986) social identity is "part of an individual's self-concept which derives from his knowledge of his membership in a social group (groups) together with the value and emotional significance attached to that membership" (Tajfel, 1978, p. 63). The basic assumption of social identity theory is that individuals strive for a positive social identity. If both a favorable and a distinct position for their ingroup cannot be achieved, then according to the theory, individuals will seek membership in a more positively valued group. In the case where individuals cannot leave their group for objective reasons (e.g., race or sex), collective action strategies gain prominence provided collective relative deprivation is experienced.

Affirmative action is a type of collective action strategy. One application of relative deprivation and identity theories, therefore, is to predict that women who strongly identify with their group and feel working women are disadvantaged relative to employed men will strongly favor affirmative action programs which materially benefit women as a group. But such an assertion fails to jibe with the observation that some women oppose affirmative action policies. Procedural justice theory provides one basis for resolving the mystery.

Procedural justice theory asserts that people value justice in general (Lerner, 1981) and procedural justice in particular (Lind & Tyler, 1988). According to procedural justice theory, people endorse collective actions that seem fair and do not endorse collective actions that seem unfair. Even when people notice an injustice such as sex discrimination, and even when they think the injustice touches their lives, they will not favor any means of redress that itself seems unfair. If a woman notices sex discrimination and knows it to affect her, she will endorse affirmative action as a remedy only if she perceives affirmative action policies and programs to be fair.

Affirmative action programs sometimes seem fair and sometimes do not. Affirmative action programs may, for example, feature preferential treatment so that female job candidates are given preference over male candidates when qualifications of the two groups are similar. To some people preferential treatment does not appear a just or fair policy (Chacko, 1982; deCarufel & Schopler, 1979; Norvell & Worchel, 1981). Some people -- including potential beneficiaries of affirmative action programs -- object to affirmative action programs because the programs seem unfair (Clayton & Tangri, Chapter 15; Nacoste, Chapter 8).

Not all affirmative action programs feature preferential treatment. In the Canadian Public Service, for example, affirmative action is designed to identify and eliminate barriers hidden in employment systems. This type of affirmative action program also provides services, such as career counseling, that help women "help themselves."

Corroborating Studies

Tougas, Dubé and Veilleux (1987) have shown that, among French Canadian women, collective relative deprivation is significantly related to collective and organizational change seeking behaviors but not to promotion of affirmative action programs. Women, according to the findings of this study, are willing to take action to promote equality of access but do not favor the policy of affirmative action when it emphasizes preferential treatment. For example, participants experiencing discontent felt ready to denounce discrimination on the basis of sex in their working environment and to participate in a group intended to improve women's situation in the work force. They did not, however, advocate affirmative action in the form of preferential treatment. The only affirmative action policy described in this study was one involving preferential treatment of women.

A second study was conducted in order to examine the possibility that support for the goals of affirmative action might be separated from the procedures employed to achieve those goals (Tougas & Veilleux, 1988.) We hypothesized that strong attachment to one's disadvantaged group engenders feelings of collective relative deprivation which in turn lead women to favor affirmative action policies if the policies omit preferential treatment. One half of a sample of francophone women in the second study were provided a description of an affirmative action policy which emphasized preferential treatment to achieve the goal of "increasing the percentage of women in the higher levels of the hierarchy as well as in job categories traditionally held by men." This description was identical to the one provided to all respondents in the previous study. The other half of the respondents were provided a description of an affirmative action policy which relied upon "eliminating discriminatory administrative practices, helping women prepare for job interviews, and giving them information about career paths leading to higher levels" in order to achieve the same goal.

The results indicated that both identification with one's group and feelings of collective relative deprivation were associated with support for affirmative action only when the procedures omitted preferential treatment. Moreover, women who were presented an affirmative action policy which included preferential treatment were significantly less in favor of the goals set forth by the program even though they were the same in the two programs.

These results show the importance of the implementing procedure on women's attitudes toward affirmative action. It could be said that women prefer programs whereby "from now on, they are treated fairly," to those "which try to compensate for past injustices." It could also be argued that results indicate that women recognize that in order to succeed where they have no experience, and where they are still a minority, they need more than a change in hiring procedures. A support system may be a necessary precondition.

Men's Responses to Affirmative Action

How can we understand men's attitudes toward affirmative action strategies? In this section we present a model (Veilleux & Tougas, 1988) and test it. The first element of our model refers to the feeling of discontent experienced by men after perceiving that women are unfairly treated in the work force; we use Runciman's (1972) terminology and call it relative deprivation on behalf of others (RDBO). While this concept has not received much attention in the literature, it is believed to motivate social behaviors that are altruistic or liberal in nature (Walker & Pettigrew, 1984). Also, the link between relative deprivation on behalf of others and promotion of another group's welfare was first confirmed in an exploratory study conducted by Tougas, Dubé and Veilleux (1987). Relative deprivation on behalf of others was associated with support for affirmative action and belief that improvement of women's circumstances should be a priority.

A predictive model which includes relative deprivation on behalf of others would be conceptually incomplete without taking into consideration men's attitudes toward their own group, especially because gender is binary. We again turn to Tajfel's theory to describe the process of identification with a group, and its consequences on attitudes and social behaviors. In the present case, the first question is: In which circumstances is membership in an advantaged group not positively valued? In Tajfel's (1978) view, individuals will question their membership, and contemplate leaving the group when its advantaged position is threatened by impending change or when the superior status seems to derive from unfair advantages, various forms of injustice, or exploitation. In these circumstances members who cannot leave the group will, according to Tajfel (1978), intensify attempts to restore positive social identity. Governments voicing their commitment to equality of access in the work force and implementation of affirmative action policies could be perceived by men as a threat to their gender group. In this case men may respond with exaggerated male dominant ideology.

The connection between social identification and relative deprivation on behalf of others is suggested by the data on women. The value of the link between social identity and relative deprivation on behalf of others must, however, be adjusted to take into account the socially recognized advantaged position of men as a group. In dichotomous intergroup situations dissatisfaction with the other group's situation will not arise when membership in the superior group is positively valued. For example, men who strongly identify with their group and embrace a

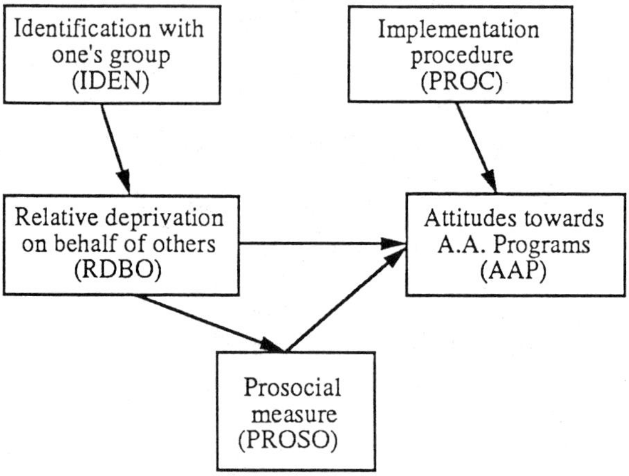

Figure 9.1
Predictive Model of Men's Attitudes Towards Affirmative Action

corollary male dominant ideology may not perceive women in the work force as a disadvantaged group, let alone feel dissatisfied on their behalf.

The predictive model presented in Figure 9.1 posits that positive social identification with a high status group has negative impact on the level of relative deprivation on behalf of others experienced which, in turn, has a direct effect on attitudes toward prosocial measures and affirmative action strategies. The model also predicts that the overall attitude toward prosocial measures influences perceptions and emotional reactions vis-a-vis affirmative action. Finally, for men as for women, the procedure of implementation must also affect reactions toward affirmative action: Compared with preferential treatment, the elimination of barriers hidden in the system will trigger more positive reactions.

Method

Participants. Two hundred and fifty names of male managers and professionals willing to participate in a study focusing on some aspects of work life were obtained from students enrolled in an introductory psychology class. Out of this pool 150 were chosen at random and 145 participated in the study. They were all francophones, ranging in age from 23 years to 61 years (M = 39.9 years), and 92.5% had attended college.

Questionnaire. Participants received a questionnaire (in French) and a pre-addressed, return envelope. Numerous questions allowed us to measure the variables in our model. Ten-point, Likert-type response continua were used for each question.

Two questions dealt with social identification (IDEN). Participants were asked whether their values, interests, attitudes, and behaviors were similar to men in general (id1), and whether they identified with men in general (id2). We also measured relative deprivation on behalf of others (RDBO). Perceptions of differences between men and women in the work force with regard to salary (rd1), chances of being hired (rd2), and promoted (rd3) measured RDBO's cognitive component. The affective component was evaluated by asking participants whether they were dissatisfied with each perceived discrepancy. Three RDBO scores were obtained by multiplying the cognitive and affective scales. This method of measuring relative deprivation is an adaptation of Fishbein and Ajzen's (1975; Ajzen & Fishbein, 1980) technique and has already been used (Tougas, Veilleux, Cere, & Boudreault, in press).

One question asked participants to evaluate their overall attitude toward prosocial measures (pm): "Do you think that the improvement of women's situation should be a social priority?"

Four questions dealt with men's attitudes toward affirmative action programs (AAP). The first three asked whether participants agreed with the program presented (aa1), its goals (aa2), and procedure (aa3). Participants also indicated their intention to participate in an affirmative action program (aa4).

Experimental Manipulation. In order to determine the influence of the procedure of implementation, two versions of the questionnaire were prepared and distributed randomly to participants. Both versions contained identical descriptions of affirmative action's goals: "Because of women's situation in the work force, institutions have decided to implement affirmative action programs. These programs aim at increasing the percentage of women in the higher levels of the hierarchy as well as in job categories traditionally held by men." Following this description, it was stated in one version that fair representation of women was achieved by eliminating discriminatory administrative practices, helping women to prepare for job interviews, and giving information as to career paths leading to higher levels. It was also stated that this program never involved preferential treatment based on gender. In the second version, the procedure was preferential treatment: "...female candidates are given preference over males when their qualifications for a particular job are similar." The variable PROC in Figures 9.1 and 9.2 refers to procedures.

Results

In order to determine whether affirmative action programs designed to eliminate barriers of the system (TYP1) yielded more positive reactions than those giving women preferential treatment (TYP2), *t*-tests were computed between the two experimental groups. As predicted respondents were significantly more in favor of the TYP1 program (*M*s = 8.76 and 5.25), $t(143) = 6.64$, $p < .001$, as well as its underlying procedure (*M*s = 8.08 and 4.74), $t(143) = 7.05$, $p < .001$. The same pattern was observed for the program's goals (*M*s = 8.70 and 7.00), $t(143) = 3.50$, $p < .001$, and intentions to participate in such a program (*M*s = 7.87 and 5.59), $t(142) = 4.29$, $p < .001$.

The general form of the proposed model was tested using LISREL VI. We employed the unweighted least squares fitting function for estimating parameters (Joreskog & Sorbom, 1986) because of the presence of a dichotomous variable. Table 9.1 reports polychoric or polyserial correlations among the various observed variables included in the LISREL VI analysis. In the specification step, Lomax's (1982) recommendations were followed: Parameters relating single observed variables (i.e., pm and typ) to underlying constructs were constrained to equal one. Similarly, the error of measurement parameters for those variables were fixed at zero.

Table 9.1
Polychoric and/or Polyserial Correlations for the Observed Variables

	RD1	RD2	RD3	PM	AA1	AA2	AA3	AA4	1D1	ID2
RD2	.648									
RD3	.695	.669								
PM	.361	.325	.375							
AA1	.245	.260	.290	.215						
AA2	.342	.307	.356	.360	.620					
AA3	.130	.123	.158	.207	.857	.625				
AA4	.294	.264	.283	.248	.693	.643	.737			
ID1	-.034	-.144	-.158	-.093	-.223	.003	-.132	-.130		
ID2	-.146	-.253	-.250	-.177	-.147	-.002	-.083	-.050	.460	
TYP	.032	.019	.063	-.006	.571	.351	.598	.415	-.127	-.119

Figure 9.2 shows the standardized parameter coefficients estimated

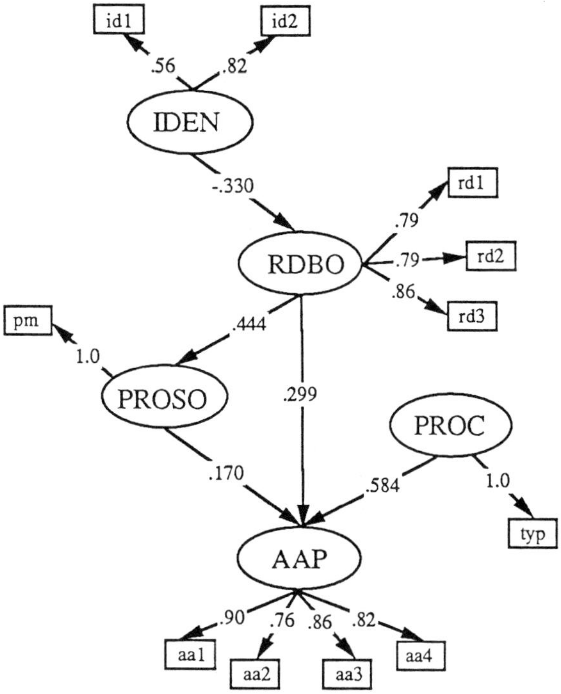

Figure 9.2
Final Obtained Model of Men's Attitudes Toward Affirmative Action (standardized solution)

for the global analysis. According to predictions, the solution obtained shows that attitudes about affirmative action are directly influenced by dissatisfaction experienced as a result of perceived inequalities (RDBO), attitudes toward prosocial measures (PROSO), and the procedure used (PROC) to implement such programs. Finally, the model indicates a negative causal link between identification with men (IDEN) and RDBO.

Correspondence between the final model and the underlying data may be estimated from various indices contained in Table 9.2. For example, the total coefficient of determination for the structural equation of .472 shows a moderate strength of relationships included in the model. Goodness of fit indices were also calculated. Because it is generally recognized that a GFI above .90 represents a good fit between the overall

Table 9.2
Indices Reflecting the Adjustment of Fit of Constructs, Structural Equations, and the Overall Final Model

Y	R^2	X	R^2	Structural Equation	R^2
RD1	0.623	ID1	0.689	RDBO	0.109
RD2	0.617	ID2	0.680	PROSO	0.197
RD3	0.745	TYP	1.0	AAP	0.504
PM	1.0				
AA1	0.813				
AA2	0.578				
AA3	0.746				
AA4	0.667				

Total Coefficient of Determination for Structural Equations	.472
Goodness of Fit Index	.980
Adjusted Goodness of Fit Index	.966
Root Mean Square Residual	.062

model and the data, statistics obtained (GFI = .980, AGFI = .966) in this case suggest that the model accounts adequately for the variability observed in the data.

Discussion

Analyses confirmed the hypothesis stating that relative deprivation on behalf of others (RDBO) is negatively influenced by a sense of positive identification with one's group (IDEN). In other words, strong attachment to the superior group is associated with a failure to recognize the disadvantageous position of the other group, a necessary precondition for support of affirmative action. This study also confirmed the role of relative deprivation on behalf of others as a motivator of altruistic or liberal social behavior. More precisely, it was shown that when men perceive sex discrimination (RDBO's cognitive component), they will more readily approve of corrective strategies (including affirmative action) if they feel dissatisfied about the perceived difference than if they do not feel dissatisfied.

The proposed model specified that the procedures of affirmative action (PROC) influence responses to the overall policy of affirmative action. This hypothesis was confirmed. As in the case of women (Tougas &

Veilleux, 1988), it was found that programs in which the primary objective is to eliminate systematic barriers are preferred by men over those using preferential treatment. Despite the existence of identical goals in both affirmative action descriptions, the male respondents favored those goals less when they were paired with the procedure of preferential treatment than when they were paired with the elimination of discriminatory barriers.

Results underscore the importance of making well known the procedure used to arrive at fair representation of women in the work place. Our findings imply that whenever possible administrators might strongly and repeatedly stress the fact that their program does not include preferential treatment. When one feels threatened by affirmative action policies, one might easily distort reality. If procedural fairness appears at risk, the advantaged group might be more inclined to feel cheated and robbed of career opportunities.

Conclusion

We will now sketch an impression of those who like affirmative action. Findings pertaining to the concept of relative deprivation show that reactions to affirmative action are influenced by beliefs about how the opportunity structure works, and to some extent how it should work. In order to favor affirmative action, one must first recognize that women as a group are unfairly treated so that their career opportunities are more limited than men. Secondly, one must express dissatisfaction with the present structure. The links between relative deprivation, the implementing procedure, and attitudes toward affirmative action lead us to believe that an equal opportunity structure would be endorsed by those who perceive undue inequalities in the present system.

Identification with one's group also plays an important role in the formation of attitudes toward affirmative action. It seems reasonable to suppose that women identifying with their group have rejected some traditional sex stereotypes because they support a program designed to increase their career opportunities in areas where they have been underrepresented at all levels of the hierarchy. Tajfel's theory gives some credence to a similar argument concerning men. Men who experience relative deprivation on behalf of others should have at least questioned traditional male stereotypes in order to recognize the disadvantageous situation of women.

Moreover, results clearly demonstrate that both men and women disapprove of preferential treatment as a means to improve women's circumstances. Everyone prefers a program intended to achieve equality of access through the elimination of systematic barriers and through the provision of support to target groups. These findings are consistent with prevailing values on individualism and equity. On the one hand, programs offering to help women acquire skills necessary to achievement are supported because they are consistent with the value of equality of opportunity. On the other hand, programs seen as promoting preferential treatment are opposed because they are seen as inegalitarian.

In sum, feelings of personal relative deprivation arise when individuals believe that their position on some social or economic hierarchy is unjustifiably low. Collective relative deprivation occurs when individuals feel upset about the position of their group, e.g., women. Relative deprivation can occur on behalf of others. People who feel deprived, on behalf of themselves, their group, or another group, do not endorse *any* means of redress. Most favored are programs that strengthen the belief that all relative positions in a given hierarchy result from demonstrated ability and individual effort.

References

Ajzen, I., & Fishbein, M. (1980). *Understanding Attitudes and Predicting Social Behavior.* Englewood Cliffs, NJ: Prentice-Hall, Inc.

Chacko, T. I. (1982). Women and equal employment opportunity: Some unintended effects. *Journal of Applied Psychology, 67,* 119-123.

Clayton, S. D., & Tangri, S. S. (1989). The justice of affirmative action. In F. A. Blanchard & F. J. Crosby (Eds.), *Affirmative action in perspective* (pp. 177-192). New York: Springer-Verlag.

Colwill, N. L. (1982). *The New Partnership: Men and Women in Organization.* Palo Alto, CA: Mayfield Publishing Company.

Crosby, F. J. (1982). *Relative Deprivation and Working Women.* New York: Oxford University Press, Inc.

deCarufel, A., & Schopler, J. (1979). Evaluation of outcome improvement resulting from threats and appeals. *Journal of Personality and Social Psychology, 37,* 662-673.

Etaugh, E., & Kasley, H. C. (1981). Evaluating competence: Effects of sex, marital status and parental status, *Psychology of Women Quarterly, 6,* 196-203.

Fishbein, M., & Ajzen, I. (1975). *Belief, Attitude, Intention, and Behavior. An Introduction to Theory and Research.* Addison-Wesley Publishing Company, Inc.

Hopkins Lattin, P. (1983). Academic women, affirmative action, and mid-America in the eighties. *Women's Studies International Forum, 6,* 223-230.

Joreskog, K. G., & Sorbom, D. (1986). *LISREL VI*. Moorville, IN: Scientific Software.

Kahn, W., & Crosby, F. (1985). Change and stasis: Discriminating between attitudes and discriminating behavior. In L. Larwood, B. A. Gutek & A. H. Stromberg (Eds.), *Women and Work, an Annual Review* (Vol. 1, pp. 215-238). Beverly Hills, CA: Sage Publications.

Kaschak, E. (1981). Another look at sex bias in students' evaluations of professors: Do winners get the recognition that they have been given? *Psychology of Women Quarterly, 5*, 767-772.

Labour Canada, Women's Bureau. (1983). *Women in the Labour Force, Part III, a Variety of Facts and Figures*. Ottawa: Ministry of Labour.

Lerner, M. J. (1981). *The belief in a just world: A fundamental delusion*. New York: Plenum Press.

Lind, E. A., & Tyler, T. R. (1988). *The social psychology of procedural justice*. New York: Plenum Press.

Lomax, R. G. (1982). A guide to LISREL-type structural equation modeling. *Behavior Research Methods & Instrumentation, 14*, 1-8.

Martin, J., Brickman, P., & Murray, A. (1983). Moral outrage and pragmatism: Explanations for collective action. *Journal of Experimental Social Psychology, 20*, 484-496.

Nacoste, R. W. (1989). Affirmative action and self-evaluation. In F. A. Blanchard & F. J. Crosby (Eds.), *Affirmative action in perspective* (pp. 103-109). New York: Springer-Verlag.

Norvell, N., & Worchel, S. (1981). A re-examination of the relation between equal status contact and intergroup attraction. *Journal of Personality and Social Psychology, 41*, 902-908.

Runciman, W. G. (1966). *Relative deprivation and social justice: A study of attitudes to social inequality in twentieth-century England*. Berkeley, CA: University of California Press.

Runciman, W. G. (1972). Postscript to the 1972 edition of Relative deprivation and social justice: Some lessons of hindsight. *Relative Deprivation and Social Justice*. Harmondsworth, Middlesex, England: Penguin Books.

Simpson, S., McCarrey, M., & Edwards, H. P. (1987). Relationship of supervisors' sex-role stereotypes to performance evaluation of male and female subordinates in non-traditional jobs. *Canadian Journal of Administration Science, 4*(1), 15-30.

Tajfel, H. (1978). *Differenciation Between Social Groups: Studies in the Social Psychology of Intergroup Relations*. London: Academic Press, Inc.

Taylor, D. M., & Dubé, L. (1986). Two faces of identity: The "I" and the "We." *Journal of Social Issues, 42*(2), 81-98.

Tougas, F., Dubé, L., & Veilleux, F. (1987). Privation relative et programmes d'action positive. *Revue Canadienne des Sciences du Comportement, 19,* 167-176.

Tougas, F., & Veilleux, F. (1988). The influence of identification, collective relative deprivation and procedure of implementation on women's responses to affirmative action: A causal modeling approach. *Canadian Journal of Behavioral Science, 20*(1), 16-29.

Tougas, F., Veilleux, F., Cere, M., & Boudreault, L. (in press). L'effet de l'information sur la privation relative collective dans une situation d'evaluation de candidat-e-s. *Revue Quebecoise de Psychologie.*

U.S. Department of Labor. (1978a). Bureau of Labor Statistics. *News.* October 12.

U.S. Department of Labor. (1978b). *Employment in Perspective: Working Women.* No. 3, Third quarter, report 547.

Useem, M. (1980). Solidarity model, breakdown model, and the Boston anti-busing movement. *American Sociological Review, 45,* 357-369.

Veilleux, F., & Tougas, F. (1988). Modele predictif des comportements d'action positive chez les hommes et les femmes. *Canadian Psychology, 29,* 809.

Walker, I., & Pettigrew, T. F. (1984). Relative deprivation theory: An overview and conceptual critique. *British Journal of Social Psychology, 23,* 301-310.

10

Administrators' Perceptions of Affirmative Action in Higher Education

Ann Tickamyer, Susan Scollay, Janet Bokemeier, and Teresa Wood

The use of affirmative action programs to implement equal opportunity policies and end employment discrimination has created controversy from its inception. Debate over the necessity, advisability, impact, and effectiveness of such programs is a longstanding theme in both the popular and scholarly literature. As mandated by law, institutions of higher education have been among the earliest organizations to adopt formal affirmative action programs and to incorporate such policies as explicit goals of the organization. Additionally, higher education is often viewed both by members of the educational establishment and the public at large as the central societal institution implementing meritocratic norms and values of equal opportunity. Paradoxically, there is a clear history of failure to meet these standards. For all these reasons the university provides an ideal setting to study issues raised in the ongoing debate over affirmative action.

In this research we investigate one aspect of affirmative action in higher education which has received little scholarly attention. This is the perceptions of administrators who are both the subject and object of affirmative action/equal opportunity (AA/EEO) policies. In particular, we examine two sets of administrators in higher education: the affirmative action officers who administer affirmative action policies and the more general group of university administrators. By comparing the opinions of these two groups on the impact of their own universities' AA/EEO programs and the need for affirmative action more generally, it is possible to evaluate the degree to which these programs are viewed as effective. It is also possible that we might discover that differing perceptions of effectiveness and need correspond with specific characteristics of administrators and their positions in the university. It is likely that the understanding of affirmative action mandates held by central players in the process can have an important impact on the design, function, and ultimate effectiveness of programs intended to achieve them.

Debates Over Affirmative Action

Two issues have dominated discussions of affirmative action in higher education: a) the need for remedial measures and b) the effectiveness of affirmative action as a remedy. Initial debates centered on the need for affirmative action in the academy with many arguments made against its relevance to colleges and universities (Gittel, 1975; Lester, 1975; Sowell, 1975, 1978). Such arguments were countered by early documentation studies. These provided ample evidence of pervasive sex and race discrimination in the hiring, retention, and promotion of women and minorities in the faculty and administrative ranks of higher education institutions (cf. Abramson, 1975; Astin, Carter, & Hirsh, 1977; Bayer & Astin, 1975; Boulding, 1976; Faia, 1977; Ferber & Westmiller, 1976; Gappa, 1977).

Less consensus exists about the impact of affirmative action in higher education. Different approaches to examining the status of women and minorities create contradictory assessments of progress. Studies which focus on the extent or percentage of change since the advent of affirmative action note positive gains in the representation and distribution of women and minorities within the professional ranks of higher education (cf. Astin & Snyder, 1982; Green, 1984; Rickard & Clement, 1984; Rickard, 1985; Tinsley, Secor, & Kaplan, 1984; Touchton & Shavlick, 1984; Watkins, 1985). Studies which examine current status rather than the alteration in that status find much less real impact or substantive change (Etaugh, 1985; Finkelstein, 1984; Hyer, 1984; Moore, 1983, 1984; Taylor, 1986).

Much of the disagreement can be attributed to differences in sampling and emphasis. It has, for example, been well-documented that more women occupy administrative and faculty positions at smaller, less prestigious institutions than at the larger, more prestigious schools (Ester, 1975; Touchton & Shavlik, 1984; Turk, 1981). Samples show larger gains for women if they include all institutions than if they are restricted to the top schools. Also, impressive percentage or absolute numerical gains often translate into very small actual representation. For example, a recent American Council of Education study of women in higher education administration (Touchton & Shavlik, 1984) used percent of change over a 10 year period as the basic measure of change. They found the number of women presidents nearly doubled during the decade (i.e., there was a 93% increase). This statistic presents one impression. Very different is the impression that comes in learning that, by the close of 1984, women presided over only 10% of the 2800 regionally accredited colleges and universities in the United States.

Problem Statement

Laws aimed at social change are not self-enforcing, and their success or failure depends on political climate, public opinion, and adequate enforcement (Burstein, 1985). Especially important in enforcing affirmative action policies in higher education are university administrators and affirmative action officers. Yet, their views are conspicuously absent from the literature on affirmative action and equal employment opportunity. The perceptions of both groups form important components of the political climate which influences current program directions and the potential for future success.

The lack of attention paid AA officers is puzzling because they are the persons who administer institutional efforts to fulfill federal mandates and achieve equity. Thus, their opinions influence how affirmative action efforts are managed, what programmatic priorities are selected, and how finite AA/EEO resources are allocated. AA officers should have the perspective, experience, and understanding necessary to make realistic assessments of relative progress within the operational context of complex, bureaucratic organizations.

The failure to investigate the views of the larger body of administrators is equally strange because these people constitute both a primary target and a major institutional context for such programs. Their views on the need for and impact of AA/EEO can condition how seriously such policies are taken, the range of resources committed to them, and the general climate for success or failure of AA/EEO programs and policies.

In addition to determining the content of views on this subject, it is important to investigate the factors which influence opinions. While there is very little research directly investigating attitudes toward affirmative action, a large literature on sources of managerial attitudes and values debates the relative influence of individual background, socialization, and position within the organization on work related attitudes and behaviors (Kanter, 1977; Kohn, Miller, Miller, Schenbach, & Schoenberg, 1983; Larwood, Gutek, & Gattiker, 1984; Mortimer & Lorence, 1979; Posner & Munson, 1981; Powell, Posner, & Schmidt, 1984; Yount, 1986). Particularly controversial is the extent to which individual traits (e.g., sex, race) either through differential inclination, socialization, or discrimination influence work attitudes and behavior compared to structural sources such as power and influence within the organization. Based on this work, we investigate how perceptions of affirmative action are influenced by sex, race, age, education, position, and length of time in the university.

Attitudes towards affirmative action selected for study are guided by the emphasis on need and impact assessment in the debates over affirmative action. We examine the opinions of the two groups of university administrators to determine how each perceives these programs. In addition, we explore how these perceptions are influenced by personal and positional characteristics associated with these administrators. The emphasis is on the comparison of the two groups and the reasons for differences which occur.

Research Methods

The data come from a study of sex differences in careers in higher education administration. Two separate data sets were used. The first is an affirmative action data base which was created from responses to a survey mailed to affirmative action officers at 252 U.S. research and doctorate granting institutions. The Carnegie classification (1976) of American post-secondary institutions was used to select schools for this study. All Research Universities I and II, Doctorate-granting Universities I and II, and a selected number of Comprehensive Universities and Colleges I were included. The questionnaire was mailed in the Spring of 1986. Usable responses were received from 60% of the surveyed institutions. The second data source is a survey of all the women and a matching number of randomly sampled men administrators at these same institutions conducted during the Summer and Fall of 1986. Names and addresses of individual administrators were obtained from the 1986 Higher Education Directory, supplemented with additional listings obtained from the survey of Affirmative Action officers. Usable responses were received for 62% of the sample of administrators. (For the purposes of clarity, we restrict the label "administrator" to this group. The affirmative action officers of the first sample are, in fact, administrators too, but we call them "officers".)

Both survey instruments included the same eight items evaluating perceptions of various features of Affirmative Action/Equal Employment Opportunity programs. Four items assessed opinions about the *impact* of AA/EEO on sex and race compositions of faculty and administrators on campus over the previous five years. The four remaining items more generally evaluated the *need* for AA/EEO programs. All eight items were presented with five-point, Likert-type response continua, ranging from "strongly disagree" to "strongly agree." The four impact items and the four need items exhibited sufficient internal consistency that they were summed to form two, four-item scales for some analyses.

Personal background and position data were collected for both groups. These included sex, race (dichotomized as White/nonwhite), age, educational background, faculty rank, and years in current position. Position levels for university administrators were determined by dividing the *1986 Directory of Higher Education* function codes into four categories. These are Chief Administrators which include top line officials of the institution; Deans which include the heads or directors of major academic units; Major Administrators which include heads and directors of major support units in the institution; and Assistants which include administrators whose position is defined as assisting any of the above categories.

Results

Table 10.1 presents descriptive characteristics of both groups of respondents. With the exception of age and years in position, there were very large differences between the two groups. Affirmative action officers had much higher female and minority representation than the general population of university administrators. This was especially noteworthy for nonwhites. Only 6.7% of the administrators were nonwhite compared to 44.0% of the affirmative action officers. Other differences occurred in education and faculty rank. The modal educational level for AA administrators was postgraduate work short of a doctorate. In fact, a large proportion were attorneys or M.B.A.s. For the general administrators, a doctorate was the modal degree. Many more university administrators held faculty rank than did affirmative action officers (52% compared to 25%). The largest group of administrators held a position

Table 10.1
Descriptive Characteristics of University Administrators and Affirmative Action Officers

	Administrators		AA Officers	
	N	%	*N*	%
Sex				
Male	864	45.6	48	32.0
Female	1030	54.4	103	68.0
Race				
White	1733	93.4	85	56.0
Nonwhite	123	6.7	66	44.0
Degree				
< College	75	4.2	2	1.3
College	270	15.1	28	18.5
Postgrad.	513	28.8	72	47.7
Doctorate	926	51.9	49	32.5
Faculty Rank				
Yes	926	48.2	114	75.0
No	862	51.8	38	25.0
Position				
Chiefs	389	21.3	NA	
Deans	583	31.9	NA	
Majors	770	42.2	NA	
Assistants	83	4.5	NA	
Age				
Md	46		44	
Range	20-72		29-67	
Years in Position				
Md	4		5	
Range	0-39		0-26	

classified as "major," followed by deans and "chiefs."

Administrators' views on the impact of affirmative action on their campus over the past five years and the need for affirmative action programs and policies are found in Tables 10.2 and 10.3. In these tables the response categories are collapsed from the original five to three categories. It is evident that the samples generally felt mildly to very positive about affirmative action.

Table 10.2 also shows that the affirmative action officers were much more likely than the administrators to believe that their programs have had an impact on their campuses. About two thirds of the AA officers but only 38% of the administrators, for example, thought that the pro-

Table 10.2

Perceptions of University Administrators (UA) and Affirmative Action Officers (AA) that Affirmative Action/Equal Employment Opportunity Has Had Substantial Impact on their Campuses

	Percent Responding							
	Disagree		Neither		Agree		N	
Program type	UA	AA	UA	AA	UA	AA	UA	AA
Sex composition								
Administrators	47.4	26.3	15.4	12.8	36.9	60.8	1800	148
Faculty	38.0	20.2	23.8	11.5	38.2	68.2	1875	148
Race composition								
Administrators	57.6	42.8	15.6	12.2	26.7	44.9	1877	147
Faculty	53.1	40.5	20.7	12.0	26.2	46.6	1876	148

grams have had an impact on the sex composition of the faculty.

A similar contrast between the administrators and the AA officers occurs concerning the need for affirmative action programs and policies. As Table 10.3 shows, AA officers strongly supported setting goals for hiring both women and minority administrators. University administrators equally strongly *disagreed* with the need for such hiring goals. Large majorities of both types of administrators disagreed with

Table 10.3

Perceptions of University Administrators (UA) and Affirmative Action Officers (AA) of Need for Affirmative Action/Equal Employment Opportunity Programs on their Campuses

	Percent Responding							
	Disagree		Neither		Agree		N	
Program type	UA	AA	UA	AA	UA	AA	UA	AA
Goals for women	63.6	25.2	15.3	13.6	21.0	61.2	1877	147
Goals for nonwhites	62.3	23.9	15.7	12.3	21.9	63.7	1880	146
Positive action	13.2	4.8	12.4	4.1	74.4	91.2	1894	148
Nothing needed	71.8	85.7	15.2	4.8	13.0	9.5	1882	148

the statement "affirmative action is not needed" and supported the idea that "positive action is necessary to overcome past discrimination." Affirmative action officers showed slightly more agreement than did administrators with the affirmative action position on both items.

We conducted a series of one-way analyses of variance to discover whether attitudes about affirmative action differed as a consequence of personal and position characteristics. From Table 10.4 it can be seen that sex, age, and years in position consistently influence attitudes about the impact of AA/EEO programs among university administrators (but not among affirmative action officers). Women administrators had lower scores than the men on the impact items. The women generally disagreed that there had been an impact at their schools. Younger administrators and those who have been in their positions for shorter periods of time also had lower scores than did older and more seasoned administrators. Interestingly enough, nonwhite administrators were more likely than their White colleagues to agree there has been progress for women, but they shared the same negative assessment of progress for nonwhites. Position level exhibited surprisingly little relationship to administrators' views of the impact of affirmative action.

A different pattern emerged from the analyses of variance of the items concerning the need -- as opposed to impact -- for affirmative action. Table 10.5 indicates that sex and race consistently and significantly differentiated groups of respondents. Women and nonwhites generally disagreed that AA/EEO is not needed, strongly agreed that positive action is needed to overcome past discrimination, and were more likely to advocate specific hiring goals for women and nonwhite administrators. As with the AA/EEO impact items, age and years in position selectively influenced views of university administrators on the need for AA/EEO. Somewhat stronger support came from younger, less senior respondents. Position level, educational degree, and possession of faculty rank showed some association with administrators' assessment of the need for AA/EEO (although not necessarily in a consistent or linear fashion). Items about the need for specific hiring goals were more likely to differ by the characteristics of the administrators than by those of the AA officers.

Finally, we combined the four impact items into one total scale, Cronbach's alpha = .78 for administrators and .77 for affirmative action officers, and the four need items into another, alpha = .79 for administrators and .83 for affirmative action officers, and submitted them to ordinary least squares regression analyses in which personal and position characteristics served as predictors. Overall the effects of the predic-

Table 10.4

Mean Differences of Perceived AA/EEO Impact by University Administrator (UA) and Affirmative Action Officer (AA) Personal and Position Characteristics

	Sex Composition				Race Composition			
	Admin.		Faculty		Admin.		Faculty	
Respondent Variable	UA	AA	UA	AA	UA	AA	UA	AA
Sex								
Male	3.06	3.48	3.12	3.43	2.68	2.91	2.74	3.04
Female	2.64	3.49	2.82	3.78	2.45	2.98	2.51	3.04
F	68.65***	.01	41.12***	2.96*	20.21***	.08	22.03***	.00
Race								
White	2.82	3.34	2.95	3.56	2.52	2.99	2.62	2.96
Nonwhite	3.06	3.64	2.95	3.56	2.52	2.99	2.62	2.96
F	5.21**	2.21	4.23**	2.06	.07	.12	1.69	.64
Age								
20-34	2.53	3.25	2.82	3.08	2.46	2.50	2.54	2.83
35-44	2.75	3.58	2.85	3.90	2.46	3.18	2.49	3.32
45-54	2.84	3.51	3.05	3.80	2.56	2.94	2.69	3.04
> 54	3.04	3.35	3.05	3.30	2.72	2.73	2.71	2.50
F	9.98***	.37	6.11***	2.98**	4.98**	1.17	5.60***	2.37*
Degree								
< College	2.65	3.50	2.87	3.00	2.47	2.50	2.61	3.00
College	2.91	3.77	3.02	3.85	2.70	3.00	2.76	3.24
Postgrad.	2.73	3.41	2.83	3.64	2.47	3.10	2.50	2.76
Doctorate	2.86	3.35	3.01	3.66	2.54	3.02	2.61	3.07
F	2.48	.74	4.08**	.46	2.43	.14	3.51*	1.05
Rank								
Faculty	2.84	3.34	3.03	3.56	2.57	2.99	2.65	2.96
Nonfaculty	2.79	3.64	2.87	3.83	2.51	2.91	2.56	2.96
F	.55	2.21	10.75***	2.06	1.18	.12	3.87*	.64
Years in Position								
0-1	2.72	3.65	2.91	3.48	2.45	3.00	2.55	3.00
2-5	2.78	3.53	2.92	3.78	2.51	3.17	2.54	3.24
6-10	2.87	3.32	3.00	3.51	2.57	2.73	2.67	2.76
11-40	3.06	3.45	3.10	3.83	2.75	2.79	2.75	3.07
F	5.69***	.41	2.51*	.84	4.59**	.93	3.48**	1.05
Position								
Chiefs	2.93	NA	3.07	NA	2.58	NA	2.67	NA
Deans	2.84		3.01		2.58		2.65	
Majors	2.79		2.87		2.51		2.56	
Assistants	2.81		3.00		2.63		2.73	
F	1.47		4.07***		.61		1.59	

Note. Higher scores convey greater impact. * $p < .10$. ** $p < .05$. *** $p < .01$.

Table 10.5

Mean Differences of Perceived Need for AA/EEO by University Administrator (UA) and Affirmative Action Officer (AA) Personal and Position Characteristics

Respondent Variable	Goals for Women		Goals for Nonwhites		Positive Action		Nothing Needed	
	UA	AA	UA	AA	UA	AA	UA	AA
Sex								
Male	2.48	1.85	2.10	3.35	2.14	3.48	3.62	4.44
Female	1.89	1.41	2.63	3.76	2.65	3.79	3.97	4.60
F	163.66***	5.50**	11.62***	2.71	96.76***	1.59	53.39***	.92
Race								
White	2.19	1.78	2.33	3.30	2.35	3.32	3.76	4.40
Nonwhite	1.65	1.25	3.23	4.07	3.29	4.22	4.48	4.74
F	32.19***	9.46***	76.12***	11.64***	82.55***	16.14***	54.78***	4.85***
Age								
20-34	2.18	1.25	2.67	3.33	2.68	3.42	3.61	4.50
35-44	2.01	1.53	2.47	3.85	2.52	3.96	3.92	4.60
45-54	2.22	1.50	2.32	3.76	2.32	3.80	3.75	4.58
> 54	2.28	1.92	2.26	3.15	2.29	3.19	3.77	4.31
F	7.12***	1.39	6.88***	1.75	8.15***	1.99	5.08***	.65
Degree								
< College	2.34	1.00	2.24	4.50	2.24	5.00	3.77	5.00
College	2.16	1.77	2.45	3.60	2.46	3.66	3.76	4.37
Postgrad.	2.19	1.61	2.49	3.61	2.52	3.68	3.75	4.50
Doctorate	2.10	1.35	2.33	3.61	2.36	3.66	3.87	4.69
F	1.82	1.17	2.93**	.26	3.05***	.57	1.84	.90
Rank								
Faculty	2.11	1.58	2.31	3.60	2.35	3.66	3.83	4.50
Nonfaculty	2.17	1.43	2.46	3.71	2.48	3.81	3.78	4.68
F	2.55	.55	7.83***	.15	6.25***	.35	.74	1.11
Years in Position								
0-1	2.00	1.13	2.45	3.42	2.51	3.52	3.87	4.69
2-5	2.10	1.54	2.46	4.02	2.48	4.11	3.84	4.76
6-10	2.24	1.56	2.33	3.53	2.35	3.59	3.78	4.34
11-40	2.42	1.86	2.20	2.01	2.21	3.21	3.63	4.31
F	10.76***	2.08	4.18***	2.56*	5.09***	3.02*	3.28**	2.37*
Position								
Chiefs	2.12	NA	2.23	NA	2.27	NA	3.95	NA
Deans	2.16		2.36		2.39		3.81	
Majors	2.19		2.49		2.52		3.73	
Assistants	1.98		2.48		2.48		3.89	
F	1.18		4.91***		4.54***		3.86***	

Note. Higher scores convey greater need. * $p < .10$. ** $p < .05$. *** $p < .01$.

tor characteristics on the dependent opinion variables were small. The best model explained 21% of the variance in the need scale among affirmative action officers, largely by sex, race, and years in position. These results tended to parallel the bivariate findings. Controlling for all other factors, women in both samples saw less impact for AA/EEO programs than men; but they perceived a greater need for AA/EEO. Nonwhites from both samples differed little from Whites on AA/EEO impact; but they too saw much greater program need. There was a very small positive effect of age on administrators' views of AA/EEO impact and a small to moderate negative effect of years in position for the views of affirmative action officers. Thus, age and length of tenure made these groups slightly more conservative. None of the position levels of university administrators proved significant predictors of impact or need.

Discussion and Conclusions

The views about affirmative action of the officers charged with overseeing and implementing these programs are very different than the views of their administrative colleagues. The former generally see a greater need for affirmative action policies and, at the same time, believe the programs they manage have had a greater impact at their universities. Perhaps, the nature of the affirmative action officer's job requires realistic assessment of the actual progress (or its lack) made by AA/EEO programs on campus. Because officers are intimately familiar with the situation of their own organizations, they should be able to identify any real changes that have occurred. It also seems very plausible that the affirmative action officers are more invested in the AA/EEO programs than are the administrators. People usually assess favorably programs in which they are personally invested.

The attitudes of the affirmative action officers do not vary much as a function of their personal characteristics. Additional research might expand the investigation of different types of influences on views about affirmative action. One recent study found some evidence that specific program and institutional characteristics influence views of affirmative action officers about the relative impact of affirmative action (Scollay, Tickamyer, Bokemeier, & Wood, 1987). For example, formal involvement of the AA/EEO program in faculty tenure decisions, frequency of contact between the affirmative action officer and the campus chief executive officer, and the actual sex and race compositions of the full time faculty and upper level administration all were found to influence the affirmative action officers' assessment of AA/EEO impact on campus. It would be useful to know whether such characteristics similarly influence the views of other administrators.

Among administrators, opinions about the need for affirmative action and especially about the impact of affirmative action are related to personal characteristics. What makes this especially interesting is that many of the theories of organizational power suggest that the attitudes and behaviors of groups targeted by discrimination can be explained by their lack of power within the organization rather than by traits associated with minority status. In this study, sex remains a significant predictor, regardless of position, of both the impact and need scales, and race remains significant under the same circumstances on the need scale. The implications of these findings are clear and important. If we are to bring about institutional change through affirmative action programs, then we must have more women and minorities in administrative positions. We must not isolate women and minorities in the position of affirmative action officer.

Finally, it is clear that to a large extent the debate on affirmative action has shifted from its initial terms. If these administrators are representative of views generally held within the academy, then there is little opposition to and widespread acceptance of the need for affirmative action. What appears to create more controversy is the type of methods used in affirmative action programs. Much greater disagreement was expressed about the necessity of specific hiring goals than about more general statements of either need for or impact of AA/EEO. This suggests mixed prospects for affirmative action in the future. The eventual outcome of such programmatic efforts to achieve equity may well depend on whether opposition to specific approaches represents reasoned debate over the most effective programs or whether it instead reflects a socially acceptable way to express a more basic uneasiness with the very existence of such programs. Whichever the case, it will be important to continue research on this topic and to monitor future developments.

References

Abramson, J. (1975). *The invisible women: Discrimination in the academic profession.* San Francisco: Josey Bass.

Astin, H., Carter, A., & Hirsh, W. (Eds.). (1977). *Women -- a challenge to higher education.* New York: Praeger.

Astin, H., & Snyder, M. (1982). Affirmative action 1972-1982: A decade of response. *Change, 14,* 26-31.

Bayer, A., & Astin, H. (1975). Sex differentials in the academic reward system. *Science, 188,* 796-802.

Boulding, E. (1976). The global macroproblem: Prospects for women and minorities. *Liberal Education, 62,* 185-207.

Burstein, P. (1985). *Discrimination, jobs, and politics.* Chicago: University of Chicago.

Estler, E. (1975). Women as leaders in public education. *Signs, 1,* 363-386.

Etaugh, C. (1985, April). *Changes in the status of women faculty and administrators in higher education since 1972.* Paper presented at the annual meeting of the American Educational Research Association, Chicago, IL.

Faia, M. (1977). Discrimination and exchange: Double burden of the female academic. *Pacific Sociological Review, 20,* 3-20.

Ferber, M., & Westmiller, A. (1976). Sex and race difference in nonacademic wages on a university campus. *Journal of Human Resources, 11,* 366-373.

Finkelstein, M. J. (1984). The status of academic women: An assessment of five competing explanations. *Review of Higher Education, 7,* 223-246.

Gappa, J. (1977). *Improving equity in postsecondary education.* Washington, D.C.: U.S. Government Printing Office.

Gittell, M. (1975). The illusion of AA. *Change, 7,* 39-43.

Green, M. F. (1984). Women and minorities ACE fellows in the ascent toward administrative posts. *Educational Record, 65,* 46-49

Hyer, P. B. (1984, April). *A ten year progress report on women faculty at doctorate-granting universities.* Paper presented at the American Education Research Association, New Orleans, LA.

Kanter, R. (1977). *Men and women of the corporation.* New York: Basic Books.

Kohn, M. C., Miller, J., Miller, K., Schenbach, C., & Schoenberg, R. (1983) *Work and personality: An inquiry into the impact of social stratification.* Norwood, NJ: Ablex.

Larwood, L., Gutek, B., & Gattiker, U. (1984). Perspectives on institutional discrimination and resistance to change. *Group and Organization Studies, 9,* 333-352.

Lester, R. (1975). The equal pay boondoggle. *Change, 7,* 38-43.

Moore, K. M. (1983). *Leaders in transition: A national study of higher education administrators.* University Park, PA: Pennsylvania State University.

Moore, K. M. (1984). Career in college and university administration: How are women affected? in A. Tinsley, C. Secor, & S. Kaplan (eds.) *Women in Higher Education Administration.* San Francisco: Jossey Bass.

Mortimer, J., & Lorence, J. (1979). Occupational experience and the self-concept: A longitudinal study. *Social Psychology Quarterly, 42,* 307-323.

Posner, B. Z., & Munson, J. M. (1981). Gender differences in managerial value systems. *Psychological Report, 49,* 867-881.

Powell, G. Posner, B. Z., & Schmidt, W. H. (1984). Sex effects on managerial value systems. *Human Relations, 37,* 909-921.

Rickard, S. T. (1985). The chief student affairs officer: Progress toward equity. *Journal of College Student Personnel, 26,* 5-10.

Rickard, S. T., & Clement, L. M. (1984). The director of admissions: Progress toward equity for women and minorities. *Journal of College Admissions, 104,* 24-27.

Scollay, S., Tickamyer, A., Bokemeier, J., & Wood, T. (1987). *The impact of affirmative action in higher education: Perceptions from the front line.* Paper presented at AERA Annual Meeting, Washington, D.C.

Sowell, T. (1975). *Affirmative action reconsidered: Was it necessary in academia?* Washington, D.C.: American Enterprise Institute for Public Policy Research.

Sowell, T. (1978). Landmark or curiosity? *Regulation, 2,* 30-34.

Taylor, B. (1986, April). *Minority (Black) faculty advancement: Recruitment, selection and promotion.* Paper presented at the American Education Research Association, San Francisco, CA.

Tinsley, A., Secor, C., & Kaplan, S. (Eds.). (1984). *Women in Higher Education, New Directions in Higher Education,* No. 45. San Francisco: Josey-Bass.

Touchton, J., & Shavlik, D. (1984). *Senior women administrators in higher education: A decade of change, 1975-1983. Preliminary report.* Washington, D.C.: Office of women in Higher Education, American Council on Education.

Turk, T. G. (1981). Women faculty in higher education. *Pacific Sociological Review, 24,* 212-236.

Watkins, B. (1985). Number of women college presidents has doubled in decade, study finds. *The Chronicle of Higher Education, 31,* 1-33.

Yount, K. (1986). A theory of productive activity: The relationships among self-concept, gender, sex role stereotypes, and work-emergent traits. *Psychology of Women Quarterly, 10,* 63-88.

Acknowledgements

This research was funded in part by grants from the University of Kentucky Research Committee and the National Science Foundation under Grant Number SLS-85 11060.

11
Reactions to Affirmative Action: A Case Study

Nancy Goldsmith, Diana Cordova, Karen Dwyer, Bergen Langlois, and Faye J. Crosby

Affirmative action is a policy that elicits strong reactions. Perhaps nowhere more than in American higher education has affirmative action stirred controversy (Bronstein & Pfennig, 1988). Letters to the editor periodically appear in national newspapers like *The New York Times* that give the impression of a substantial number of educators worrying about reverse discrimination and about the diluted standards of education that are thought to come with affirmative action. Scrutiny of *The Chronicle of Higher Education* might also lead one to think that varied constituencies on college campuses object to affirmative action (Goldsmith, 1987).

At odds with the impression of opposition to affirmative action are the findings of Tickamyer, Scollay, Bokemeier, and Wood (Chapter 10). In their samples containing approximately 150 affirmative action officers and 1700 other administrators at colleges and universities across the country, Tickamyer et al. have found a generally positive attitude toward affirmative action. College and university administrators generally believe that there is a need for affirmative action programs and sometimes also believe that the programs have had a positive impact on their own institutions. Affirmative action officers feel even more positively than do the other administrators.

How can we reconcile the generally positive opinions found by Tickamyer et al. with the general impression of negativity given in the *Chronicle*? Part of the answer has to do, no doubt, with the respondents' degree of involvement in affirmative action. As with the affirmative action officers and administrators in Tickamyer et al.'s study, so perhaps with all groups: the more involved, the more positive.

The proposition linking involvement and positive attitudes leads us to the next question: How do various constituencies on a college campus feel about affirmative action? What do students, faculty, and support staff, none of whom typically have much to do with the implementation of affirmative action policies, feel and know about affirmative action? How do these groups compare with each other and with administrators?

To explore these questions, we conducted a case study. The central purpose of our study was to examine the attitudes toward and knowledge of affirmative action among various constituencies at a single institution. In addition to looking at the distribution of scores among four different groups, we also looked at the relationship -- across all groups -- between knowledge and attitudes. We asked, in essence: How do people's feelings relate to their thoughts about affirmative action? Finally, following the lead of Tickamyer et al., we compared the attitudes of men and women. Tickamyer et al. found that female administrators were more convinced about the need for affirmative action at their institutions than were male administrators. Would we find similar patterns among different constituencies at one college campus?

Our study took place at a liberal arts college for women located in Massachusetts. In September, 1987, the president of the college announced that it was to become an affirmative action institution. Considerable fanfare attended the process: Racial incidents at the college and at neighboring schools had occasioned some publicity, and officials at the college were eager to correct both wrong impressions and past injustices. When the college was about to hire its first affirmative action officer, in the Spring of 1988, a group of students protested their apparent exclusion from the decision making process; and the entire campus plunged into a series of informational meetings about the institution's racial policies generally and about affirmative action specifically.

Given the publicity surrounding the issue of affirmative action at the college in our study, one might have expected people from all constituencies on campus to feel and to be well informed about affirmative action. It also seemed plausible that there might be a positive association between knowledge and attitudes. Those who were the best informed might have also favored affirmative action the most strongly.

To test our predictions, we interviewed a representative sample of middle-level students, faculty, support staff, and administrators. Our analyses look first at the distribution of knowledge and feelings among the different groups. We then look at the relationship between knowledge and feelings -- examining, more specifically, the intercorrelations among self-proclaimed attitudes and self-assessed knowledge, on the one hand, and, on the other, feelings and knowledge as assessed by an outside rater. We end with a look at the question of gender differences in attitudes toward affirmative action.

Method

Sample

Participants in our study all worked or studied at the college. We identified four constituencies on campus: students; faculty; support staff (clerical and service); and administrators and obtained lists of each. Using the school directory, we obtained a list of 374 faculty names and 2908 student names. The personnel department supplied us with a list of 312 administrators (ranging from the president of the college to all the administrative assistants); 204 clerical staff workers; and 435 service staff workers. For each category of respondent, we randomly selected names.

A personal letter was sent to each potential participant explaining the nature of our study and requesting an interview. Eighty-nine percent of the students contacted agreed to participate in the study as did 83% of the faculty, 77% of the staff, and 84% of the administrators. The final sample included 15 students, 15 faculty; 17 support staff (8 service and 9 clerical); and 15 administrators, mostly from the middle management ranks. Only two respondents in the study were persons of color.

Measures

Three female interviewers conducted all the interviews during April and May, 1988. Two of the interviewers were Anglos, one Hispanic. The interviews typically lasted a half hour and included many open ended questions. A few close-ended questions were also included. We were interested in four variables concerning self-assessed attitudes and knowledge and also attitudes and knowledge as assessed by others.

Self-proclaimed attitudes. One item asked respondents to assign a number between 0 (extremely negative) and 10 (extremely positive) "that reflects your feelings" toward affirmative action.

Rated attitudes. The typescripts, denuded of identifying information and of answers to the self-rated attitude item, were given to an independent rater. This rater was told only a small amount about the study and was asked to assign a rating from -3 to +3 to reflect how positively the respondent felt about affirmative action. A score of -3 meant the respondent actively disliked the policy of affirmative action and located the origin of campus problems in the minority group. A score of +3 meant the respondent actively endorsed affirmative action and located the origin of campus problems in institutional practices.

The rater's assessment was based on her reading of the entire transcript for each respondent. Especially informative was the respondent's evaluative language in answering the open-ended questions. Among the open-ended questions were these: (a) "Imagine that a friend from out of town learned that [this] college has become an affirmative action institution and asked you: What is affirmative action? Based on the information you have gathered, what would you say?" (asked at the beginning); (b) "What, if anything, is the difference between being an equal opportunity employer and being an affirmative action employer?" (asked in the middle); and (c) "It is obvious from this interview that there are reasons to be in favor of affirmative action and reasons to be cautious about it. Why might you be in favor of affirmative action? Why might you be an opponent?" (asked at the end).

Respondents' answers to certain close-ended questions were also considered. Among these questions was one that asked the respondent to select, from a 38-item list, all the adjectives (e.g., annoyed, hopeful, proud, unhappy) that applied to his or her feelings about the institution becoming an affirmative action institution. Also important was the respondent's reaction to the statement "affirmative action is really just reverse discrimination."

A second rater scored a sub-set of the transcripts. The two raters agreed entirely half of the time and were within one point of each other (on the seven point scale) the other half of the time.

Self-assessed knowledge. One item, the second question in the interview, asked the respondent: "Would you say that you know a lot or a little about what affirmative action is and how it operates?" Each respondent gave herself or himself a number between 0 (know very little) and 10 (know very much).

Rated knowledge. We gave the typed transcripts of the interviews, denuded of identifying information and of the respondent's self-assessed level of knowledge, to an expert rater, who was well versed in affirmative action. The expert rater scored each transcript from -3 (extremely misinformed about affirmative action) to +3 (extremely well informed) primarily on the basis of how the respondent answered all of the open-ended questions. Also informative were the respondent's answers to some close-ended questions, such as one about whether or not certain practices (e.g., the hiring of an affirmative action officer) were always, sometimes, or never part of an affirmative action program.

A second rater scored a sub-set of transcripts, and the two raters agreed absolutely half of the time, were within one point of each other (on the seven point scale) 40% of the time, and were within two points of the remaining 10% of the time.

Findings and Discussion

We conducted a series of one-way analyses of variance (ANOVAs) to look for an effect due to the interviewer. There was none. We therefore combined the data from all three interviewers.

Comparison among constituencies

How did students, faculty, staff, and administrators compare with each other in their attitudes toward and knowledge of affirmative action? Table 11.1 presents the mean scores of the four constituencies of the campus for self-rated attitudes and knowledge. It is apparent from the table that administrators and faculty were more knowledgeable about affirmative action than were students or staff. One-way ANOVAs of self-assessed and other-rated knowledge revealed the effects due to constituency to be reliable. In contrast to knowledge, attitudes did not vary as a function of constituency. All groups on the campus were moderately positive about affirmative action.

Interrelationships

How did knowledge relate to attitudes? Given the events at the institution where we conducted our study, we expected to find a positive correlation between knowledge and attitudes. Official sources at the college were educating people to see why affirmative action was a good policy, and so we thought that the most positive attitudes might be found among the most knowledgeable people. It also seemed likely that the people with the most positive feelings about affirmative action would be the most active in seeking out information.

Our expectations of a strong relationship between attitudes and knowledge were not totally confirmed. As Table 11.2 shows, there were moderate relationships between attitudes and knowledge. The table also shows a substantial relationship between self-assessed knowledge and the expert's rating of knowledge and a strong relationship between self-

Table 11.1
Mean Scores on Attitudes toward and Knowledge of Affirmative Action for Students, Faculty, Support Staff, and Administration

Variable	Students	Faculty	Support Staff	Adminis-tration	Statistical Effects
Attitudes					
Self-proclaimed	7.6	8.6	7.1	8.7	n.s.
Rated	0.7	1.5	0.4	1.3	n.s.
Knowledge					
Self-assessed	3.6_a	5.8_b	2.8_a	$4.7_{a,b}$	$F(3, 57) = 5.66$ *
Rated	-0.2_a	1.1_b	-1.1_c	$0.5_{a,b}$	$F(3, 58) = 13.90$ **

Note. $N = 62$. * indicates significant at $p < .01$. ** indicates significant at $p < .001$. Means with different subscripts are significantly different. Self-proclaimed attitudes could range from 0 (negative) to 10 (positive). Rated attitudes could range from -3 (negative) to +3 (positive). Self-assessed knowledge could range from 0 (not knowledgeable) to 10 (very knowledgeable). Rated knowledge could range from -3 (misinformed) to +3 (well informed).

proclaimed attitudes and other-rated attitudes.

Gender

Were women more positive and perhaps even more knowledgeable about affirmative action than were men? On the one hand, Tickamyer et al.'s findings suggest the possibility of sex differences. Certainly, more males than females might think they have something to lose from affirmative action; and more females than males might think they have something to gain. On the other hand, the connection between self-

Table 11.2
Correlations among Affirmative Action Attitude and Knowledge Measures

	Rated Attitudes	Self-assessed Knowledge	Rated Knowledge
Self-proclaimed attitudes	.68	.26	.38
Rated attitudes		.26	.32
Self-assessed knowledge			.49

Note. $N = 62$. All correlations are significant at $p < .05$.

interest and attitudes toward significant social issues is often weak (Clayton & Crosby, 1986; Crosby & Clayton 1986) even when the issues concern gender politics (Crosby & Herek, 1986).

In evaluating the influence of gender, we restricted the sample to faculty, support staff, and administrators. We eliminated students from the analyses because all the students were female. We then conducted four 2 x 3 ANOVAs in which we crossed gender of the respondent (male, female) with constituency (faculty, staff, administrator). As Table 11.3 shows, women had more positive attitudes than did men, but men and women were equally knowledgeable about affirmative action.

Table 11.3

Significance Tests for Analyses of Variance of the Effects of Constituency and Gender on Attitudes toward and Knowledge of Affirmative Action among Faculty, Staff, and Administrators

Dependent Variable	Main Effect for Gender	Main Effect for Constituency
Attitudes		
Self-proclaimed	$F(1, 36) = 10.24$*	n.s.
Rated	$F(1, 40) = 11.63$*	n.s.
Knowledge		
Self-assessed	n.s.	$F(2, 36) = 7.78$*
Rated	n.s.	$F(2, 40) = 18.94$**

Note. Students were excluded from these analyses. All tabled *F*-values are significant. * indicates $p < .01$. ** indicates $p < .001$. No interactions were significant.

Implications

Our case study carries implications for other institutions, especially other educational institutions. First, it is interesting to note the generally positive attitudes toward affirmative action at the college we studied. Some of the more vociferous detractors of affirmative action would have us believe that many people in higher education are up in arms against what they perceive to be an unfair and unworkable system. Our data challenge such a view. Second, the lack of a strong association between attitudes and knowledge suggests that the advocates of affirmative action ought not to equate education about affirmative action with persuasion. One can make people more informed about affirmative action without making them feel more positively about it; and one can make people feel more positively about affirmative action without informing them. Finally, the connection between gender and support for affirmative action merits notice. If firmly positive attitudes among individuals in institutions make a difference in the success of affirmation action programs in the institutions, then programs may be needed to help men feel more positively about affirmative action.

References

Bronstein, P., & Pfennig, J. (1988). Misperceptions of women and affirmative action principles in faculty hiring. *American Psychologist, 43,* 668-669.

Clayton, S., & Crosby, F. (1986). Postscript: The nature of corrections. *Journal of Social Issues, 42*(2), 189-194.

Crosby, F., & Clayton S. (1986). Introduction: The search for connections. *Journal of Social Issues, 42*(2), 1-10.

Crosby, F., & Herek, G. (1986). Male sympathy with the situation of women: Does experience make a difference? *Journal of Social Issues, 42*(2), 55-66.

Goldsmith, N. (1987). Affirmative action and higher education. Unpublished paper, Smith College, Northampton, MA.

Tickamyer, A., Scollay, S. Bokemeier, J., & Wood, T. (1989). Affirmative action in higher education administration. In F. A. Blanchard & F. J. Crosby (Eds.), *Affirmative action in perspective* (pp. 125-138). New York: Springer-Verlag.

Acknowledgement

We would like to acknowledge the excellent help of Ann Pufall, stalwart statistician.

III: Why Bother?

12

Labor Market Discrimination in the United States

Christopher J. Ruhm

One important argument in favor of affirmative action programs is that, despite apparent changes in American attitudes about race and gender since World War II, race and sex discrimination persist. Labor market discrimination exists if equally productive workers receive systematically unequal treatment, by employers, on the basis of ascriptive characteristics such as race or gender. Economists commonly gauge discrimination by observing the gap in earnings between, say, Blacks and Whites or females and males, that cannot be accounted for by differences in observed characteristics such as education, experience, or seniority. Virtually every empirical study shows that nonwhites and females earn less than White males with similar observable characteristics and most scholars have concluded that discrimination is a feature of the American labor market.

Conventional methods for estimating discrimination have several limitations, however. Most problematically, the degree of wage discrimination against nonwhites and women could be overestimated if these groups differ from White males in ways that are not known by the researcher. Housing segregation, for example, prevents many nonwhites from receiving the quality of education typically obtained by Whites, even when the two groups attend schools for the same number of years. Quality of education affects productivity, as does quantity, but researchers are able to assess only the quantity and not the quality of schooling. Firms may, thus, pay nonwhites less than Whites because of the relatively low productivity of the former. Because labor market discrimination includes only the unequal treatment of equally productive workers, the appearance of wage discrimination on the basis of race, in this instance, would be false (see Daymont & Andrisiani, 1984; Filer, 1983; and Goldin & Polachek, 1987).

What is needed is an alternative measure of earnings discrimination. This chapter presents one. Instead of focusing on cross-sectional earnings, I select a sample of workers who experience involuntary permanent job terminations (i.e., who have been laid off) and examine how earnings change between pre- and postseparation employment. By focusing on *changes* rather than *levels* of wages, time-invariant individual effects are held constant, thereby eliminating the bias caused by correlation between race or gender and unobserved productive attributes. In the absence of discrimination, we have no reason to anticipate systematic gender or ethnic differences in wage growth (once preseparation earnings are controlled for).

Consider, for illustration, a nonwhite man earning the same predisplacement wage as a White male with identical observed characteristics. Because their earnings are equal, absent discrimination we expect the two workers to have equal unmeasured attributes (e.g., quality of education) as well as measured ones (e.g., years of education) and further anticipate that, on average, they will obtain equivalent postlayoff employment. Conversely, if there is discrimination, the good fortune of obtaining a job with a relatively non-discriminating employer will generally be required for the nonwhite to obtain equal preseparation earnings. To the extent this early luck is not replicated after the job loss, his postseparation earnings will fall below those of the White counterpart. Further, if discrimination limits his reemployment possibilities, the man's relative wages will decline even if the initial (preseparation) position was not unusually favorable. (See Ruhm, 1988 for a more technical discussion of these issues.)

The principal advantage of using wage *changes* rather than *levels* to measure discrimination is that the former hold constant all time-invariant individual characteristics, where the latter do not. For example, if females earn ten percent less than seemingly comparable males because (unbeknownst to the researcher) they are less attached to the labor force and so invest in less training, differences in wage levels spuriously indicate discrimination. Since their earnings would be equally depressed in both the pre and postseparation jobs, however, there is no reason to expect systematic differences in wage changes.

Several factors, other than discrimination, could explain relative wage losses of females and nonwhites following permanent layoffs.

First, they could be more heavily invested in skills specific to their predisplacement firm than are White males. This explanation, however, is not consistent with the hypothesis that women earn low wages because of weak attachments to the labor force. If this were the case, they would concentrate investments in general rather than firm-specific skills, or simply refrain from any investment. Similarly, given the relatively greater vulnerability of nonwhites to involuntary layoffs, it is unlikely that their investments will be disproportionately firm-specific. Second, the relative wages of *all* women or minorities (whether displaced or not) could be declining. Race and gender wage differentials have remained fairly constant during the time period studied, however, and previous research indicates that job stability is more important for the wage growth of nonwhites and women than for White males. Therefore, this explanation is probably not important. Finally, the relative earnings of minorities and females will decline, as a consequence of displacement, if they are relatively "overpaid" prior to it. After presenting the basic model, I examine and generally reject the possibility that affirmative action hiring represents an important source of such overpayments.

The Data

The data were obtained from the special "Displaced Worker Supplements" (*DWS*) which the Bureau of Labor Statistics appended to the regular monthly Current Population Survey (*CPS*) in January of 1984 and 1986. Individuals are included in the sample if, during the previous five years, they had lost or left a job because of a plant closing, slack work, or position or shift abolishment. To avoid persons whose earnings would frequently be influenced by non-economic considerations, I eliminated those under the age of twenty-five or over fifty-five. In addition, workers displaced in the thirteen months prior to the survey date were excluded because of their very high rates of unemployment and because wages received during short-lasting training and probationary periods might poorly indicate long-run earnings. Self-employed and agricultural workers were also dropped from the sample as were persons leaving temporary or seasonal jobs.

Sample means, presented in Table 12.1, generally conform to the cross-sectional comparisons reported by others. Although displaced nonwhites are slightly less experienced and educated than Whites, and females have slightly less time on the preseparation job than men, the average values for these variables are surprisingly similar. On the other hand, minorities are much less frequently married and have consider-

Table 12.1
Means of Selected Variables

Variable	All Workers	Males	Females	Whites	Non-Whites
Age in years	35.8	35.5	36.3	35.9	35.2
Experience	16.5	16.2	17.0	16.6	16.1
Preseparation tenure	4.2	4.5	3.6	4.2	4.2
Education in years	12.8	12.8	12.8	12.8	12.4
% married	65.9	68.5	61.8	68.5	42.0
% household head	62.9	84.7	27.5	63.2	60.9
% moved	18.5	22.0	13.0	19.2	13.9
% government	5.2	3.4	8.0	4.8	7.6
Weeks out of work	26.1	25.8	26.7	24.9	34.8
% reemployed	60.6	58.4	64.2	61.9	52.0
% part-time					
Preseparation	8.1	2.8	16.8	8.2	7.5
Postseparation	13.5	6.7	23.4	13.2	15.4
Economic reasons	9.2	5.3	14.5	8.7	13.1
Weekly wage (log)					
Preseparation	5.70	5.89	5.39	5.72	5.55
Postseparation	5.54	5.74	5.25	5.56	5.37
% wage change	-16.8	-17.6	-15.6	-16.5	-19.8
N	6166	3817	2349	5393	773

Note. Percent reemployed includes only those for whom wages were reported.

ably greater difficulty finding new jobs following displacement. For example, compared to Whites they are: unemployed five extra weeks; reemployed at the time of the survey only five-sixths as often; fifty percent more likely to involuntarily work in part-time jobs; and suffer twenty percent larger wage losses upon reemployment.

Displaced women are less likely than men to be married or household heads. This is expected given the somewhat higher labor force participation rates of single (than married) females and the convention of classifying males as the head of most two adult households. Somewhat surprisingly, the period of postdisplacement joblessness is quite similar for men and women, and a slightly higher percentage of the latter are reemployed at the time of the survey. This results, in part, because women more frequently accept part-time work when full-time jobs would be preferred. For example, they are almost three times as likely as men to work part-time for economic reasons in the survey year and have much higher probabilities of working part-time (for any reason) both prior and subsequent to the termination.

Compared to White males, nonwhites and women receive relatively low wages both before and after displacement, less frequently change geographic regions for economic reasons, and disproportionately terminate from government jobs. Individuals surveyed in 1984 and 1986 have virtually identical personal characteristics but, because of the severe recession in the earlier year, 1984 respondents: are less likely to report survey year wages (50.9% vs. 72.0 %); experience greater joblessness (28.1 vs. 23.9 weeks); and suffer larger earnings losses (18.8% vs. 15.2%) than their 1986 peers.

Demographic Group Differences in Wage Changes

In this chapter labor market discrimination is measured by the residual difference in postdisplacement earnings changes which remains after individual characteristics and preseparation earnings are held constant. Dummy variables indicating household head and marital status, race, gender, and the survey year are included in the wage regressions, as are continuous linear and quadratic variables for the number of years of schooling. The dependent variable is the natural log of weekly wages. Dichotomous regressors controlling for part-time status in pre- and post-separation employment and for economically motivated geographic mobility are incorporated in most of the estimates. The inverse Mills Ratio from a probit reemployment equation is also included to correct for sample selection bias.

Holding constant preseparation wages, household heads and married persons -- with their greater family responsibilities -- are expected to experience smaller wage losses than single individuals and non-heads. The anticipated coefficient on mobility is ambiguous. Dislocated individuals are likely to move if they receive (or expect to obtain) favorable wage offers; however, this may be offset by more probable relocation out of depressed local labor markets or by workers whose skills have been rendered obsolete. Weekly wages increase with hours worked. Therefore, earnings changes should be more (less) positive when the predisplacement (postlayoff) position is part-time.

Whites and males change regions more often and work part-time less frequently than nonwhites and females. This suggests that the additional controls for work hours and geographic mobility may explain a portion of the wage change differential. Although the data do not indicate the reason for previous part-time work, we can determine whether part-time employment in the postseparation job occurs for personal or economic reasons. Since involuntary part-time employment is likely to be one consequence of discrimination, the survey year dummy variable is set to one only for individuals who voluntarily work less than full-time. The absence of more detailed information on work hours precludes use of a continuous hours variable.

Econometric Findings

Postdisplacement earnings increase with the number of years since the layoff, years of schooling, and preseparation wages, while changes in seniority have a small and non-linear effect. As expected, married persons and household heads have more favorable postdisplacement experiences than their single or non-head peers.

The presence of labor market discrimination is strongly indicated by the slower wage growth of nonwhites and females, as compared to White males receiving equivalent pay prior to the layoff. For example, in a model which excludes controls for hours of work and economically motivated geographic mobility, the relative wage losses of White females, nonwhite males, and nonwhite females are a statistically significant -10.4, -11.6, and -20.8 percent, respectively.

Sex and race are not the only variables that affect wage change. Although geographic mobility has no systematic impact on wage changes, voluntary reemployment of less than thirty-five hours per week is associated with a forty-one percent reduction in wages, while part-time work prior to the separation is correlated with 13.3 percent faster earnings growth. Inclusion of these additional controls reduces the relative loss of White females by almost a quarter (to eight percent) but has essentially no impact on nonwhite differentials.

The postdisplacement earnings of White males grow relative to other groups, partly because they are less often forced to accept part-time employment. Thus, controlling for involuntary part-time work reduces the wage change differentials of White females, nonwhite males, and nonwhite females from -8.0, -12.2, and -20.1 percent to -5.8, -10.2, and -16.1 percent, respectively.

Table 12.2 shows results of wage change regressions estimated on subsamples stratified by race and sex. The race coefficients in the first two columns indicate that the relative wages of nonwhites of both sexes fall approximately thirteen percent below those of comparable Whites following displacement. Although White females lose more than nine percent compared to their male counterparts, the sex differential for nonwhites is a statistically insignificant three percent. Compared to full sample regressions, these stratified results suggest slightly more severe

Table 12.2
Postdisplacement Wage Change Percentages by Race and Sex

Variable	Males	Females	Whites	Non-Whites
Household head	9.3	12.4	14.1	18.9
	(2.5)	(2.4)	(5.5)	(2.4)
Married	16.0	6.6	10.3	18.9
	(5.5)	(1.4)	(5.2)	(2.8)
Changed location	2.2	1.0	0.2	17.5
	(0.9)	(0.3)	(0.1)	(2.0)
Part-time job				
Predisplacment	12.3	12.4	13.9	12.6
	(1.8)	(2.6)	(3.6)	(1.1)
Postdisplacement (voluntary)	-43.8	-40.0	-42.9	-22.6
	(-8.5)	(-12.3)	(-15.9)	(-1.9)
Nonwhite	-12.6	-13.0		
	(-3.7)	(-3.0)		
Female			-9.2	-3.3
			(-3.6)	(-0.5)

Note. *t*-statistics in parentheses. Coefficients show the difference in predicted wage changes compared to persons without the specified characteristic. Estimates are obtained by taking the exponent of the regression coefficient because the natural log of wages is the dependent variable. Controls are also included for the change in experience and seniority, years of education (and squared terms for each), the survey year, and the inverse Mills ratio from a probit reemployment equation.

discrimination against White females and nonwhite males, but less evidence that nonwhite women suffer from "double discrimination" based upon both race and sex.

Household and marital status have more influence on the postdisplacement wage changes of nonwhites than Whites, while the pattern is mixed across gender groups. Interestingly, nonwhites are the only group to benefit from economically motivated geographic mobility and the resulting gains are quite large. Conversely, voluntary part-time work, subsequent to displacement, has a relatively small negative impact on their wages. Further research is needed to determine the causes of these differences.

Affirmative Action

Race and gender differences in general wage trends cannot explain the relative erosion in postlayoff earnings suffered by nonwhites and females. Although such reductions could occur if the earnings of *all* nonwhites and females (job stayers as well as job changers) were falling relative to White males, the relative wages of these groups have, if anything, been slightly improving over time. Similarly, previous research indicates that involuntary job change hurts nonwhites and women more than White men (see Borjas, 1984; Maxwell & D'Amico, 1986; and Ruhm, 1987). Taken together these findings suggest that the relative earnings reductions observed for females and nonwhites result from displacement rather than secular changes in relative wages.

On the other hand, displaced females and nonwhites might have been previously paid more than equally productive White males (and so suffer larger wage reductions when changing jobs) if they terminate from affirmative action jobs where pay is deliberately set above market wages. Although the *DWS* does not contain direct information on the affirmative action status of predisplacement jobs, affirmative action positions are probably most common in the public sector, from which a disproportionate share of women and nonwhites are also displaced. If job-specific wage premiums in affirmative action employment explain post-displacement earnings differentials, we would expect females and ethnic minorities leaving government jobs to lose more than those terminating from private sector employment (relative to corresponding White males).

The data do not support these predictions. In earnings change regressions which are stratified by the sector of employment, the wages of nonwhite males leaving government jobs grow eight percent compared to their White counterparts, whereas those departing from private sector positions suffer a relative earnings reduction of at least twelve percent. Similarly, nonwhite females gain almost fifteen percent, relative to White males, when displaced from government employment, but lose twenty-two percent when laid-off from non-government positions. These differences between government and non-government workers provide strong evidence against the hypothesis that nonwhites suffer post-displacement wage reductions due to the loss of "overpaid" affirmative action jobs.

As the affirmative action hypothesis predicts, White females suffer larger relative wage losses when departing government than when leaving private sector employment. The differences are quite small, however, and even for the latter group, the unexplained wage gap is almost nine percent (compared with 11.4 percent for the former). Thus, even for White females, affirmative action could explain at most only a small proportion of the relative wage loss which follows layoffs.

The evidence that minorities leaving government jobs fare better than those departing private sector employment suggests two further possibilities. First, employers may carefully screen nonwhites, only selecting those of exceptional quality for affirmative action jobs; being unusually productive, these individuals are then able to replicate their relatively high wages following displacement. Second, affirmative action may impart training which raises earnings in future employment. Distinguishing between the screening and training explanations is important since the second indicates a highly desirable characteristic of affirmative action while the first does not. Even if screening is prevalent, however, there is no evidence that affirmative action stigmatizes program participants.

Conclusions

Economists commonly estimate the extent of labor market discrimination from the residual difference in wage *levels* which remains after controlling for observed characteristics. Such estimates are upwardly biased, however, if unobserved traits such as educational quality or labor force attachment correlate with race or gender. Moreover, the potential list of unmeasured characteristics is unlimited. Having adopted the conventional approach, the scrupulous researcher might dig ever deeper into alternative explanations for the appearance of labor market discrimination. To overcome this problem, I offer a measure of discrimination which depends upon the relative difference in wage *changes* following involuntary job terminations. Because time-invariant individual characteristics are held constant in pre- and postdisplacement employment, the estimated race and gender coefficients are likely to represent true discrimination rather than unobserved heterogeneity.

After controlling for preseparation earnings and a variety of observed characteristics, the wages of White females fall nine percent in postlayoff employment relative to White males. The corresponding differentials for nonwhite males and females are approximately thirteen percent. These figures represent lower bound estimates of the discrimination. Because nonwhites and females are compared to White males with equivalent observed characteristics, any discriminatory mechanisms which prevent the former from obtaining the same levels of education, experience, and seniority as the latter are excluded. This measure also ignores any "network" effects. For example, women in high paying jobs may be able to find roughly equivalent positions following displacement. Yet, females may still have more difficulty in initially obtaining such work if they are excluded from the networks which facilitate access to "good" jobs.

The wage change differentials observed in this chapter can probably not be explained by the loss of affirmative action positions which carry job-specific wage premiums. Were this the case, we would expect nonwhites and females to suffer larger relative losses when leaving government positions (where affirmative action is prevalent) than when terminating from private sector jobs (where it is not). Although such a pattern is observed for White females, the differences are small and a considerable differential remains even among private sector job leavers. For nonwhites, exit out of government employment is actually associated with more favorable relative outcomes. This not only confirms the presence of discrimination but also provides evidence suggesting that affirmative action programs may bestow training which is useful in future employment.

References

Borjas, G. J. (1984). Race, turnover, and male earnings. *Industrial Relations, 23*, 73-89.

Daymont, T. N., & Andrisiani, P. J. (1984). Job preferences, college major, and the gender gap in earnings. *Journal of Human Resources, 19*, 408-428.

Filer, R. K. (1983). Sexual differences in earnings: The role of individual personalities and tastes. *Journal of Human Resources, 18*, 82-99.

Goldin, C., & Polachek, S. (1987). Residual differences by sex: Perspectives on the gender gap in earnings. *American Economic Review, 77*, 143-151.

Maxwell, N. L., & D'Amico, R. J. (1986). Employment and wage effects of involuntary job separation: Male-female differences. *American Economic Review, 76*, 373-377.

Ruhm, C. J. (1987). The economic consequences of labor mobility. *Industrial and Labor Relations Review, 41*, 30-42.

Ruhm, C. J. (1988). *A new test of labor market discrimination*, unpublished manuscript, Boston University, Department of Economics Working Paper 149.

13

Affirmative Action and Aggregate Data: The Importance of Patterns in the Perception of Discrimination

Catherine Twiss, Susan Tabb, and Faye J. Crosby

Discrimination exists as a pattern of unjustifiably negative treatment of persons by virtue of their group membership. This fact is clear to many. Less well understood is the fact that discrimination does not necessarily involve conscious awareness of differential treatment. One can discriminate against women and minority groups without having the conscious or unconscious intention of placing them at a disadvantage. "Knowing" their own intentions to be good, people assume that they are not acting in any way that perpetuates discrimination. Assuming, by extension, the motives of others in the organization to be equally good, people mistakenly conclude that the organization is untroubled by discrimination.

The difficulty of recognizing discrimination is compounded by the nature of its disclosure. Invariably, examples of discrimination emerge in isolated, anecdotal form. Typically one hears (often at second hand) of an adverse decision concerning a woman or a person of color. Perhaps a month or two later, another story surfaces. Then, later that year, one encounters perhaps a third example. In each case, circumstances may differ: Different departments are affected, say, or, gender and ethnicity of the victim of discrimination varies. In such circumstances, a pattern of discrimination is difficult to discern. It is easy to see how individual cases of discrimination may not convince employees of a systematic pattern of, if unintentional, organizational discrimination.

In the workplace, a number of attributes are considered to be relevant "input variables" for any given outcome (Adams, 1965). Because any two individuals are likely to differ on a number of input characteristics, a comparison between the outcomes of, say, one female and one male seldom provides sure proof of disparate treatment. As long as the male in the comparison surpasses the female on just one input attribute, we may have a plausible explanation of any outcome decision that favors the male. As long as the female can be considered inferior on just one relevant input characteristic, we can theoretically justify an outcome decision that adversely affects the female (Crosby, 1984).

Imagine, for example, an academic institution in which one all-male department fails to hire a woman candidate on the grounds that her research, although excellent, overlaps too much with the research of someone who is already in the department. Is this discrimination? It is hard to say. Certainly, departments do need diversity and too much overlap could pose a problem. Now imagine another all-male department in the same institution that justifies its failure to hire an otherwise well-qualified woman on the grounds that her research area is inappropriately divergent from those already represented in the department. Again, in isolation the decision appears fair. Only when one looks at the two individual departmental decisions together does one begin to suspect the institution of discrimination.

Because the mechanisms of discrimination are so very difficult to perceive, affirmative action is needed. The most basic service to an organization of an affirmative action program is that such a program forces an organization to monitor itself. By systematizing the information that would otherwise remain anecdotal, an institution can recognize disparate outcomes and then move to identify the often subtle factors that produce disparate outcomes. Without monitoring systematic documentation, even those organizations with the best of intentions can fail to make inroads on discrimination.

Cognition and Emotion

Some scholars would quarrel with our line of reasoning. It may seem ingenious to claim that people in charge of organizations fail to correct injustices simply because they fail to see the injustices. Perhaps those in charge of organizations know the injustices exist but are too callous and greedy to correct them. No doubt, villains do exist. But a mass of literature shows that the average American citizen, including presumably many heads of organizations, do care about justice as well as profit (Deutsch, 1985) and avow an interest in ending racial and sexual discrimination (Kahn & Crosby, 1985).

The present line of reasoning may be assailed in another way. Perhaps we have pointed the causal arrow in the wrong direction. Perhaps the failure of corrective action does not spring from a failure to perceive the problem. Maybe the failure to perceive the problem of discrimination results from an unwillingness or inability to entertain the idea of correcting it (Lerner, 1981). Could it be, in other words, that it is emotional factors that motivate a blindness to discrimination (Crosby, Pufall, Snyder, & O'Connell, in press)? Have we overemphasized the importance of cognitive factors?

It matters whether the failure to perceive sex discrimination is cognitively or emotionally driven. When the failure to perceive discrimination is due to cognitive factors, then the way to make people see the injustice is to present them with additional, more convincing information. But when the failure to perceive discrimination results from an emotional resistance, then the cogency of one's arguments and the completeness of one's information may produce limited change.

Have we overemphasized cognitive, as opposed to emotional or motivational, factors? One test of our position would be to see if people process information differently when they encounter the information in aggregated (systematic) form than when the same people encounter the same information in less systematic form. If people who are unable to perceive discrimination in anecdotal form are then able to perceive discrimination when the information is presented to them systematically, then we can infer that it is something about the information and not something about the people that accounts for their original misperceptions. If, on the other hand, emotional factors -- including deep-seated attitudes or prejudices -- are the cause of people's blindness, then changing the format of the information should have little effect on people's perceptions.

A preliminary test of the cognitive position occurred in an experiment conducted by Crosby, Clayton, Alksnis, and Hemker (1986). The researchers presented male undergraduates with a set of materials about a fictitious Company Z, comprised of ten different departments. The materials were constructed so that the women in the company, on average, earned significantly less money than the men in the company who were equal, on average, to the females in terms of the three input characteristics that had been stated to be relevant to salary. The information given to the students, in short, should have allowed them to perceive the presence of sex discrimination in Company Z.

Half of the students received the information first in aggregated form. In the aggregated form, the information was all gathered systematically on one page showing the education, management level, and supervisor rating of a typical man and a typical woman in each of ten departments. The page also showed the salaries earned by the men and women. The students were asked to make a determination about whether or not sex discrimination existed and then to judge the likelihood and the seriousness of the discrimination. They were instructed to weigh each department equally in making their determination. After assessing discrimination from the aggregated information, the students then encountered the same information department by department and were asked to make serial judgments about each department.

For the other half of the subjects in the experiment, the process was essentially the same except that the order was reversed. This group of students first made serial judgments, based on information about each department, and then made judgments of the whole company, based on the aggregated information.

Of central importance in the Crosby, Clayton, Alksnis, and Hemker (1986) experiment was the question: Would the subjects perceive discrimination as readily when they encountered the information serially, department by department, as when they encountered the information in aggregate form? In other words, would the format of the materials make a difference in the subjects' judgments of the amount, likelihood, or seriousness of sex discrimination in Company Z? To answer this question, the researchers contrasted the sum of the discrimination scores of the ten departments with the discrimination scores given to Company Z as a whole. Because each of the ten departments was to weigh equally in the judgment, the two scores ought to have been very similar -- if subjects were not influenced by the formatting of the information.

Crosby, Clayton, Alksnis, and Hemker (1986) found that the formatting of the information was extremely important. When the subjects encountered the information serially, they perceived significantly less discrimination than when they encountered a single fact sheet systematically summarizing the ten different departments. By and large, the order of presentation (serially first or aggregate first) made little difference. Nor did the judgments of discrimination bear any relation to self-labeled feminism. Anti-feminist subjects scored as high as feminist subjects in aggregate judgments; just as both anti-feminists and feminists scored equally low in detecting discrimination in the anecdotal format.

The original experiment with Company Z illustrates that people fail to perceive sex discrimination when the relevant information dribbles in, but does the experiment prove that cognitive factors are as important in the perception of discrimination as we claim? One criticism of the original experiment with Company Z is that the experimental materials used the words "sex discrimination" and contrasted males and females. In today's world, goes the argument, any discussion of sex discrimination is bound to arouse emotions. Perhaps the imperfect information processing that was evident in the experiment occurred because of (or only in the presence of) the emotionally arousing words "sex discrimination."

There is a logical test of the proposition that the emotionally arousing labels accounted for the phenomenon. One need only change the labels and see if the phenomenon persists. The purpose of the present experiment was to test the possibility that information formatting influences judgments only when the topic is an arousing one. We replicated and extended the experiment by Crosby, Clayton, Alksnis, and Hemker (1986). Like the earlier researchers we presented the subjects with information in both an aggregated form and a non-aggregated form. Half of our subjects received materials about sex discrimination in which male and female managers were contrasted. The other half received information about managers from Plant A and Plant B, and no mention was made of sex discrimination.

We expected to find that subjects were able to perceive patterns when the information came to them in aggregated form and were unable to perceive patterns when the same information came to them serially. We expected further that the phenomenon might be the same for the emotionally bland materials (plant A and B) as for the emotionally arousing materials (sex discrimination). If both of our expectations proved correct, then we have increased confidence in the earlier findings and in the assertion that non-emotional, purely cognitive factors can account for people's failure to perceive sex discrimination.

Method

Subjects

The subjects were forty female undergraduates at Smith College, recruited from the dormitories. Subjects were randomly assigned to conditions.

Independent Variables and Design

The materials and procedures were patterned on earlier work. First the subjects were given a brief glance at a fact sheet containing all the data they were to analyze later so that they would have an idea of how much information they would be called upon to process. The subjects then read a cover story that asked them to act as if they had been hired to find out whether or not there was discrimination at Company Z. To make this determination, the subjects were instructed to consider both the relevant "input" variables (job level, seniority, education, and supervisor's motivational rating) and the one relevant "outcome" variable: salary. Subjects were told that salary was supposed to vary only according to the input factors.

Each subject received the information in two formats, and Format constituted the first independent variable. In the Aggregate Information Condition, subjects encountered the information about inputs and outcomes systematically arranged on a single fact sheet. Following the single fact sheet came a page of questions about the extent of discrimination in Company Z. In the Single Instance Condition, subjects encountered the information one department to a page. The pages were presented one at a time, with a set of questions about discrimination in the department given at the bottom of each page. The order of departments was randomized.

The second independent variable was Order. Format and Order constitute exact replications of Crosby, Clayton, Alksnis, and Hemker (1986). All subjects encountered both the aggregated and the unaggregated information. Half of the subjects encountered first the aggregated information and then the individual departments; for the other half, the order of presentation of materials was reversed.

The final independent variable, a between-groups factor, was introduced to test whether the earlier findings would also occur with neutral materials. The final independent variable, Label, had two levels: a) Sex Discrimination Condition; and b) Plant Condition. Subjects in the former condition received information about female and male managers in Company Z. This presentation exactly replicated the earlier experiment. Subjects in the latter condition received information about Plant A and Plant B. The information given for Plant A managers was the same as that given for female managers; the information given for Plant B managers was the same as that given for male managers. Females and Plant A managers had, on average, exactly the same inputs as males and Plant B managers. Males (and Plant B managers) enjoyed significantly higher salaries than females (and Plant A managers).

The design was a 2 (Format) x 2 (Order) x 2 (Label) factorial design. The independent variables were Format, Order, and Label. We predicted that subjects would be better able to perceive (veridically) discrimination in the Aggregate Information Condition than in the Single Instance Condition, regardless of Order and Label.

Dependent Variables

Three measures of perceived discrimination were used. First, subjects were requested to rate whether there was discrimination in terms of pay evident in the information they had seen. This was the Overall Rating. When subjects rated each department separately, the Overall Rating item was worded: "Would you say there is (sex) discrimination in terms of pay?" Concerning the entire company, the Overall rating measure read: "All ten departments are equally important in the company. Weighing the departments equally in your evaluation, would you say there is (sex) discrimination in terms of pay in the company as a whole?" Both versions of the Overall Rating were followed by a scale from 1 (no) to 10 (yes). The second measure of perceived discrimination asked how probable it was that there was discrimination, with response options ranging from 0 to 100%. The third measure, seriousness of the discrimination, was assessed with an 11-point scale where 0 meant there was no discrimination and 10 meant discrimination was very serious. In the anecdotal information format total scores on the three dependent variables were calculated by averaging the scores for the ten departments. In the Aggregate Information Format, Overall Rating, Probability, and Seriousness ratings were taken directly from the ratings given to the company as a whole. After assessing perceived discrimination, the subjects were asked an open-ended question about why they thought there was or was not discrimination.

After viewing all the material and completing all the dependent measures, subjects received a new sheet asking them to estimate the average level, seniority, education, motivation, and salary for employees in Company Z and to recall their own average ratings on the three dependent variables. The final sheet also asked the subjects if they considered themselves feminist on a 5-point scale and if they had (contrary to instructions) emphasized any of the factors that were supposed to predict salary. Subjects were debriefed at the end of the experimental sessions.

Results

To test the hypothesis that the format of the information presented would influence the perception of discrimination, three 2 x 2 x 2 analyses of variances on subjects' Overall Ratings, Likelihood Ratings and Seriousness Ratings of discrimination were conducted. In the Overall Rating of discrimination, there were two significant effects. First, the predicted main effect for format, $F(1, 39) = 6.04$, $p < .05$, was observed. Subjects perceived more discrimination in the aggregate format than in the single instance format. There was also a significant, two-way interaction involving Format and Label, $F(1, 39) = 4.40$, $p < .05$. The magnitude of the effect of Format on the Overall Ratings of discrimination was greater when the task involved comparisons between Plant A and Plant B than when it explicitly invited subjects to evaluate sex discrimination.

Second, the hypothesized main effect for Format was also obtained for the Seriousness Ratings, $F(1, 39) = 4.29$, $p < .05$. Again, the discrimination appeared more serious when the subjects encountered the information in aggregate form than when they encountered the information serially, department by department. No other effects on Seriousness Ratings were found.

Concerning Likelihood, there were no main effects. There was, however, a significant interaction effect between Format and Order, $F(1, 39) = 5.18$, $p < .05$. Subjects perceived discrimination to be most likely in the Aggregate Information Condition when the department-by-department information was followed by the aggregate fact sheet.

Discussion

The present experiment -- like earlier studies (Crosby, Burns, Censor, & MacKwethan, 1986; Crosby, Clayton, Alksnis, & Clayton, 1986) -- demonstrates how heavily the detection of discrimination can depend on the format of the information. When subjects read materials on a case by case basis, they perceived less discrimination than when they read the same information in aggregate form. Examining the components individually and serially leads subjects to underestimate the extent of discrimination. The phenomenon applies to emotionally neutral materials as fully as to emotionally charged ones. Indeed, the interaction on overall ratings indicates that the phenomenon is stronger for emotionally neutral materials than for emotionally charged ones.

The present study has far reaching implications. Even when one searches for evidence of discrimination, one may fail to perceive the situation accurately. The problem could lie primarily in the nature of the materials and not, as some assert, in the attitudes of the people running organizations. Accurate perceptions are necessary if people are to reduce the level of discrimination, and until organizations gather aggregate data, they may continue to discriminate against women and minorities. That's the bad news.

The good news is that even the most rudimentary affirmative action programs can help organizations change. If the difficulty perceiving discrimination is -- as our data indicate -- informational rather than attitudinal or emotional, then organizational change can come from a change in the information available to decision makers and need not await a change in underlying attitudes. Where attitudes are already egalitarian -- as is more generally true today than ever before (Kahn & Crosby, 1985) -- affirmative action programs can help organizations put their liberal attitudes into action.

References

Adams, J. S. (1965). Inequity in social exchange. In L. Berkowitz (Ed.), *Advances in Experimental Social Psychology* (vol. 2, pp. 267-299). New York: Academic Press.

Crosby, F. (1984). The denial of personal discrimination. *American Behavioral Scientist, 27*, 38-386.

Crosby, F., Burris, L., Censor, C., & MacKwethan, E. R. (1986). Two rotten apples spoil the justice barrel. In H. Bierhoff, R. Chen, & J. Greenberg (Eds.), *Justice: Views from the social sciences* (pp. 267-281). New York: Plenum Press.

Crosby, F., Clayton, S., Alksnis, O., & Hemker, K. (1986). Cognitive biases in the failure to perceive discrimination. *Sex Roles, 14*, 637-646.

Crosby, F., Pufall, A., Snyder, R. C., O'Connell, M., & Whalen, P. (in press). The denial of personal disadvantage among you, me, and all the other ostriches. In M. Crawford & M. Gentry (Eds.), *Gender and Thought*. New York: Springer-Verlag.

Deutsch, M. (1985). *Distributive Justice: A Social-Psychological Perspective*. New Haven: Yale University Press.

Kahn, W., & Crosby, F. (1985). Change and stasis: Discriminating between attitudes and discriminatory behavior. In L. Larwood, B. A. Gutek, & A. H. Stromberg (Eds.), *Women and work, an annual review* (vol. 1, pp. 215-238). Beverly Hills, CA: Sage Publications.

Lerner, M. (1981). *The justice motive: The fundamental delusion*. New York: Plenum Press.

14

Affirmative Action and the Challenge of the Color-blind Perspective

Bernardo M. Ferdman

Affirmative action programs take many different forms, but they are all alike in one respect. All affirmative action programs require an organization to take notice of people's ethnic group and gender. All affirmative action programs, in other words, require organizations to notice categorical information about people.

Affirmative action may appear an odd policy in an age when many organizations are trying to correct past injustices by remaining scrupulously color-blind and gender-blind. Is it not, after all, racist to insist on knowing the racial composition of a work force or sexist to insist on knowing the gender composition? Is it not discriminatory to take into account a person's ethnic group in evaluating that person? Should not an organization be interested only in what makes individuals unique -- their individuating information -- and ignore categorical information?

In her ethnographic research at a desegregated school, Janet Schofield found that most of the teachers, both Black and White, acted as if they ascribed to the color-blind perspective. Even though she found ample evidence that race influenced how the teachers reacted to people, the teachers were unwilling to recognize explicitly the importance of race. On the contrary, the teachers seemed to believe that to acknowledge the race of a pupil or a fellow teacher was an indication of prejudice (Schofield, 1986a, 1986b).

Prominent conservative leaders in the United States have transformed the color-blind perspective into an ideology. Members of President Reagan's administration, for example, have often claimed that it is racist and discriminatory simply to notice race or ethnicity in making hiring decisions. Such claims have been used to justify conservative attempts to dismantle affirmative action as a national policy (Taylor, Chapter 3).

The claims and counter-claims of politicians and policy makers are based, in part, on certain assumptions about the nature of stereotyping and prejudice. For example, advocates of the color-blind perspective base their views on the presumption that reducing the salience of other people's group memberships will also reduce the degree to which judgments are clouded by negative beliefs about the group. The assumption may seem initially plausible. Common sense tells us that most people, much of the time, notice each other's gender and race and ethnicity. Further reflection, however, makes us realize that there is no evidence that taking formal cognizance of another's race or gender or ethnicity increases a person's tendencies toward prejudice. We need to document what happens when people of the dominant social group -- say, White managers in a corporation -- are asked to take account of categorical information -- say, about ethnicity -- as well as individuating information about a minority person. Do they like the target person less than when they attend only to individuating information? Or do members of the dominant group like the minority person as well or even better when ethnicity is taken into account than when it is purportedly ignored? From the color-blind perspective, we would predict that making people in the dominant group pay attention to categorical information about people in the subordinate group increases social distance and disliking. From the perspective of affirmation action, however, we hope not.

It was to explore these questions that I conducted a study in the XYZ Corporation, a traditionally Anglo business. White managers there evaluated a Hispanic manager depicted in a videotape. Sometimes the Hispanic's ethnicity was highlighted in the introductory materials and sometimes it was not. According to the color-blind perspective, the White managers would show less positive attitudes when ethnicity was salient than when it was not. The group-sensitive perspective, in contrast, predicts that categorical information need not make evaluations more negative and can in fact make them more positive.

Methods

The study was conducted at the XYZ Corporation between December, 1985 and July, 1986. This company has 13,000 employees including approximately 3,000 managers. Among the managers were 46 self-identified Hispanics.

The research proceeded in two phases: an interview phase and an experiment. In the first phase, I interviewed 27 Hispanic and 19 Anglo (nonhispanic White) managers about their jobs and about how they normally handled situations in the course of their work. The interviews suggested that many of the Hispanic managers handled conflict and approached work tasks in a manner consistent with the norms of Hispanic culture (e.g., Albert, 1986; Herrera Ramirez, 1984; Moore & Pachon, 1985; Morris, 1981; Nine Curt, 1976a, 1976b; Poyatos, 1983; Westfried, 1985) and different from those of their Anglo peers.

On the basis of the information obtained during the initial interviews, I created video-tape presentations of a man called Eduardo Soldano in four different management situations. For each scene there were two versions: a normative version and a non-normative or Hispanic version. In the former, Eduardo Soldano behaved in a manner consistent with the majority norms at XYZ. In the latter, his behavior was consistent with Hispanic norms and deviated from the majority norms at XYZ, but it could be plausibly interpreted in a positive manner. Ratings provided by an independent group of Hispanic professors, graduate students, and managers (not from XYZ) provided validation that the differences between the two versions reflected cultural differences between Hispanics and Anglos.

During the second phase of the research, an experiment was conducted. Eighty-four nonhispanic White managers viewed the video-tape of Eddie in the four situations. Before they saw the video-tapes, study participants read a fact sheet that included excerpts from an interview with Eddie. For one third of the participants, individuating features -- such as hobbies -- were highlighted. For another third, Eddie highlighted his ethnicity, focusing on how being Puerto Rican was very important to him and how he belonged to a number of Hispanic organizations. The last third of the participants received fact sheets that included both ethnic group information and individuating information. Thus, the first independent variable, Information, had three levels: individuating, categorical, and combined.

The second independent variable, Version, was manipulated when participants viewed the film clips. Half of the managers saw the Anglo version in which Eddie behaved in the normative fashion. Half saw the Hispanic version. The resulting experimental design was thus a 2 x 3 factorial.

After reading the fact sheet and viewing the video-tape, each White manager in the experiment filled out a questionnaire. Four dependent variables were coded from the questionnaire. They included a measure of social distance, an evaluation of Eddie's handling of the situation, and two similarity ratings. All four indicated how favorably the White managers rated Eddie.

Seven items combined to form the social distance scale. Participants were asked to rate their "feelings about Eddie as a manager and a person" and to indicate how they would feel about various types of associations with him, for example being in the same work group, getting to know him personally, working as his subordinate, or living next door. The second dependent variable was scored by averaging participants' responses over the four scenes to the question: "How well did Eddie handle the situation?" Scores could range from 7 (very positive) to 1 (very negative). Participants were also asked to rate how similar Eddie was "to yourself" and "to most XYZ management people." These ratings, which could vary from 7 (very similar) to 1 (very dissimilar), made up the third and fourth dependent variables.

Results and Discussion

The color-blind perspective predicts that the White managers would have the most positive ratings when the videotape about Eddie had been preceded by individuating information alone. Visual inspection of the data and statistical analyses both cast serious doubt on the color-blind perspective. In all four analyses of variance, a main effect was obtained for the independent variable Information. The actual statistics were: for social distance, $F(2, 66) = 3.29, p < .05$; for situational evaluations, $F(2, 59) = 3.39, p < .05$; for similarity to self, $F(2, 60) = 3.80$, $p < .05$; for similarity to most XYZ managers, $F(2, 66) = 11.79, p < .001$. As Figures 1, 2, 3, and 4 show, the White managers evaluated Eddie most positively when they were presented with both individuating and categorical information and least positively when they were presented with individuating information alone. The lack of any statistically significant interaction between Information and Version showed that the effect of Information was the same whether Eddie behaved normatively or non-normatively.

The effects of the Information manipulation should hearten the proponents of affirmative action, for they very thoroughly disconfirm the color-blind perspective. How people enter an organization no doubt affects their eventual acceptance. Some detractors of affirmative action hint that the very use of categorical knowledge in having people enter an

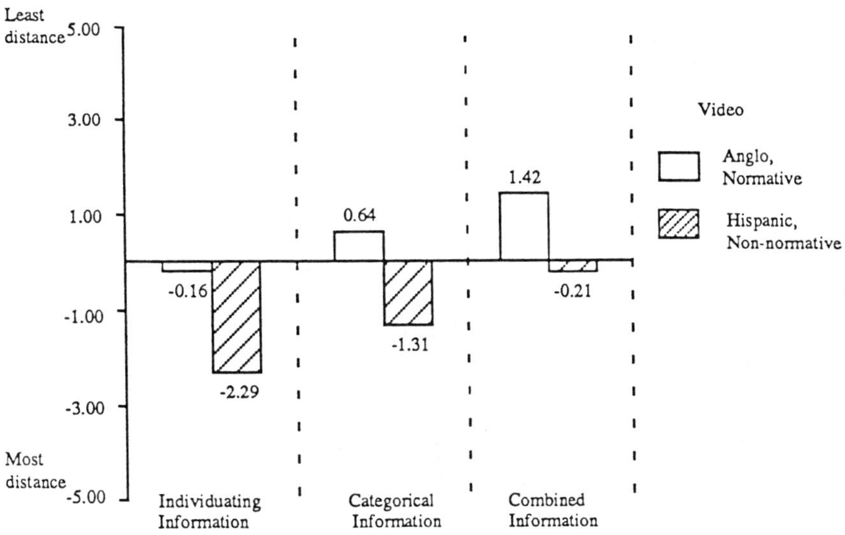

Figure 14.1
Social Distance Ratings

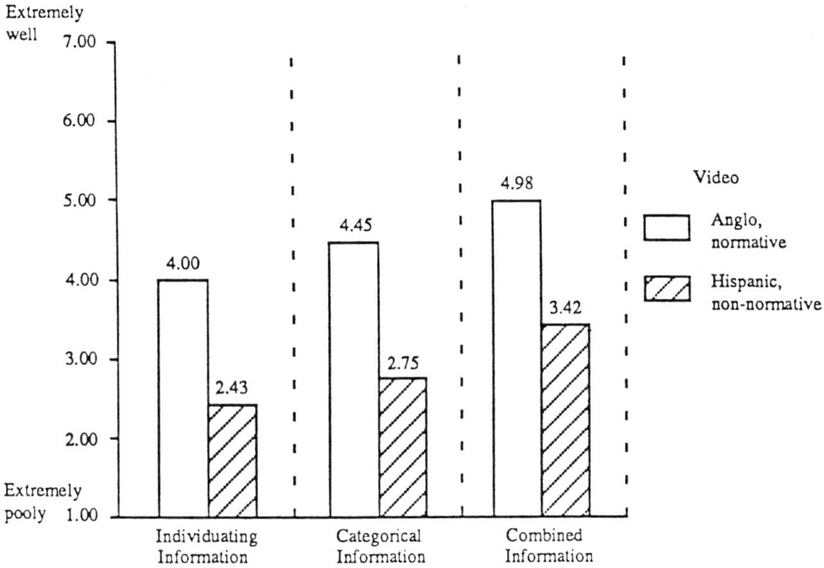

Figure 14.2
Evaluation of "How Well Eddie Handled the Situation"

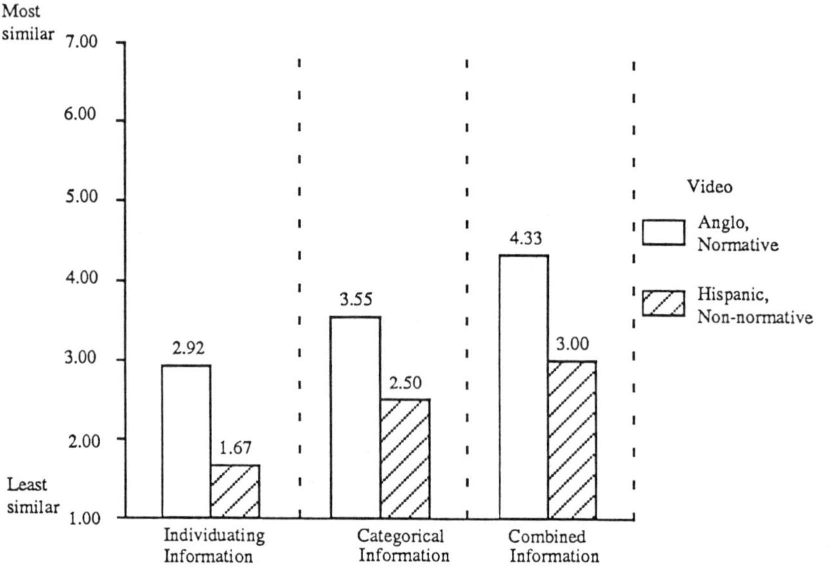

Figure 14.3
Ratings of Similarity to Self

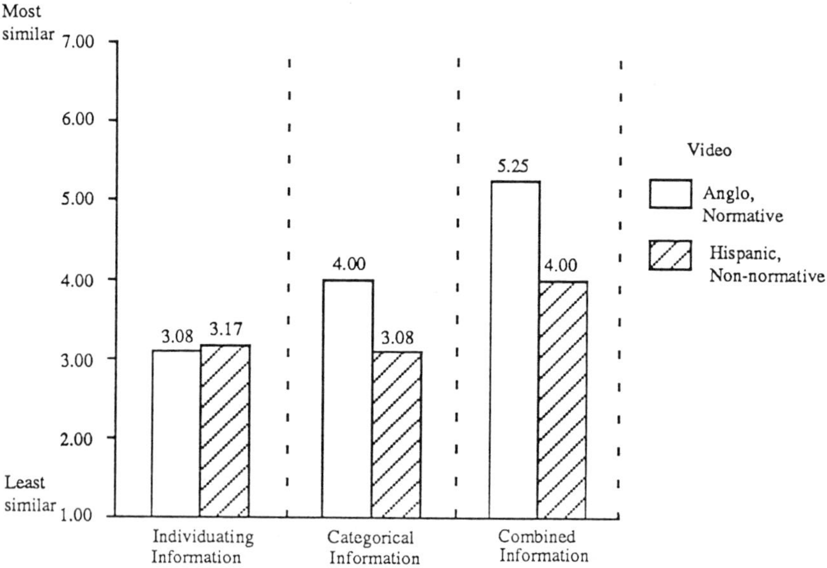

Figure 14.4
Ratings of Similarity to "Most XYZ Management People"

organization will interfere later with their acceptance. The data presented here do not support this view.

If some of the data can reassure the proponents of affirmative action, some contain cause for alarm. On all four variables, the White managers at XYZ reacted significantly more negatively to the non-normative Eddie than to the normative Eddie. The patterns are visible in Figures 1 through 4, and statistical analyses revealed that the patterns are reliable. White managers felt more distant from Eddie when they viewed the Hispanic clips than when they viewed the Anglo clips, $F(1, 66) = 4.92, p < .01$. The White managers also evaluated Eddie's handling of the situations less positively when they viewed the non-normative behavior than when they viewed the normative behavior, $F(1, 50) = 27.20, p < .001$. Finally, White managers felt the non-normative Eddie to be more dissimilar to themselves and to most managers at XYZ than the normative Eddie, $F(1, 60) = 9.06, p < .01$ and $F(1, 66) = 6.95, p < .01$, respectively.

The impact of Version on the study participants' evaluations of the stimulus person hold important implications for affirmative action. The opponents of affirmative action are wrong, as we have seen, to propose that White people always become more negatively biased when they notice ethnicity. But other differences and misunderstandings between groups must be surmounted to avoid heightening or confirming prejudices. The challenge to the color-blind perspective must include attention to the effects of cultural dissimilarities as well as to those of group labels.

Organizational researchers often distinguish between entry into an organization and acceptance within it (Pettigrew & Martin, 1987). Acceptance includes retention and promotion. An affirmative action program may be quite successful in increasing the number of women and minorities who enter an organization and yet unsuccessful in terms of retention and promotion. Typically people in organizations evaluate favorably those whose behavior conforms to the norms of the organization. Newcomers whose behavior does not conform to the old norms are likely to encounter resistance.

How to deal with the clash between new modes of behavior and existing organizational norms is a matter of some importance for affirmative action. It does not suffice simply to bring new groups of people into organizations. A good affirmative action program helps the newcomers become acculturated to the organization. And perhaps an excellent affirmative action program helps the organization to see how some of its normative practices might be made more flexible and diverse in ways that do not sacrifice but rather promote the goals and aims of the organization. Perhaps the best affirmative action programs develop an iterative process in which no one pretends to be blind to the color, gender, or ethnicity of others or is permitted to remain blind to the color, gender and ethnicity of the self.

References

Albert, R. D. (1986). Conceptual framework for the development and evaluation of cross-cultural orientation programs. *International Journal of Intercultural Relations, 10,* 197-213.

Herrera Ramirez, R. Y. (1984). Hispanic managers in U.S. organizations: The cultural experience of authority. Pre-dissertation research, Yale University, New Haven.

Moore, J., & Pachon, H. (1985). *Hispanics in the United States.* Englewood Cliffs, NJ: Prentice-Hall.

Morris, M. (1981). *Saying and meaning in Puerto Rico: Some problems in the ethnography of discourse.* Oxford: Pergamon Press.

Nine Curt, C. J. (1976a). *Non-verbal communication.* Cambridge, MA: National Assessment and Dissemination Center for Bilingual/Bicultural Education.

Nine Curt, C. J. (1976b). *Teacher training pack for a course on cultural awareness.* Cambridge, MA: National Assessment and Dissemination Center for Bilingual/Bicultural Education.

Pettigrew, T., & Martin, J. (1987). Shaping the organizational context for Black American inclusion. *Journal of Social Issues, 43*(1), 41-78.

Poyatos, F. (1983). *New perspectives in nonverbal communication: Studies in cultural anthropology, social psychology, linguistics, literature and semiotics.* Oxford: Pergamon Press.

Schofield, J. W. (1986a). Causes and consequences of the color-blind perspective. In J. F. Dovidio, & S. L. Gaertner (Eds.), *Prejudice, discrimination, and racism* (pp. 231-253). Orlando, FL: Academic Press.

Schofield, J. W. (1986b). Black-white contact in desegregated schools. In M. Hewstone & R. Brown (Eds.), *Contact and conflict in intergroup encounters* (pp. 78-93). Oxford: Basil Blackwell.

Westfried, A. H. (1985). *Three Puerto Rican families.* Salem, WI: Sheffield Publishing Company.

15

The Justice of Affirmative Action

Susan D. Clayton and Sandra S. Tangri

There is greater consensus in the United States on the goal of social equality than on the means to achieve that goal. Affirmative action, one legally mandated path to social justice, meets widespread resistance. Title VII of the Civil Rights Act refers to affirmative action as a compensatory procedure directed at victims of discrimination by employers who were guilty of discriminatory practices. Executive Order 11246, issued a year later, widens the field by suggesting that affirmative action is taken in order to avoid potential discrimination. Affirmative action goals have been operationalized in a variety of ways, including hiring and promotion of qualified women or minority group members over equally qualified White males, setting goals and timetables for hiring and promoting to be implemented, and active recruitment of underrepresented groups. Such policies are perceived to violate two basic principles underlying individual achievement in American society: equal access to opportunities and equitable assignment of rewards based on individual merit rather than on immutable status characteristics. It is this appearance of incompatibility with equality of opportunity and equity of rewards which has led some to conclude that affirmative action policies are fundamentally unfair.

Laws reflect as much as they shape public attitudes. Law can neither shape opinion nor effectively alter behavior in an environment of widespread skepticism about its value. For this reason, an examination of the reasons for the resistance to affirmative action is crucial. Some who resist affirmative action may be expressing "symbolic" (Kinder, 1986; Kinder & Sears, 1981) or "aversive" (Dovidio, Mann, & Gaertner, Chapter 7) racism or sexism. Others, expressing self-interest, may feel merely that they will lose out under affirmative action programs. Still other objections are made by people who strongly assert their lack of biases, and for whom there is every reason to credit such assertions. Finally, objections to affirmative action are sometimes voiced by members of groups who would benefit from the programs (e.g., Taylor & Dubé, 1986) and even by those who have themselves benefited (Nacoste, 1987)

The seemingly irrefutable basis for many objections is that affirmative action programs are unfair. Affirmative action, it is argued, perpetuates the very discrimination that it intends to eliminate. Race- and sex-conscious goals and timetables, according to this position, are antithetical to the goal of eliminating these characteristics as bases for decisions regarding individuals' organizational entry and progress. Moreover, their use penalizes White males who did not personally discriminate and should, therefore, not be made to pay the price of restitution for past discrimination by others. The argument is eloquently stated by Guzzardi (1981):

> For the federal government to continue to dole out prizes and penalties on the basis of racial and sexual categories, which are the old enemies that inflicted the stigmata on the unfortunate in the first place, is to apply the disease as cure...To favor some groups is not a free-floating act: It means less justice and freedom for others...Who should pay that price? On which sons should the sins of the fathers be visited? And for how many generations? (pp. 100-101).

While Guzzardi's simplistic argument has initial appeal, it is ultimately unsatisfactory. It is not that concerns of justice should be abandoned in favor of more pragmatic considerations. Research has documented that justice is very important to people -- so much so that they will change their attitudes about a person in order to maintain the belief that justice has occurred (Lerner, 1981), adjust their input to a task in order to calibrate it with their outcome (Walster, Berscheid, & Walster, 1973), or passively accept negative outcomes if these outcomes are perceived to have been justly obtained (Tyler & McGraw, 1986). Research has also shown that justice concerns are exceedingly complex. Determinations of fairness (which we consider synonymous with justice) depend on whether the focus involves the distribution of benefits (Deutsch, 1975), retribution for wrongdoing (Hogan & Emler, 1981), or the procedures that guide decision-making (Thibaut & Walker, 1975;

Tyler, 1987) and whether the assessment is made at an individual or at a societal level (Brickman, Folger, Goode, & Schul, 1981). We contend that a precise analysis of fairness, one that acknowledges the complexity of the multifaceted construct of justice, yields the conclusion that affirmative action is fair under any principle of justice.

Distributive Justice

Whenever societies or organizations allocate goods and services, issues of distributive justice arise (Deutsch, 1975). Three principles of distributive justice have been articulated: equity, equality, and need. Equity refers to the correspondence between inputs and outcomes. A relationship is equitable when all participants obtain equal relative outcomes -- when, that is, the ratio of outcome to input is equal for all individuals (Walster et al., 1973). If, for example, Person A has twice as much training and skill as Person B, then equity obtains if A earns twice as much as B.

While equity appears to be the fundamental rule in our economic system, two other principles often complement equity-based rules of distribution. By the principle of equality everyone is allotted the same amount of given resources. By the principle of need everyone is allotted the resources they need: Those who start with the least are given the most.

Affirmative action programs have been criticized for their apparent violation of the norms of distributive justice. The criticisms are ill founded in two ways. First, they assume that affirmative action programs are necessarily incompatible with the norms of equity. Second, they presume that equity is the only relevant principle of distributive justice.

Calculating Equity

The strength of the equity model is demonstrated by the variety of people's reactions to inequity. Those who are relatively advantaged by inequity typically respond by reducing their outcomes or increasing their inputs, in actuality or in their evaluations. Those who are relatively disadvantaged under inequity often do the opposite. An inability to restore equity leads to distress and, for the disadvantaged person, a feeling of relative deprivation (Adams, 1965; Crosby, 1976, 1982). Although inequity is perceived negatively by all parties, victims are typically more distressed than beneficiaries.

Some people feel that affirmative action policies violate equity because an irrelevant characteristic, such as race or gender, is factored into the equation. (There is little disagreement, at least overtly, that such characteristics should be irrelevant in an ideal world.) White males who believe that they are being underrewarded relative to a less-qualified other are especially likely to raise cries of "reverse discrimination."

In fact, affirmative action is justifiable in terms of equity. The primary problem for equity theory has always been defining and assessing the relevant inputs. Because of this difficulty, "color-blind" decisions that do not include affirmative action adjustments lack the objectivity which they are believed to demonstrate. Even among decision-makers who feel no hostility or intent to discriminate, color-blind decisions handicap members of disadvantaged groups in two ways.

The first problem lies in defining the input. "Relevance" has been defined for generations by White males, and merely extending the boundaries to include other groups does not mean that the relevant inputs will be the same for them. How is one to evaluate the history of accomplishments of a middle-aged woman relative to a middle-aged man given that the former had a ten-year hiatus in her career while she raised two children? Or compare a Black manager to a White manager given that the former made it up through the ranks in an era of overt racism? And how do we weigh the assets that minorities and women bring with them, simply by virtue of being different, the value of diversity? Fairness requires the recognition that individuals bring with them into the organization not merely different amounts of the same things, but also different kinds of things that may make them valuable to an organization.

The second problem lies in evaluating what appear to be the "same" inputs. A perfect example is that of standardized scholastic test scores. Such scores have a certain amount of predictive value for Whites; their accuracy in predicting the future academic success of students of color is far less. Nonwhite students also tend to receive lower scores on average. Using such test scores as admissions criteria may seem objective but is, in fact, discriminatory. Although the differential validity of selection tests may be less of a problem in employment than in education (Anastasi, 1982), the underestimation of minority and female abilities remains widespread. We must find or create new criteria relevant to females and minority people. If equity is to obtain, we must calibrate the inputs of females and minorities with as much sensitivity as we calibrate the inputs of White males.

In the case of non-standardized tests the evaluation of performance is more subject to obvious bias. Research by Dovidio et al. (Chapter 7) shows clearly that the same performance by Blacks and by Whites is evaluated in a manner that is biased toward Whites. We all think we are capable of objectively assessing performance. But time and again, the data show that we are not. In addition, as Heilman and Guzzo (1978) argue, the allocation of rewards at work reflects not only actual performance, but also attributions about the cause of the performance. Employers who expect weak performance attribute unexpectedly strong performances to unstable causes such as luck or effort. Strong performances that are attributed to luck or effort are less often rewarded with promotions than are strong performances attributed to ability.

The bias against disadvantaged groups in an "objective" calibration of outcomes to inputs argues for weighting the equity equation by adding minority or female group membership to the input side of the model. Including such a factor does not unbalance an equitable state, but rather restores balance by adjusting for the positive weighting of majority group membership that is ingrained within the system.

Other norms

Different social arrangements appear to call for different norms of distributive justice; equity may not be the most appropriate principle of resource allocation in all situations. Equity works best when both the input and the outcome are continuous variables whose values can fluctuate proportionately (Deutsch, 1985). The calibration of inputs to outputs under principles of equity -- always a formidable exercise -- becomes especially difficult when continuous inputs (e.g., years of experience) are paired with dichotomous outcomes (e.g., either to admit, hire, promote or not). Such dichotomous outcomes invite the artificial imposition of thresholds on continuous input variables, seriously impairing the efficiency of the equity model. Discontinuous outcomes imprecisely reflect both decreases in input below a threshold necessary for receiving the outcome and increases above that threshold.

Non-equity models are not only more efficient for optimizing certain kinds of goals, they are also perceived as more legitimate than equity under some circumstances. The principles of equality and need are more appropriate than equity in situations where social relations and human growth are of paramount importance. Deutsch (1975) found that even task-oriented groups chose equality or need principles over equity principles for distributing rewards between one-third and two-thirds of the time and those who reported feeling more cooperative with fellow group members were particularly likely to do so. Prentice and Crosby

(1987) found some preliminary evidence in interviews to suggest that, although equity norms are the strongest determinants of deservingness in the workplace, need was more often the operative principle in the home. They discuss several reasons for this, one of which is that homes are involved in distributing rather than producing resources. Educational admission and academic promotion decisions also concern the distribution rather than the production of resources (although they are preliminary and integral to production concerns); the claim may thus be made that equity should not be seen as the only guiding principle in such situations.

Indeed, even in the workplace, need has been recognized as a legitimate principle for the distribution of jobs. It is the need to "catch up" that we accept as justifying the institutionalized preference given to veterans for hiring into civil service jobs (Glasser, 1988). This is the same need that justifies preferential hiring of minorities and women.

Retributive Justice

One of the objections made to affirmative action is that it penalizes the innocent rather than the guilty. Such an argument acknowledges that there has been discrimination, but protests that affirmative action policies do not punish those responsible, or even those who have benefited from discrimination; they unfairly penalize others who have done nothing to deserve such punishment. This argument is based on the erroneous assumption that the goal of affirmative action is retribution.

Retribution is a powerful human motive. Although infrequently acknowledged and little studied, its strength can be discerned in any debate about capital punishment or prison conditions. "An eye for an eye, a tooth for a tooth" reads the Biblical algebra. Retributive justice can be seen as a type of distributive justice, but one that involves the allocation of punishments rather than rewards. An important difference between retribution and distribution is, however, that the amount of punishment to be allocated is theoretically infinite: No resources are needed in order to distribute punishment. Powerless and low-status people cannot easily reward those above them in the hierarchy but the low-status can more easily exact retribution (Hogan & Emler, 1981). This asymmetry may create the illusion that those who would benefit from affirmative action are trying to exact retribution -- an illusion that is further fostered by the fact that, no doubt, some victims of discrimination would like retribution for their past sufferings.

Another factor that may promote the illusion of affirmative action as retribution concerns the relative nature of felt deprivations. A small reward can seem like a punishment compared with a large reward. Social comparison and relative deprivation theorists have long argued that dissatisfaction results when one receives less than one believes one deserves, and that one gauges one's desert by establishing a reference point (Crosby, 1976, 1982). White males have two reference points by which to judge their current outcomes: their own, previous, privileged access to resources (or the privileged access of their White, male reference group); and the new, improved access of women and people of color to those resources, which if not better than that of White men, is better now than it was previously. The gap between White men and everybody else has narrowed, and White men accurately perceive this as a decrease in advantage. Affirmative action policies usually concern finite resources (positions or money), and thus the gain for minority group members and women is experienced as a cost to those in the majority. The situation can seem doubly unfair because it appears to penalize the innocent rather than the guilty.

Retribution is not the goal of affirmative action. Affirmative action programs are not punishment. They do not take away from any individuals money or positions they already have. They only adjust what people can expect. If affirmative action derived from principles of retributive justice, it would apply only where a victim and villain have been identified. While the criminal portions of the civil rights laws personalize both the problem of discrimination by specifying the perpetrator and victim and the remedy by specifying punishment, affirmative action personalizes neither the problem nor the remedy.

There is one circumstance in which an "innocent" party may lose a job as a result of an affirmative action plan. Seniority systems (which tend to favor Whites) may be overridden in order not to reinstate the employment pattern established by past discrimination so that a more senior White or male employee may loose his job, while the junior minority person or woman may retain her job. Even here, it may be more fair to place the burden on the employer who discriminated in the first place, rather than on the displaced employee, although the latter benefited unjustly from the discrimination (Glasser, 1988).

Procedural Justice

Distributions and retributions aside, does affirmative action violate the ideals of procedural justice? Procedural justice refers to the process preceding the distribution. It focuses on the means rather than the ends. Interestingly, although a reliance on merit in the form of equity seems to be the method of choice in distributive justice, equality is the predominant value under procedural justice (e.g., Nacoste, 1987). Equal opportunity -- an equal position at the starting gate -- is the *sine qua non* of the American dream. Affirmative action policies, although intended to ensure such equality of opportunity, are resisted because at least some of the time they are seen as moving in the opposite direction.

The American concern with procedural justice is pronounced. A series of studies by Tyler and his colleagues (Tyler & McGraw, 1986) has demonstrated that judgments of procedural fairness matter as much as, if not more than, judgments of distributive fairness in evaluating political and legal issues. In a way, this is appropriate: It is more difficult to assess objectively the fairness of outcomes than to determine whether the proper procedure was followed. But an overemphasis on procedural issues can be misleading if the criteria used to define a just procedure are inappropriate. A just procedure, presumably, is one that produces a just outcome, or at least a desirable outcome. However, Tyler, Rasinski, and Spodick (1985) found that the ability to have input into a decision was an important criterion for procedural fairness independent of one's ability to affect the outcome. If the procedure appears fair according to this criterion, one may accept passively an unfair outcome, or even fail to evaluate the outcome at all.

Consider the overriding concern with procedural justice in the criminal justice system. Does everyone have equal access to lawyers and other resources? Does everyone have an equal chance for his or her day in court, and thus an equal opportunity to be heard? Anyone who reads the newspaper knows that an unfair outcome is occasionally reached: A guilty man goes free because of a "loophole" or an innocent person is freed after serving ten years in prison. Our faith in the fairness of the procedures, however, allows us to believe that the majority of court decisions are just.

This complacency may be misplaced. Various forms of systematic bias sometimes influence criminal cases in ways that can only be discovered by examining the outcomes rather than the process. Examples include the racial bias demonstrated in capital punishment cases, such that murderers of Whites are more likely to be executed than murderers of Blacks; and the conviction-proneness of death-qualified juries (Cowan, Thompson, & Ellsworth, 1984). Legal appeals are typically based on the process rather than the outcome of a case, yet appeals concerning these biases have used evidence about the distribution of outcomes to infer that the process is not as just as we think it is.

Examination of disparate outcomes can alert us to the mechanisms that introduce inequalities into the procedures of "equal opportunity." Braddock and McPartland (1987) and Pettigrew and Martin (1987) outline, for those who believe in equal opportunity, the sociological and psychological barriers that prevent minorities from having equal access to jobs and promotions. Such barriers include segregated social networks used in job recruitment; closed internal markets, whereby minorities enter jobs that do not have equal potential for advancement; the handicap of being the only minority group member in a workplace; and the pressures of being exposed to prejudice from one's fellow employees. These barriers exist as well for women (Laws & Tangri, 1979; Laws, 1980).

It is important to note, so that the point does not appear merely academic, that Americans' concern with procedural justice has not barred acceptance of many forms of preferential selection. The most noteworthy one -- because it has similarities with affirmative action -- is veterans' preference. As Glasser (1988) points out:

> ...veterans receive preference when they apply for certain civil service jobs...whether they were drafted or not...saw combat or not, whether they specifically can be shown to have been disadvantaged by their military service or not....[Nonveterans] are discriminated against even if, as individuals, they may be more disadvantaged in some way or arguably more qualified. This preferential system, which is not based strictly on individual merit, has not been seen by American society as unfair or immoral. (p. 349)

As head of a government office, one of the authors (ST) experienced directly the privileging of veterans over nonveterans for vacancies in her office, which most often presented a barrier to women candidates. The justification for the preference was based on a social judgment that, "because all veterans, as a group, had been taken out of the race (for jobs)...by being conscripted...all veterans, as a group, were entitled to various economic and educational benefits to get them even" (Glasser, 1988, p. 347). This is no different from the moral justification for affirmative action.

Other preference systems depart from either equity, need or equality rules. For instance, colleges and universities have long incorporated preferences for state residence and for children of alumni into their admissions procedures. Although the preferential treatment of the children of alumni may perpetuate past discriminatory advantages, none of these preferential systems is generally perceived by Americans as unfair or immoral (Glasser, 1988).

We do not argue that procedural justice is unimportant, merely that it is insufficient because the means may not justify the ends. To assure ourselves that a procedure which looks fair actually is fair, its outcomes must be assessed. In the case of minority and female access to jobs, promotions, and education, standard procedures have not been just. Affirmative action programs provide the means for monitoring the outcomes of procedures so as to make the decision process more fair. The most controversial aspects of affirmative action, goals and timetables, are merely indicators of the degree to which the procedural adjustments are working (Sawhill & Tangri, 1981).

Micro- and Macrojustice

The distinction between micro- and macrojustice reflects a difference in level of analysis. Microjustice concerns the appropriateness of individual outcomes, while macrojustice concerns the fairness of the distribution of outcomes within a society (Brickman et al., 1981). Objections to affirmative action are usually made at the microjustice level: Affirmative action led to an unfair outcome for *this* qualified White man or for *that* unqualified Black woman. The reasons for affirmative action, however, are strongest at the macro level. In support of this, Jemmott and Tebbets (1980) analyzed a number of newspaper articles and editorials concerning the Bakke "reverse discrimination" case, coding for both valence of position and type of information presented. Pro-Bakke articles were significantly more likely to refer to micro-level data about the qualifications of Bakke. Anti-Bakke articles, more sympathetic to the goals of affirmative action, relied more on what Jemmott and Tebbets term "anchoring information": discussion of the wider, macro-level legal, social, or moral issues.

Affirmative action programs deserve to be evaluated on the macro level for three reasons. First, equity principles normally operate to exacerbate pre-existing differentials in resources. Since the equity rule rewards those who contribute the most, those with the most to contribute also receive the most rewards. Thus, classes of individuals who start out advantaged, become progressively more advantaged. This is easily seen in the financial arena where larger investors "earn" disproportionately larger returns. But equity is also relevant in other spheres such as education where, in general, students from better high schools gain admittance to better colleges and later to better graduate schools. In the transfer of resources from education to employment, an alma mater can open or close doors. Equity reinforces existing patterns of resource distribution in society; affirmative action policies can change this macro-level pattern.

Second, the effects of discrimination are more clearly perceived at the societal level than at the individual level. Crosby (1982, 1984) has shown that women often do not perceive themselves as suffering from discrimination on the job, despite objective evidence that they are paid less than equivalent male employees. This distorted perception might arise from self-defensive avoidance among women; it is unpleasant to perceive oneself as a victim or to cast one's associates and co-workers as villains. Even among those who are not defensive, however, discrimination can be difficult to see in an individual case. Crosby, Clayton, Hemker, and Alksnis (1986) demonstrated that uninvolved, outside raters were more likely to detect discrimination when an aggregate of cases was presented than when the same cases were presented seriatim. There is often a plausible alternative explanation to discrimination in a single case of apparent inequity. Parsimony makes alternative explanations less likely when a pattern of differential outcomes is shown across a number of cases. (See also Twiss, Tabb, & Crosby, Chapter 13.)

In addition, some of the most harmful and long-lasting effects of discrimination reside at the societal level (Laws & Tangri, 1979). The systematic exclusion of whole categories of people from positions of power and authority does more than limit the attainments of those individuals. It restricts the perspectives of those who occupy these positions, to the detriment of their effectiveness. It also limits the expectations and achievements of future generations who, deprived of role models to encourage them to strive for high goals, continue to suffer from the stereotypes of the past.

The third reason for focusing on macrojustice is that the focus on the micro level erroneously personalizes the issue. Not only does it frame the situation in terms of the effects on individuals; it encourages the belief in individuals as causes, villains who maliciously perpetuate discrimination because of their own prejudices against outgroup members (cf. Crosby & Gonzalez-Intal, 1984). This way of framing the problem is misleading. It sustains the assumption that discrimination exists only when there is intention to discriminate. It has been extensively documented that discriminatory practices are so institutionalized -- and so self-perpetuating -- that intent is necessary, not to discriminate, but to avoid discrimination.

That our society emphasizes issues of microjustice is not surprising. Americans in general have an individualistic orientation, and endorsement of macrojustice principles is associated with degree of collective consciousness within a culture (Brickman et al., 1981). Even for those who do accept the principles of macrojustice -- and minorities may be more likely to do so if they have strong group identities -- there is bound to be a conflict between these values and those of microjustice. Nacoste (1987) points out that even those who feel that macro-level changes are necessary perceive microjustice strategies to be the fairest ways of achieving those changes. The connection between the individual and societal level is difficult to see and perhaps even more difficult to maintain (Crosby & Clayton, 1986).

Nevertheless, individuals do sometimes accept macrojustice rather than microjustice as a fair basis for resource distribution. Brickman and colleagues (1981) show that lotteries are an example of a popular system that is concerned with the shape of the resource distribution rather than the input of an individual. That is, lotteries prescribe how many "winners" there should be but not who they shall be. Brickman also found that macrojustice principles were more likely to be endorsed for certain categories of issues than for others. In education, for example, colleges and universities take into account in their admissions and scholarship decisions such factors as geographic representation, diversity of intended major, and athletic prowess. People understand the value of having a student body that is balanced in certain ways. And people typically do not object to infringing on the rights of this or that intellectually gifted student from New York or Massachusetts in order to assure the well-being of the larger academic community.

At a psychological level, one reason that people feel so strongly about justice seems to be that it increases their feeling of control over the environment (Lerner, 1981). In thinking about justice, a focus on macrojustice rather than microjustice takes control out of the hands of the individual. Perhaps affirmative action programs are objected to because they explicitly give weight to uncontrollable factors (race, sex), thus presumably reducing the input of controllable factors. What objectors do not realize is that, generally speaking, controllable factors had less input than they were believed to have; uncontrollable factors have always strongly influenced hiring and promotion decisions. Affirmative action programs aim to reverse the weight that was previously given to individual variables such as race and sex, and by doing so, ultimately to neutralize their effect in such decisions.

Further Considerations

Although we have addressed the central, philosophical objection to affirmative action, we have left untouched further objections. Two complaints relate to the issue of fairness. First, some scholars have wondered if there is any limit to the number of groups that can legitimately claim preferential treatment as a targeted affirmative action group (Newton, 1973). After all, many groups have suffered past discrimination. In response we would reiterate that affirmative action is not intended as retribution. It is not so much the historical character as the present consequences of longstanding discrimination which entitles affirmative action. The Irish may have suffered many injustices in America one hundred years ago; but they no longer do. It would be inappropriate to declare the Irish a protected group.

A second objection centers on the problem of deciding when affirmative action is no longer necessary. The answer lies in our consideration of outcomes as a criterion for procedure. If resources such as jobs, wages, and promotions are still inequitably distributed between groups, then affirmative action procedures are still necessary; if not, they may be phased out.

A final question remains: How effective is affirmative action as a policy? The answer is: very. Proponents (Glasser, 1988) and opponents (Glazer, 1988) alike now accept the effectiveness of affirmative action. Even so, estimates of effectiveness tend to be biased downwards because they do not measure the indirect effects of the legal requirements on organizational behavior. That is, the mere existence of the law and the risk of being found in noncompliance at some point in the future may be sufficient to induce a change in hiring or utilization patterns, even when no specific governmental action is involved. Anti-trust and many other laws work in much the same way. One does not need a cop on every corner to deter crime, and one should not measure the effectiveness of legal sanctions by comparing the crime rate on corners with and without the presence of police (Sawhill & Tangri, 1981).

Beyond this lies a subtler point about external sanctions. Law can induce a change in behavior because they redefine what is considered socially acceptable. What may start as an externally-imposed set of requirements may eventually become internalized in the form of a new set of values. Laws reflect society's conscience, and few people deviate far from the social norm.

Justice is not an objective concept but is a socially constructed idea about what would constitute the best system (cf. Rawls, 1971). The closest we can come to objectivity is to evaluate situations or programs according to abstract principles, rather than by determining what persons or groups benefit in a particular instance. This paper has examined affirmative action programs in just such a way. We have tried, not to propose radical new standards of justice, but to articulate the ways in which affirmative action accords with the widely accepted norms of distribution and procedure that define justice in our society. A fully-informed perspective, cognizant of the complexity of these norms of justice as well as of the pervasive effects of past discrimination, will, we believe, lead one to discern the justice of affirmative action.

References

Adams, J. S. (1965). Inequity in social exchange. In L. Berkowitz (Ed.). *Advances in experimental social psychology* (Vol. 2, 267-299). New York: Academic Press.

Anastasi, A. (1982). *Psychological Testing* (5th ed.). New York: MacMillan.

Braddock, J. H., & McPartland, J. M. (1987). How minorities continue to be excluded from equal employment opportunities: Research on labor market and institutional barriers. *Journal of Social Issues, 43*(1), 5-39.

Brickman, P., Folger, R., Goode, E., & Schul, Y. (1981). Microjustice and macrojustice. In M. Lerner & S. Lerner (Eds.), *The justice motive in social behavior* (173-202). New York: Plenum.

Cowan, C. L., Thompson, W. C., & Ellsworth, P. C. (1984). The effects of death qualification on jurors' predisposition to convict and on the quality of deliberation. *Law and Human Behavior, 8*, 53-79.

Crosby, F. (1976). A model of egoistic relative deprivation. *Psychological Review, 83*, 85-113.

Crosby, F. (1982). *Relative deprivation and working women*. New York: Oxford University Press.

Crosby, F. (1984). The denial of personal discrimination. *American Behavioral Scientist, 27*, 371-386.

Crosby, F., & Clayton, S. D. (1986). Introduction: The search for connections. *Journal of Social Issues, 42*(2), 1-9.

Crosby, F., Clayton, S. D., Hemker, K., & Alksnis, O. (1986). Cognitive biases in the perception of discrimination. *Sex Roles, 14*, 637-646.

Crosby, F., & Gonzalez-Intal, M. (1984). Relative deprivation and equity theories: Felt injustice and the undeserved benefits of others. In R. Folger (Ed.), *The sense of injustice: Social psychological perspectives*, New York: Plenum.

Deutsch, M. (1975). Equity, equality and need: What determines which value will be used as the basis for distributive justice? *Journal of Social Issues, 31*(3),

137-149.

Deutsch, M. (1985). Experimental studies of the effects of different systems of distributive justice. In *Distributive Justice: A Social-Psychological Perspective* (pp. 133-163). New Haven, CT: Yale Press.

Dovidio, J. F., Mann, J., & Gaertner, S. L. (1989). Resistance to affirmative action: The implications of aversive racism. In F. A. Blanchard & F. J. Crosby (Eds.), *Affirmative action in perspective* (pp. 83-102). New York: Springer-Verlag.

Glasser, I. (1988). Affirmative action and the legacy of racial injustice. In P. A. Katz & D. A. Taylor (Eds.), *Eliminating racism: Profiles in courage* (pp. 341-358). New York: Plenum Press.

Glazer, N. (1988). The future of preferential affirmative action. In P. A. Katz & D. A. Taylor (Eds.), *Eliminating racism: Profiles in courage* (pp. 329-340). N.Y.: Plenum Press.

Guzzardi, Walter, Jr. (1981, March 9). The right way to strive for equality. *Fortune*, 98-115.

Heilman, M. E., & Guzzo, R. A. (1978). The perceived cause of work success as a mediator of sex discrimination in organization. *Organizational Behavior and Human Performance, 21*, 346-357.

Hogan, R., & Emler, N. P. (1981). Retributive justice. In M. Lerner & S. Lerner (Eds.), *The Justice Motive in Social Behavior* (pp. 125-143). New York: Plenum.

Jemmott, J. B., & Tebbets, R. (1980). Applying social cognition: A content analysis of the Bakke case. *Personality and Social Psychology Bulletin, 6*, 30-36.

Kinder, D. R. (1986). The continuing American dilemma: White resistance to racial change 40 years after Myrdal. *Journal of Social Issues, 42*(2), 151-171.

Kinder, D., & Sears, D. (1981). Prejudice and politics: Symbolic racism versus racial threats to the good life. *Journal of Personality and Social Psychology, 40*, 414-431.

Laws, J. L. (1980). *Problems of access and problems of success in women's career advancement*. Paper presented at the National Institute for Education Conference on Attitudinal and Behavioral Measurement in Social Processes and Women's Research. Washington, D.C.

Laws, J. L., & Tangri, S. S. (1979). *Institutional sexism*. Paper presented at the annual convention of the American Psychological Association, New York.

Lerner, M. (1981). *The belief in a just world: A fundamental delusion*. New York: Plenum.

Nacoste, R. (1987). Social psychology and affirmative action: The importance of process in policy analysis. *Journal of Social Issues, 43*(1), 127-132.

Newton, L. (1973). Reverse discrimination as unjustified. *Ethics, 83*, 308-312.

Pettigrew, T. F., & Martin, J. (1987). Shaping the organizational context for Black American inclusion. *Journal of Social Issues, 43*(1), 41-78.

Prentice, D. A., & Crosby, F. (1987). The importance of context for assessing deservingness. In J. C. Masters & W. P. Smith (Eds.), *Social comparison, social justice, and relative deprivation* (pp. 165-182). Hillsdale, NJ: Erlbaum.

Rawls, J. (1971). *A theory of justice.* Cambridge, MA: Harvard University Press.

Sawhill, I., & Tangri, S. (1981). *Affirmative action in the 1980's: Dismantling the process of discrimination.* Comments prepared for the U.S. Commission on Civil Rights. Washington, D.C.

Taylor, D., & Dubé, L. (1986). Two faces of identity: The "I" and the "we". *Journal of Social Issues, 42*(2), 81-98.

Thibaut, J., & Walker, L. (1975). *Procedural justice: A psychological analysis.* Hillsdale, NJ: Erlbaum.

Twiss, C., Tabb, S., & Crosby, F. J. (1989). Affirmative action and aggregate data: The importance of patterns in the perception of discrimination. In F. A. Blanchard & F. J. Crosby (Eds.), *Affirmative action in perspective* (pp. 159-167). New York: Springer-Verlag.

Tyler, T. (1987). Procedural justice research. *Social Justice Research, 1*, 41-65.

Tyler, T., & McGraw, K. (1986). Ideology and the interpretation of personal experience: Procedural justice and political quiescence. *Journal of Social Issues, 42*(2), 115-128.

Tyler, T., Rasinski, K., & Spodick, N. (1985). Influence of voice on satisfaction with leaders: Exploring the meaning of process control. *Journal of Personality and Social Psychology, 48*, 72-81.

Walster, E., Berscheid, E., & Walster, G. W. (1973). New directions in equity research. *Journal of Personality and Social Psychology, 25*, 151-176.

16

Effective Affirmative Action Programs

Fletcher A. Blanchard

Over the last three centuries members of the major U.S. minority groups -- Blacks, Hispanics, Asian Americans, and Native Americans -- and women experienced both formal and informal barriers to their occupational and educational participation in American life. Over the last twenty-five years all Americans have experienced the elimination of many of the legal prohibitions which supported the exclusion of minorities and women from equal employment opportunity and equal protection under the law. Equal opportunity policies and civil rights legislation constitute the legal framework by which the *formal* barriers have been dismantled.

Although the legal barriers are generally gone, the clear and present consequences of historic patterns of exclusion remain. White Americans today grow up and live in settings that are numerically dominated by Whites. Their close friends are Whites and their workmates tend to be Whites, as well. Few men have been supervised by women. Few Whites have been supervised or taught by members of minority groups. Neighborhoods are sufficiently segregated by race that in 1980 four out of every five Black families living on minority blocks in the urban core would have had to move to a nonminority block (and be replaced by a nonminority family) before a random housing pattern would be achieved (Farley, 1984). If the largely favorable trends toward integrated housing patterns which have occurred since the 1970s were to continue on their present course, random housing patterns for Blacks and Whites would not be achieved until the twenty-second century (Pettigrew,

1988).

In 1986 over two-thirds of the people living in the United States had lived during the period of Jim Crow rules which dominated the behavior of Whites and Blacks in some parts of the country (Dovidio & Gaertner, 1986). And, in our democratic nation, where equality constitutes a core value, an even greater proportion of currently living Americans witnessed the defeat of the Equal Rights Amendment to the Constitution of the United States. The residue of centuries of discrimination against minorities and women guides the lives of all Americans today. Informal procedures and unintentional patterns of behavior constitute the challenge we now face as we move toward the achievement of an inclusive society.

The policy of affirmative action was born of the recognition that the passive procedures of Equal Employment Opportunity had failed to yield the anticipated outcome of broad inclusion of minorities and women in the institutions of American society. Simply removing the formal barriers which constituted the old mechanisms of discrimination had not produced full representation of those who had been denied access to business and educational organizations. The emphasis on procedural fairness in the policy of equality of opportunity has shifted toward an emphasis on distributive fairness reflected in the policy of affirmative action (Clayton & Tangri, Chapter 15). The overarching goal of affirmative action is to ensure that minorities and women achieve full representation at all levels of the institutions from which they once were barred.

In the broadest sense affirmative action invites all manner of positive efforts to include minorities and women in the labor markets and institutions from which they have been historically excluded (Holloway, Chapter 2). Affirmative action programs also seek to promote the inclusion of the physically handicapped and Vietnam era veterans. Although the doors of exclusion had been unlocked by equal opportunity legislation, it is the policy of affirmative action which now holds those doors open and beckons that the newcomers enter. Much of the current debate regarding the positive efforts of affirmative action policies centers around the propriety of the color- and sex-conscious focus of these invitations (Glazer, 1988).

Support for Affirmative Action today is mixed. While 90% of Americans agree that "affirmative action programs that help Blacks and other minorities to get ahead should be supported," only slight majorities agree that educational institutions and employers "should set aside a certain number of places to hire qualified Blacks and other minorities" (Kluegel & Smith, 1983). Even some of those who favor such "set aside" policies still perceive them to be unfair (Kluegel & Smith, 1983). Generally, the more explicit the emphasis upon what is perceived to be the preferential treatment of women and minorities, the less the public support for affirmative action (Chertos, 1983). Yet, Glasser (1988) reports that over 95 percent of American corporations indicate that they would persist with numerical hiring and promotion goals for minorities even in the absence of federal requirements that they do so.

The loudest critics of the results-oriented emphasis of affirmative action programs misunderstand two fundamental and inextricably intertwined features of American society today. First, they believe that race and sex discrimination turn on the intention and malevolence of individuals (Kluegel, 1985). They do not. Second, they believe that racism and sexism have been eliminated or so substantially reduced as to be inconsequential as a cause for current patterns of disadvantage (Kluegel, 1985). They have not.

Contemporary Conceptions of Racism and Sexism

Although reviews of the research literature regarding the racial attitudes and stereotypes of Americans consistently indicate widespread and favorable changes over the last 25 years, caution has been raised regarding the meaning of these changes for contemporary race relations (Dovidio & Gaertner, 1986; Dovidio, Mann, & Gaertner, Chapter 7; Gaertner & Dovidio, 1986; Kinder, 1986; Schuman, Steeh, & Bobo, 1985; Sears, 1988). There is little doubt that Americans today much less frequently display the virulent forms of prejudice against minorities and open forms of discrimination that were once the norm in this country. However, modern forms of prejudice and discrimination may be no less problematic for the attainment of equal opportunity by women and minorities.

Sears (1988) suggests that there has been overwhelming rejection of old-fashioned racist positions and doctrines of racial inferiority, formal discrimination, and legalized segregation. Yet, there remains widespread opposition to programs which advance the cause of racial equality. Bobo (1988) describes current American attitudes as reflecting an ideology of bounded racial change which allows support for abstract egalitarian principles while simultaneously denying real access to employment and educational opportunities. Dovidio and Gaertner (1986) suggest that what may have changed most over the last quarter century is the sensitivity of White Americans to norms which proscribe discrimination and outward expressions of prejudice, not the ability of

Whites to behave in a nondiscriminatory manner.

Gaertner and Dovidio (1986) describe the most common form of contemporary prejudice as aversive racism. Their research documents the prevalence of a paradoxical combination of values, attitudes, and behaviors reflecting a generalized commitment to equality and the self-perception of being nonprejudiced, on the one hand, and the performance of unintentionally discriminatory behavior, especially in the absence of clear norms to judge appropriate behavior, on the other. These Whites find interacting with members of minority groups uncomfortable in part because of the risk that they and others might detect instances of discrimination in their own behavior. It should not be surprising in light of the continuing history of segregation in housing, schools, and employment that few Whites who reach a commitment to nonprejudice and equality have enjoyed the opportunity to rehearse the appropriate behaviors and thereby acquire the interpersonal skills necessary for them to fulfill their commitment to equality.

It is likely that the prevalence of naive prejudice contributes to the difficulties that organizations face in achieving high rates of minority inclusion. Imagine a social setting which consists of 15 people. If one of those people is Black (about six percent) and fourteen are White, this setting would correspond to a numeric representation of Blacks and Whites across a range of settings commonly encountered in contemporary American life. Now imagine that none of the Whites is an old-fashioned racist. All are committed to equality and perceive themselves to be nonprejudiced. Yet, it is very likely that none of them will have gained sufficient experience interacting with Blacks to be sensitive to the effects of their actions on the feelings of others. Now imagine that each of the Whites makes only one racially insensitive "mistake" per month. Certainly, this would constitute a low enough rate that the Whites might feel pretty good about realizing their personal commitment to equality and nondiscrimination. The genuine social reality for each of them consists of a very low incidence of discrimination in that social setting. But, the arithmetic of contemporary racism indicates that the social reality for the numerically underrepresented Black person is a painful instance of discrimination nearly every other day because each of those fourteen Whites targets the same Black person. The largely unintended patterns of insensitivity and discrimination which arise out of the combination of extreme numeric imbalance and a history of discrimination have been carefully documented for both women (Kanter, 1977) and minorities (Pettigrew, 1987a).

Contemporary Patterns of Exclusion

Recent research describes the ways in which seemingly benign institutional practices, rather than individuals *per se*, contribute to the exclusion of minorities (Braddock & McPartland, 1987a) and women (Benokraitis & Feagin, 1986; Benokraitis & Gilbert, Chapter 6) from employment opportunities. An analysis of a survey of the employment practices of 4078 public and private employers in the United States conducted by Braddock and McPartland (1987a) illustrates some of the processes which account for the widely observed inequities in pay between Whites and minorities (Ruhm, Chapter 12). Braddock and McPartland found three stages in the contemporary employment process during which Blacks encounter significant barriers to the attainment of equal opportunity: the job candidate stage, the job entry stage, and the promotion stage.

During the job candidate stage, qualified person's opportunities for employment are fundamentally controlled by finding out about openings and becoming part of the candidate pools. Braddock and McPartland (1987a) found that convenience and low cost so dominate employer's contemporary approaches to recruitment that unsolicited walk-in applications, informal referrals from current employees, and phone calls to public employment agencies constitute the primary means of filling vacancies. Employers rely on these informal procedures to fill lower and upper level jobs, although there is a greater variety in the approaches used to fill upper level positions. Employer reliance on procedures such as these magnifies the role of informal social networks at the job candidate stage. To the extent that Whites and Blacks enjoy access to social networks that are dominated by other Whites and Blacks, respectively, predominantly White employment settings tend to stay White because other Whites hear of the openings and Blacks do not. The use of segregated social networks by Black high school graduates results in lower-paying, segregated jobs; the use of desegregated networks, available to Blacks who attend less segregated schools and employed by firms with less segregated workforces, results in higher-paying, less segregated jobs for Black job-seekers (Braddock & McPartland, 1987a).

During the job entry stage, the decision to hire is fundamentally controlled by employers' judgments of applicants' qualifications, abilities, and experience. Braddock and McPartland (1987a) found that employers differ widely in the information they use to inform hiring decisions and the manner in which the information is used differs depending upon whether the applicant is White or Black. For example, such attributes as being a quick-learner, showing good judgment in complex situations, skill at client and customer relations, ability to function as a good team member, and providing supervisory leadership and direction were frequently nominated by employers as important in their hiring decisions and tended to be emphasized by employers who favored Whites in their work force. Moreover, they found that only two sources of information about applicant qualifications are highly valued and frequently used by employers. These are impressions gained from personal interviews and application forms and recommendations from previous employers (where available). Thus, these key qualities are evaluated in a fashion which requires a level of objective and unbiased judgment of which many employers may not be capable.

There is overwhelming evidence which documents the unreliability of employment interviews in general and the frequently unintentional racial biases which result when inferences drawn from personal interviews are emphasized in employment decisions. For example, Kraiger and Ford (1985) show reliable and significant effects attributable to the race of the rater when performance of Whites and Blacks is evaluated. Their meta-analysis of the results of 88 separate studies of this issue indicates that Whites rate Whites significantly more favorably than Blacks, and that Blacks rate Blacks significantly more favorably than Whites. Unless personnel offices across the country are staffed with minority interviewers (they're not) and unless minority supervisors and managers write the letters of recommendation for minority employees (they don't), these patterns constitute a considerable barrier to minority employment opportunities.

During the job promotion stage, internal recruitment procedures constrain the opportunities of Black employee promotion. Braddock and McPartland (1987a) report that private employers post and circulate written vacancy notices much less frequently (50% of the time) than public employers (80% of the time). When employers go directly to specific employees without broad notification of a vacancy, the probability of appointing a White candidate is significantly higher than the probability of appointing a minority candidate (Braddock & McPartland, 1987a). They also present evidence showing that when minority employees are promoted from within the organization, the wages they receive in their new positions are significantly higher than when a minority job candidate is appointed from outside the organization.

Features of Effective Affirmative Action

Effective Affirmative Action starts with the commitment to employ all manner of positive action to succeed at the recruitment and retention of minorities and women. Clearly, success must be measured first by appeal to the numbers of historically excluded persons who are recruited and retained at all levels of an organization (VanderWaerdt, 1982). The setting of numeric hiring goals provides an objective basis for an organization to evaluate the effectiveness of its programs for enhancing equal opportunity. Moreover, numeric hiring goals have been empirically demonstrated to contribute directly to enhanced rates of inclusion of minorities and women (Freeman, 1984; Leonard, 1985). Over the long term, no measure of good faith effort should substitute for numerically quantifiable success in this endeavor. An organization should treat failure to achieve significant inclusion as evidence that more effort, resources, and different tactics are required. After all, it was the formal patterns of discrimination which for centuries allowed the hiring of less qualified people by barring or severely limiting the employment of members of the groups now protected by equal opportunity legislation (Sandler, 1975; VanderWaerdt, 1982). It is current informal patterns which conspire to maintain the restricted applicant pools which eventuate in the exclusion of qualified people.

Among the most widely cited prerequisites of effective affirmative action programs is strong and public commitment from the top levels of management (Astin & Snyder, 1982; Hitt, Keats, & Purdum, 1983; Hitt & Keats, 1984; Larwood, Gutek, & Gattiker, 1984; Marino, 1980; Simas & McCarrey, 1979; VanderWaerdt, 1982). Commitment by those in leadership is important for three reasons. First, it is these people who control the allocation of resources and wield the decision-making authority required for the broad dissemination of equal opportunity procedures throughout the organization (Clark, 1953). Second, firm leadership by those in authority especially influences persons whose prejudice is embedded in a constellation of beliefs and values which often includes deference to authority (Weigel & Howes, 1985). Third, top management can favorably influence organizational norms which subtly guide egalitarian interpersonal behavior (Brewer & Miller, 1984; Cook, 1984; Weigel & Howes, 1985) and, thereby, reduce the incidence of unintentional discriminatory behavior (Dovidio & Gaertner, 1983; Dovidio et al., Chapter 7). For affirmative action to succeed, however, all levels of the organization must support the effort (Chertos, 1982; Ledvinka & Hildreth, 1984; VanderWaerdt, 1982). One of the ways to ensure the broadest emphasis on the goals of affirmative action is for top management to treat violation of affirmative action policy as seriously as violation of other corporate policies (Marino, 1980).

A second important feature of successful affirmative action programs is the presence of effective and credible grievance procedures for handling individual instances of discrimination (Hitt & Keats, 1984; Hitt et al., 1983; Marino, 1980; VanderWaerdt, 1982). The availability of due process provides the opportunity both to uncover discriminatory behavior and to deter individual instances of discrimination (Hitt et al., 1983). Procedures which fairly and expeditiously resolve complaints of discrimination must be a prominent goal of affirmative action; a substantial decrease in charges of discrimination is a measure of success (VanderWaerdt, 1982). Just as the systematic compilation of employment data organized by sex and minority group status facilitates the detection of patterns of discrimination (Twiss, Tabb, & Crosby, Chapter 13), regular review of the incidence, character, and disposition of grievance complaints should alert the organization to patterns of mistreatment (Kahn & Robbins, 1985).

Aggressive recruitment of minorities and women constitutes a third major feature of effective affirmative action. Marino's (1980) analysis of the views of a sample of federal contract compliance officers indicates that community outreach and seeking community support in the recruitment of members of protected classes provides convincing evidence of compliance with the good faith requirements of affirmative action. Among the outreach activities judged important by compliance officers are regular tours of the organization for representatives of minority community organizations, attention to issues of transportation to and from work, encouraging minority employee referrals, and direct contact by the Affirmative Action Officer with minority community organizations, especially those which offer recruitment and placement services. Others have emphasized the crucial role that minority and civil rights organizations can play in identifying potential new employees (Braddock & McPartland, 1987b; Cook, 1987; Pettigrew & Martin, 1987b). Some have gone so far as to suggest that recruitment is sufficiently important to justify relaxing some of the record-keeping requirements of affirmative action to allow a redirection of resources into developing more effective recruitment processes (Astin & Snyder, 1982).

Retention and promotion of minorities and women is at least as important as the initial recruitment successes. Hoffman (1985) presents convincing evidence that broad and careful attention to terminations, transfers, and promotions within an organization can produce representation proportions which not only exceed availability figures, but which surpass simple linear predictions derived from an organization's successes in initial hiring. Clearly, an orientation toward first discovering and then creating the conditions under which women and minorities can thrive at all levels of an organization constitutes a major requirement for effective affirmative action. Among the policies advocated by Hoffman (1985) are rotating supervisory positions in order to expose new employees to different management styles and supervisors to a range of employee skills and concerns, hiring entry level people with a breadth of skills and experience which will enhance their opportunities for advancement, and providing a basic level of encouragement, training, and support to all new employees.

Retention of those hired under the guidance of affirmative action will invite review of policies and practices throughout the organization, many of which appear to have nothing to do with the hiring or promotion of employees (Buonocore & Crable, 1986). As new people join the organization, informal customs and practices which had been comfortable for Whites and males may require change in order to incorporate the styles and preferences of new employees (Feagin, 1988; Ferdman, Chapter 14; Huckle, 1985). New practices might include flexible work scheduling, work at home, paternity and maternity leave, and on-site childcare (Kahn & Robbins, 1985). There is every reason to believe that some of the formal procedures of operation will also require review and change as new people bringing new strengths join the organization (Bocher, 1982; Norris & Reardon, Chapter 5).

It is unlikely that these changes will be made until appreciable numbers of new people arrive to raise new questions and offer guidance from new perspectives. Wise proponents of the goals of affirmative action in top management will do everything possible to ensure that minorities and women reach positions of power throughout the organization and that they do so in numbers which are large enough to interrupt the burdens of solo and token status (Pettigrew & Martin, 1987a). Numeric representation must also be sufficiently high at the top levels to disrupt the token gate-keeper phenomenon (Laws, 1975) where, in order to maintain personal identification with other high level executives (who are nonminority or male), numerically distinctive managers sometimes feel pressured to keep others like themselves from reaching the same level of status and authority which they personally have achieved (Larwood et al., 1984). Only then will the concerns of new members of the organization be heard. Smith (1987) argues that changes of this kind reduce to power. When minority managers gain power over significant arenas of decision-making, substantive changes will occur (Green, 1981).

New initiatives

Perhaps the most important shortcoming of current approaches to affirmative action is the failure to recognize that nonminorities and males can also be hired, promoted, and terminated in ways that directly affect the success of affirmative action efforts toward the inclusion of minorities and women. There are three areas ripe for new initiatives. First, a great deal more attention to the hiring of nonminorities and men is warranted. The criteria for evaluating nonminority candidates for employment might be expanded to include evidence which predicts their contribution to an organization's affirmative action and equal opportunity goals and evidence which predicts their abilities to function effectively in an organization which is achieving those goals. These new, additional criteria might include the extent and favorability of their experience working in multicultural settings, being supervised by minority managers, collaborating in multicultural workgroups, or living in racially integrated neighborhoods. Premiums might be placed on new skills and knowledge like facility with relevant languages other than English and substantial college course-work in the study of non-Western and nondominant cultures.

The criteria for evaluating male job candidates might be expanded to include successful experience with direct supervision by female managers, first-hand experience with the provision of childcare, and the successful juggling of employment and family responsibilities. Admission criteria for college students might be expanded to include recognition of substantial experience and success in equal status, interracial school settings, experience being taught by minority teachers, and membership in clubs and groups in which minorities are substantially represented. Recommendations provided by women and minorities might be accorded special weight in the evaluation of these experiences and skills. Not only would accomplishment in these areas predict favorable contributions to future school and employment settings by nonminorities and men, but powerful new incentives for the desegregation of employment settings, schools, and perhaps even housing patterns might result.

Second, the evaluative criteria for the promotion of current employees might be expanded to include recognition of contributions to conditions which lead all employees to thrive. Credit for finding, hiring, promoting, encouraging, and sponsoring minorities and women should become part of the formal basis for employee evaluation at all levels. Students who contribute to the recruitment and retention of minority students should be acknowledged and rewarded. Clear policies regarding the discipline and termination of those who engage in discriminatory behavior which undermines the ability of the organization to achieve its affirmative action goals and, thereby, its other goals are a necessary component of the total effort. At a minimum such policies constitute a business necessity: Employers minimize civil liabilities when they effectively prohibit racial and sexual harassment.

Finally, hiring and retention goals, traditionally set so that they approximate availability data, are often too low. Research is accumulating to indicate that, in order to create the optimal conditions for new members of an organization to thrive, inclusion rates must sometimes exceed the targets derived by appeal to workforce proportions of qualified minorities and women. Pettigrew and Martin (1986a) argue that the only way to substantially reduce the systematic patterns of the real, but subtle discrimination which attends low numeric representation of women and minorities is to surpass a minimum inclusion target of about twenty percent in any one employment setting. Although this one-in-five floor pertains separately to each minority group, it does not demand that organization-wide proportions must surpass a twenty percent inclusion rate where real unavailability constitutes an absolute barrier. Instead, at least at the earliest stages of initial affirmative action success, organizations should consider clustering members of the same minority group in particular workgroups, departments, or offices (Pettigrew & Martin, 1986a).

Clustering should never substitute for appointments to high-level positions of power and authority. However, so long as clustering remains a transitional procedure to support new employees as they distribute themselves throughout the parts and levels of the organization, it can contribute to the favorability of the work conditions for members of particular minority groups and women and to the interruption of naive and unintentionally discriminatory behavior performed by nonminorities and men. So long as clustering occurs in offices and departments characterized by high status and wages, high levels of centrality to the mission of the organization, and high levels of access to career ladders within the organization, this temporary strategy will contribute to the creation of work settings which are as comfortable for minorities and women as the customary, numerically dominant setting is for Whites and men. To the extent that clustering interrupts the exaggerated scrutiny and hypercritical evaluation characteristic of extreme numeric minority status (Pettigrew & Martin, 1986a), it promises to enhance employee performance and retention.

Affirmative action is a young policy around which the opportunity for much innovation remains. Experimentation with procedures and programs will continue until the residue of informal patterns of discrimination is eliminated and all Americans enjoy the full range of rights, privileges, opportunities, and responsibilities of citizenship. In its recent report regarding patterns of discrimination and disadvantage in America, the Commission on Minority Participation in Education and American Life (1988), jointly sponsored by the American Council on Education and the Education Commission of the States, recognized that affirmative action remains an essential tool for achieving social and individual justice. The Commission called upon the American people and their leaders to open a public debate through which a new national consensus on affirmative action might be achieved. Until full participation is accomplished, the policy of requiring positive action to achieve numerically quantifiable levels of inclusion in all arenas of American life offers the best hope of attaining those democratic ideals.

References

Astin, H. S., & Snyder, M. B. (1982, July/August). Affirmative action 1972-1982: A decade of response. *Change*, 26-31, 59.

Benokraitis, N. V., & Feagin, J. R. (1986). *Modern sexism: Blatant, subtle and covert discrimination*. Englewood Cliffs, NJ: Prentice-Hall.

Benokraitis, N. V., & Gilbert, M. K. (1989). Women in federal government employment. In F. A. Blanchard & F. J. Crosby (Eds.), *Affirmative action in perspective* (pp. 65-80). New York: Springer-Verlag.

Bobo, L. (1988). Group conflict, prejudice, and the paradox of contemporary racial attitudes. In P. A. Katz & D. A. Taylor (Eds.), *Eliminating racism: Profiles in controversy* (pp. 85-114). New York: Plenum Press.

Bocher, R. B. (1982). Does tradition affect affirmative action results? How Pennsylvania achieved changes at the middle management level. *Public Administration Review, 42*, 475-478.

Braddock, J. H., & McPartland, J. M. (1987a). How minorities continue to be excluded from equal employment opportunities: Research on labor market and institutional barriers. *Journal of Social Issues, 43*(1), 5-39.

Braddock, J. H., & McPartland, J. M. (1987b). Social science evidence and affirmative action policies: A reply to the commentators. *Journal of Social Issues, 43*(1), 133-143.

Brewer, M. B., & Miller, N. (1984). Beyond the contact hypothesis: Theoretical perspectives on desegregation. In N. Miller & M. B. Brewer (Eds.), *Groups in contact: The psychology of desegregation* (pp. 281-302). Orlando, FL: Academic Press.

Buonocore, A. J., & Crable, D. R. (1986, August). Equal opportunity: An incomplete evolution. *Personnel Journal*, 65, 32-35.

Chertos, C. H. (1983). Hard truths for strategic change: Dilemmas of implementing affirmative action. *Women's Studies International Forum*, 6, 231-241.

Clark, K. (1953). Desegregation: An appraisal of the evidence. *Journal of Social Issues*, 9(4), 2-76.

Clayton, S. D., & Tangri, S. S. (1989). The justice of affirmative action. In F. A. Blanchard & F. J. Crosby (Eds.), *Affirmative action in perspective* (pp. 177-192). New York: Springer-Verlag.

Commission on Minority Participation in Education and American Life. (1988). *One-third of a nation*. Washington, D.C.: American Council on Education.

Cook, S. W. (1984). Cooperative interaction in multiethnic contexts. In N. Miller & M. B. Brewer (Eds.), *Groups in contact: The psychology of desegregation* (pp. 155-185). Orlando, FL: Academic Press.

Cook, S. W. (1987). Behavior-change implications of low involvement in an issue. *Journal of Social Issues*, 43(1), 105-112.

Dovidio, J. F., & Gaertner, S. L. (1986). Prejudice, discrimination, and racism: Historical trends and contemporary approaches. In J. F. Dovidio & S. L. Gaertner (Eds.), *Prejudice, discrimination, and racism* (pp. 1-34). Orlando, FL: Academic Press.

Dovidio, J. F., & Gaertner, S. L. (1983). Race, normative structure, and helpseeking. In B. M. Depaulo, A. Nadler, & J. P. Fisher (Eds.), *New directions in helping: Vol. 2. Help-seeking* (pp. 285-302). New York: Academic Press.

Dovidio, J. F., Mann, J., & Gaertner, S. L. (1989). Resistance to affirmative action: The implications of aversive racism. In F. A. Blanchard & F. J. Crosby (Eds.), *Affirmative action in perspective* (pp. 83-102). New York: Springer-Verlag.

Farley, R. (1984). *Blacks and whites: Narrowing the gap?* Cambridge, MA: Harvard University Press.

Feagin, J. R. (1987). Changing black Americans to fit a racist system? *Journal of Social Issues*, 43(1), 85-89.

Ferdman, B. M. (1989). Affirmative action and the challenge of the color-blind perspective. In F. A. Blanchard & F. J. Crosby (Eds.), *Affirmative action in perspective* (pp. 169-176). New York: Springer-Verlag.

Freeman, R. B. (1984). Affirmative action: Good, bad, or irrelevant? *New Perspectives*, 16(2), 23-27.

Gaertner, S. L., & Dovidio, J. F. (1986). The aversive form of racism. In J. F. Dovidio & S. L. Gaertner (Eds.), *Prejudice, discrimination, and racism* (pp. 61-

89). Orlando, FL: Academic Press.

Glasser, I. (1988). Affirmative action and racial injustice. In P. A. Katz & D. A. Taylor (Eds.), *Eliminating racism: Profiles in controversy* (pp. 341-358). New York: Plenum Press.

Glazer, N. (1988). The future of preferential affirmative action. In P. A. Katz & D. A. Taylor (Eds.), *Eliminating racism: Profiles in controversy* (pp. 329-340). New York: Plenum Press.

Green, P. (1981). The new individualism. *Christianity and Crisis, 41,* 79-80.

Hitt, M. A., Keats, B. W., & Purdum, S. (1983). Affirmative action effectiveness criteria in institutions of higher education. *Research in Higher Education, 18,* 391-407.

Hitt, M. A., & Keats, B. W. (1984). Empirical identification of the criteria for effective affirmative action programs. *Journal of Applied Behavioral Science, 20,* 203-222.

Hoffman, C. (1985). Affirmative action programs that work. *New Perspectives, 17*(3), 16-23.

Holloway, F. A. (1989). What is affirmative action? In F. A. Blanchard & F. J. Crosby (Eds.), *Affirmative action in perspective* (pp. 9-19). New York: Springer-Verlag.

Huckle, P. (1985). Whatever happened to affirmative action? Employment of women in the Los Angeles City Department of Water and Power, 1973-1983. *Review of Public Personnel Administration, 6,* 44-58.

Kanter, R. M. (1977). Some effects of proportions on group life: Skewed sex ratios and responses to token women. *American Journal of Sociology, 82,* 965-991.

Kahn, E. D., & Robbins, L. (1985). Social-psychological issues in sex discrimination. *Journal of Social Issues, 41*(4), 135-154.

Kinder, D. R. (1986). The continuing American dilemma: White resistance to racial change 40 years after Myrdal. *Journal of Social Issues, 42*(2), 151-171.

Kluegel, J. R. (1985). If there isn't a problem, you don't have to fix it: The basis of contemporary affirmative action attitudes. *American Behavioral Scientist, 28,* 761-784.

Kluegel, J. R., & Smith, E. R. (1983). Affirmative action attitudes: Effects of self-interest, racial affect, and stratification beliefs on whites' views. *Social Forces, 61,* 797-824.

Kraiger, K., & Ford, J. K. (1985). A meta-analysis of ratee race effects in performance ratings. *Journal of Applied Psychology, 70,* 56-65.

Larwood, L., Gutek, B., & Gattiker, U. E. (1984). Perspectives on institutional discrimination and resistance to change. *Group & Organization Studies, 9,* 333-352.

Laws, J. L. (1975). The psychology of tokenism: An analysis. *Sex Roles, 1,* 51-67.

Ledvinka, J., & Hildreth, W. B. (1984). Integrating planned-change intervention and computer simulation technology: The case of affirmative action. *Journal of Applied Behavioral Science, 20*, 125-140.

Leonard, J. S. (1985). What promises are worth: The impact of affirmative action goals. *Journal of Human Resources, 20*(1), 3-20.

Marino, K. E. (1980). A preliminary investigation into the behavioral dimensions of affirmative action compliance. *Journal of Applied Psychology, 65*, 346-350.

Norris, W. L., & Reardon, M. (1989). Employment screening qualifications, and gender discrimination: A case study of the New York City Firefighters. In F. A. Blanchard & F. J. Crosby (Eds.), *Affirmative action in perspective* (pp. 51-63). New York: Springer-Verlag.

Pettigrew, T. F. (1988) Integration and pluralism. In P. A. Katz & D. A. Taylor (Eds.), *Eliminating racism: Profiles in controversy* (pp. 19-30). New York: Plenum Press.

Pettigrew, T. F., & Martin, J. (1987a). Shaping the organizational context for black American inclusion. *Journal of Social Issues, 43*(1), 41-78.

Pettigrew, T. F., & Martin, J. (1987b). The fruits of critical discussion: A reply to the commentators. *Journal of Social Issues, 43*(1), 145-156.

Ruhm, C. J. (1989). Labor market discrimination in the United States. In F. A. Blanchard & F. J. Crosby (Eds.), *Affirmative action in perspective* (pp. 149-158). New York: Springer-Verlag.

Sandler, B. (1975). Affirmative action on campus: Progress, problems and perplexity. In *Affirmative action in employment in higher education*. Washington, D.C.: U.S. Commission on Civil Rights.

Schuman, H., Steeh, C., & Bobo, L. (1985). *Racial attitudes in America: Trends and interpretations*. Cambridge, MA: Harvard University Press.

Sears, D. O. (1988). Symbolic racism. In P. A. Katz & D. A. Taylor (Eds.), *Eliminating racism: Profiles in controversy* (pp. 53-84). New York: Plenum Press.

Simas, K., & McCarrey, M. (1979). Impact of recruiter authoritarianism and applicant sex on evaluation and selection decisions in a recruitment interview analogue study. *Journal of Applied Psychology, 64*, 483-491.

Smith, A. W. (1987). Racial trends and countertrends in American organizational behavior. *Journal of Social Issues, 43*(1), 91-94.

Twiss, C., Tabb, S., & Crosby, F. J. (1989). Affirmative action and aggregate data: The importance of patterns in the perception of discrimination. In F. A. Blanchard & F. J. Crosby (Eds.), *Affirmative action in perspective* (pp. 159-167). New York: Springer-Verlag.

VanderWaerdt, L. (1982). *Affirmative Action in Higher Education: A Sourcebook.* New York: Garland Publishing.

Weigel, R. H., & Howes, P. W. (1985). Conceptions of racial prejudice: Symbolic racism reconsidered. *Journal of Social Issues, 41*(3), 117-138.

Acknowledgements

I am indebted to Stuart W. Cook, Samuel L. Gaertner, and Russell H. Weigel for the helpful comments they provided on previous versions of this chapter.

Index